T0295634

# Policy Solutions for Economic Growth in a Developing Country

First of its kind, comprehensive and illuminating insight into Afghanistan with concrete recommendations on how the country can thrive and help itself reform its trade and trade relations with the world.

Immersing myself in the pages of this book, I journeyed through the world of Afghanistan's global trade, concluding with enriched insights essential for academics and policymakers.

I highly recommend this book for its in-depth exploration of Afghanistan's international trade journey, especially post-2001. It provides valuable insights for policymakers and scholars, offering innovative trade proposals and insights into Afghanistan's global trade role. Essential for understanding Afghanistan's trade potential.

This book provides a timely and profoundly insightful exploration into a fundamental question that has bedevilled economic policy planning for decades – how should developing countries achieve economic growth? Straddling the topics of international trade, globalisation, economic development, state policy planning and private sector development, Wani diagnoses the impediments to export-oriented growth and proposes ambitious recommendations that may serve as correctives. His focus on Afghanistan provides a rich site for exploring these challenges. Using extensive quantitative analysis alongside well-established theoretical models, Wani positions Afghanistan vis-à-vis its regional neighbours as well as concerning ASEAN and SAARC nations and the European Union, thereby evincing opportunities for enhanced international trade. While optimistic, he also raises the trade-offs of different policy choices. The book draws on Wani's decade of scholarly engagement with Afghanistan's economy, ultimately succeeding in providing lessons on economic growth that may be applied to much of the developing world.

# Policy Solutions for Economic Growth in a Developing Country: Perspectives on Afghanistan's Trade and Development

BY

**NASSIR UL HAQ WANI**

*Kardan University, Afghanistan*

United Kingdom – North America – Japan – India – Malaysia – China

Emerald Publishing Limited
Emerald Publishing, Floor 5, Northspring, 21-23 Wellington Street, Leeds LS1 4DL

First edition 2024

**Reprints and permissions service**
Contact: www.copyright.com

**British Library Cataloguing in Publication Data**
A catalogue record for this book is available from the British Library.

ISBN: 978-1-83753-431-9 (Print)
ISBN: 978-1-83753-430-2 (Online)
ISBN: 978-1-83753-432-6 (Epub)

INVESTOR IN PEOPLE

*Dedicated to ...*

*The Humble People of Afghanistan*
*&*
*My Beloved Parents (Gh. Mohi Ud Din Wani and Sara Parveen)*
*My Wife (Amina Hamid)*
*Our Daughter (Ummat-Un- Nafiyah) and Son (Ahmad Ehaan Wani).*

# Contents

# List of Figures and Tables

**Chapter 2**

**Chapter 3**

**Chapter 4**

# List of Abbreviations

| | |
|---|---|
| ADF | Augmented Dickey–Fuller |
| AFTA | ASEAN Free Trade Area |
| APPTA | Afghanistan Pakistan Preferential Trade Agreement |
| APTTA | Afghanistan–Pakistan Transit and Trade Agreement |
| ARDL | Auto Regressive Distributed Lag |
| ASEAN | Association of South East Asian Nations |
| ATP | Afghanistan Trade Policy |
| BFTAs | Bilateral Free Trade Agreements |
| BIMSTEC | Bengal Initiative for Multi-Sectoral Technical and Economic Cooperation |
| BOP | Balance of Payments |
| BTA | Bilateral Trade Agreement |
| BSA | Bilateral Security Agreement |
| CAB | Current Account Balance |
| CAD | Current Account Deficit |
| CAR | Central Asia Region |
| CES | Constant Elasticity of Substitution |
| CCE | Commodity Composition Effect |
| CIF | Cost Insurance and Freight |
| CL | Civil Liberties |
| CMS | Constant-Market-Share |
| COR | Changes in Official Reserves |
| CSE | Commodity Structure Effect |
| DAB | Da Afghanistan Bank |
| ECA | Europe and Central Asia |
| ED | Export Survival |
| ES | Export Sophistication |
| ESCAP | Economic and Social Commission for Asia and the Pacific |

| | |
|---|---|
| EU | European Union |
| FMOLS | Fully Modified Ordinary Least Square |
| FOB | Free on Board |
| GATT | General Agreement on Trade and Tariffs |
| GDP | Gross Domestic Product |
| GFI | Global Financial Integrity |
| HHI | Herfindahl–Hirschman Product Concentration Index |
| HOS | Heckscher–Ohlin–Samuelson |
| HS | Harmonised Standards |
| IARTII | Intra-Regional Trade Intensity Index |
| IERTII | Inter-Regional Trade Intensity Index |
| IMF | International Monetary Fund |
| IRTS | Intra-Regional Trade Share |
| LF | Lafay Index |
| MDE | Market Distribution Effect |
| MENA | Middle East Nations |
| MFN | Most Favoured Nation |
| MNNA | Major Non-NATO Ally |
| NAC | Net Acquisition of Non-Bank Private Short-Term Capital |
| NAFA | Net Acquisition of Foreign Assets |
| NAFTA | North America Free Trade Agreement |
| NFDI | Net Foreign Direct Investment |
| NTBs | Non-Tariff Barriers |
| NTMs | Non-Tariff Measures |
| ODA | Official Development Assistance |
| PTA | Preferential Trade Arrangement |
| RCA | Revealed Comparative Advantage |
| RCF | Reverse Capital Flow |
| RDE | Residual Competitiveness Effect |
| REER | Real Effective Exchange Rate |
| RTA | Regional Trading Agreements |
| SA | South Asia |
| SAARC | South Asian Association for Regional Cooperation |

| | |
|---|---|
| SAE | Structural Adaptation Effect |
| SAFTA | South Asian Free Trade Agreement |
| SAPTA | South Asia Preferential Trade Agreement |
| SBC | Schwarz Bayesian Criterion |
| SIGAR | Special Inspector General for Afghanistan Reconstruction |
| SITC | Standard International Trading Classification |
| SPS | Sanitary and Phytosanitary |
| TBT | Technical Barriers to Trade |
| TC | Trade Costs |
| TCI | Trade Complementarity Index |
| TO | Trade Openness |
| TP | Tariff Preferential |
| TR | Tariff Rate |
| UN | United Nations |
| UNCLOS | United Nations Conventions of Law of Sea |
| UNCTAD | United Nations Conference on Trade and Development |
| WEF | World Economic Forum |
| WITS | World Integrated Trade Solution |
| WTO | World Trade Organization |

# About the Author

**Dr Nassir Ul Haq Wani** is the Dean of the Department of Research and Development and a Professor at the School of Graduate Studies, Kardan University, Kabul, Afghanistan. He also serves as an Adjunct Professor at Lovely Professional University, Punjab, India; and Director of Kashmir Research Information System (KRIS), J&K, India. He is the Chief Editor of the *Kardan Journal of Economics and Management Sciences*, *Afghanistan Development Review* and the Managing Editor of *Kardan Journal of Social Sciences and Humanities*.

# Preface

This book combines my writings on international trade and development at Kardan University (KU) since joining KU in 2017. All the papers aim to develop concepts and ideas concerning trade and development in Afghanistan. This book provides a longitudinal study of Afghanistan's involvement in multilateral trade negotiations, highlights the policy propositions for enhancing and expediting trade ties with the region and other trading partners and presents policy discourse on key elements akin to trade escalation and growth.

This book offers a detailed analysis and explores the possibility that economic globalisation may finally deliver to developing countries what they had failed to achieve in five decades of multilateral negotiations – an opportunity to climb the industrialisation ladder and achieve development. The book offers a proposal for revising the format of trade negotiations in a way that helps overcome stalemates and deadlocks. Perspectives on trade and development will interest students and scholars of international trade, trade and development, negotiation, global governance, political economy, international relations and economics.

The volume thus addresses several issues and challenges fairly novel to the Afghanistan economy in general and the trade sector in particular. This book will be most suitable for applied courses on international trade and development for graduate and undergraduate students and for policy and decision-makers in the government.

I benefitted from a personal association with Dr Ahmad Khalid Hatam (Chancellor and Professor) at KU. It is hoped his influence on my work will have prevented detection. I benefited greatly from other faculty members at many presentations, conferences and workshops at KU and abroad. A special thanks to Dr Jasdeep Kaur Dhami (Professor and Dean R&D, CT University, Punjab, India), Dr Nafay Choudhary (British Academy Postdoctoral Research Fellow at the Centre for Socio-Legal Studies [CSLS], University of Oxford), Dr Amruta Deshpande (Assistant Professor, Indira School of Business Studies PGDM, Maharashtra, India) and Dr Suhailah Akbari (Postdoctoral Researcher at Humboldt Universität zu Berlin), for motivating and helping me with the research materials and offering conducive feedbacks whenever needed.

Mr Mirwais Rasa, Mr Muhammad Elyas Naseri and Mr Sadiq Zazai helped finalise the manuscript. For permission to reprint material from which material has been adapted, I am happy to acknowledge the *South Asian Economic Journal*, *Kardan Journal of Economics and Management Sciences* and *Kardan Journal of Social Sciences and Humanities*.

Dr Nassir Ul Haq Wani

# Acknowledgement

*Ahlamdulillaahi Robbil"Alamiin.* All praise would only be bestowed to Allah *subhanahu wa ta"ala*, because only with His blessing finally this book could be finished. In this connection, I would like to express my gratitude to a number of people whose admission, permission and assistance contributed to a great deal of the process of finishing this book.

I BLAME ALL OF YOU. Writing this book has been an exercise in sustained suffering along with great learning, and finally, that learning outweighs the suffering. The casual reader may perhaps exempt themself from excessive guilt, but for those of you who have played the larger role in prolonging my agonies with your encouragement and support as well...you know who you are, and you owe me but anyway...

All praises and thanks to Almighty Allah who bestowed me with the potential, ability and opportunity to work on this book. It is a matter of great pleasure to express my cordial gratitude to KU's top leadership including Mr Roeen Rahmani and Ms. Meena Rahmani for the support and encouragement that they have given throughout this research work. The support extended by them throughout the course of writing this book is beyond words.

I express my gratitude to Dr Ahmad Khalid Hatam (*Chancellor, KU*), Dr Jasdeep Kaur Dhami (*Professor and Dean R&D, CT University, Punjab, India*), Dr Nafay Choudhary (*British Academy Postdoctoral Research Fellow at the Centre for Socio-Legal Studies [CSLS], University of Oxford*), Dr Amruta Deshpande (*Assistant Professor, Indira School of Business Studies PGDM, Maharashtra, India*), Dr Suhailah Akbari (Postdoctoral Researcher at Humboldt Universität zu Berlin), the team of DRD (Mr Muhammad Elyas Naseri, Mr Sadiq Zazai and Mr Mirwais Rasa) of KU and Senior Research Fellows (Dr Inam Ul Haq, Dr Imran Ibn Gani and Dr Sheeraz Ahmad Sofi) at Kashmir Research Information System (KRIS) for their kind support, encouragement and motivation. During the initial stages of book assembly, discussions with them influenced the structure and content of the publication. Their contributions transcend the realm of the book chapters. I express my gratitude for their time, intellect and assistance; however, their passion is what I value the most. I am also thankful to staff members of the library and all other teaching and non-teaching staff of KU for their kind care and cooperation.

Thank you to Dr Daniel Ridge, the Commissioning editor, at Emerald Publishing for guiding and providing kind feedback always. Hemavathi Rajendran and Lydia Cutmore of Emerald Publishing were consistently encouraging and forbearing in light of the delays caused by relocations, new employment and other stuff. Additionally, I appreciate Sangeeta Menon's introduction of Dr Daniel Ridge. You are an extraordinary connector.

I would like to express my gratitude to every academic with whom I have collaborated throughout the years and who have imparted invaluable knowledge. There are times when the bureaucracy – forms, deadlines, evaluations and spreadsheets – becomes overwhelming. Simply hearing about how someone's research is assisting in the transformation of circumstances for communities, industries and individuals across the globe, particularly in Afghanistan, is sufficient to remind me why I adore my profession.

Finally, I respectfully offer thanks to my beloved parents (Gh. Mohi Ud Din Wani and Sarah Parveen), for their love, mellifluous affection and sincerity which hearten me to achieve success in every sphere of my life. I am highly indebted to my wife Aamina Hamid for her frequent help, care and encouragement during the course of writing this book. A big thank you to my daughter (Ummatun Nafiyah) and son (Ahamd Ehaan Wani) for making my work easier, by having a cute smile always on their faces. That cute smile is like an energy booster always.

I also pay thanks to my beloved brothers, the most beloved sister and brother-in-law (Khursheed Ahmad Wani, Tanveer Ahmad Wani, Massarat Jan and Shahnawaz Ahmad Zarger) regarding their love, moral support and constant encouragement. Without their encouragement and support, the present study would have been a mere dream.

Part I

# Introduction

# Introduction to the Book

## 1. Background

This book examines Afghanistan's participation in international trade and evaluates its involvement in global trade. The post-World War II trading framework did not accommodate, and in some circumstances excluded, the developmental goals of newly independent nations, and the emergence of this book provides a thorough examination of the following topics. This book does not discuss the economic fragility that doomed Afghanistan before 2001; however, a sincere effort to discuss the trading mechanism and other phenomena is vigorously discussed post-2001. This book further examines the prospect that economic globalisation would finally provide underdeveloped nations with what they have been unable to accomplish during five decades of international negotiations: a chance to climb the industrialisation ladder and attain development. The book proposes altering the framework of trade talks to avoid stalemates and deadlocks. The collection of papers offers Afghanistan numerous policy options and options for positioning itself to obtain entrance into international markets to position itself as a reliable and appealing trading partner on a global scale.

Gauging the present situation of the export industry reflects fundamental constraints that need to be addressed via policy dialogue. The export sector faces serious impediments, as identified in the preceding chapters, such as a dearth of the exceptional workforce for managing endeavours in a rapidly evolving global marketplace, a deficiency of creative operations that impede export firms' capacity for acquisition in implementing advancements in technology in both manufacturing and service procedures, a scarcity of financing for export firms, and inefficient affordable infrastructures.

Afghanistan's export performance is additionally constrained by the government's anti-export prejudice, which prohibits resources from being reallocated from the import-competing economy to the country's export sector. Excessive domestic market protection, especially for exporting-oriented businesses, results in inefficiencies, waste and reduced product and service quality; consequently, the export sector bears the burden of protection. The prevalence of allowances and exceptions for non-traded manufacturing has shifted native producers' interest from quality products as well as the export market; the incentive and incidence of

Policy Solutions for Economic Growth in a Developing Country, 3–9

Copyright © 2024 Nassir Ul Haq Wani

Published under exclusive licence by Emerald Publishing Limited

doi:10.1108/978-1-83753-430-220241001

fleeing the capital and bypassing import taxes contributed to trade mis-invoicing, undermining trade policy's goal; and an unsupportive credit policy for trade and other economic reforms was never implemented.

The export revenues have varied drastically because of a shortage of significant exportable commodities and a relatively limited production and export base. Export concentration has increased the danger of fluctuating export revenues. Afghanistan's principal export items suffer trade restrictions in overseas markets, limiting export capability. The export base is undiversified and focused on relatively low-value-added items; exports concentrate in marketplaces in which growth in imports is slow, generating limited possibilities for export growth; trade costs are high because of the absence of global links and trade facilitation; and export tactics has always concentrated on merchandised exports while ignoring exports of services that might substitute for them.

Given the poor pace of the export sector and economy, Afghanistan must brace itself for a significant policy commitment to begin on a growth path to re-energise its economy and exports. By adopting trade policy decisions, the nation may assure long-term growth, expand possibilities for residents and methodically obtain a larger share of the expanding global wealth. The chapters in this book evaluate the national, international, and regional trading platforms to launch a consistent and long-term set of policies to encourage exports. These studies emphasise that besides macroeconomic stability, governance and private sector development, technical advancement, socio-economic balance, trade liberalisation and export revitalisation may all play an important role in Afghanistan's wealth generation. These chapters discuss the worldwide trade and economic consequences of Afghanistan. The study is carried out utilising cutting-edge models and estimate approaches.

## 2. The Perspective

The primary goal of this introductory chapter is to synthesise the findings of all of the investigations in this collection. The chapters are succinct, energetic, and profound. The book has eight chapters covering critical aspects of Afghanistan's foreign trade and economic growth. The book is further divided into four parts, with part two focusing on the nexus between Trade and Development, part three hinges on determinants of trade costs, export supply, diversification and growth and part four discusses the policy discourse analysis by offering policy insights with an international perspective and offering a gateway for the stage of development.

The paper included in Chapter 1 discusses *Afghanistan's Regional Integration with Central Asia: Identifying Trade Linkages, Economic Recital, and Future Latency.* Using different trade indices spanning 2018–2021, this paper investigates Afghanistan's current patterns, prospects and barriers for intra- and inter-regional trade perspectives, emphasising the various pathways by which Afghanistan trades with Central Asian economies. The empirical findings reflect that the potential value of trade between Afghanistan and Central Asia is about twice as high as the actual level. Furthermore, the analysis categorises industries that range from sector diversification across resource-intensive, labour-intensive and technology-intensive industries. The study further augmented Afghanistan's trade potential with Central Asia and vice versa by highlighting the comparative advantage, diversification, complementarity and similarity in trade. The findings suggest that larger economies are rated higher than smaller ones as size and development level are essential factors in regional trade development. The most effective channels of regional trade development are price competitiveness measures, intra-industry trade and trade complementarities. These results significantly impact the crafting of various trade policy initiatives to promote trade within and between the two regions. These policy initiatives could be implemented to encourage investment and trade in and between the two regions.

Chapter 2 evaluates the trade potential of Afghanistan with SAARC and the European Union by employing the Gravity Model Approach. The impact of trade on economic growth has been phenomenal. Thus countries reaping the trade dividends diversify their trade destinations. Against this backdrop, this study investigates the trade potential of Afghanistan with the SAARC and European Union by employing an augmented Gravity Model approach. The model used the latest Economic and Social Commission for Asia and the Pacific (ESCAP) dataset with the base year 2016. The study used panel data for seven years, from 2015 to 2021. The results of the study satiate that out of the chosen 15 countries of the European Union, the magnitude of Afghanistan's trade potential is high with three EU countries (Germany, France and Spain), whereas in the case of SAARC, Afghanistan's trade potential is highest with Pakistan, followed by India and Bangladesh. Results show that simple average tariff imposition and partner countries' GDP positively impact Afghanistan's trade value.

Chapter 3 highlights the determinants/drivers of export supply in selected South Asian economies, primarily focusing on Afghanistan. Given the significance of international trade and export performance in economic development, this research investigates the drivers of exports in SAARC countries from 2008 to 2021, utilising pooled time series and cross-section data. This research aims to determine if classic trade model elements, developing trading realities or macroeconomic variables influence export supply choices. The approach used is the export demand model and the augmented-exports supply model, which are provided with relevant variables. The model with fixed effects (country-specific intercepts) examines the connection between exports and their possible drivers. Traditional export supply models show that production capacity, variable cost and relative price significantly impact South Asian export supply performance. Changes in trade, for example, have a substantial impact on export supply, demonstrating that the trade reform process promotes export growth, import compression and technological innovation. The deterioration of the energy sector and rising levels of corruption have proven to be significant impediments to export supply selections. According to the research, FDI has a favourable but modest influence on export growth. GDP, GDP growth, official development aid, development expenditures, indirect taxes, labour force and real exchange rate benefit exports. Furthermore, the findings demonstrate that an increase in savings considerably impacts exports. The report recommends that concerned governments reassess their export policies and develop new approaches that align with changing realities to grow and improve export performance.

Chapter 4 explains export diversification in ASEAN and SAARC regions by empirically investigating the trends and factors. Emerging countries have experienced export product concentration primarily due to manufacturing and exporting raw materials and semi-manufactured goods. While these products do not often have market access issues, they have inelastic demand in foreign markets, and close replacements are easily accessible. In developed markets, finished manufactured goods exported by underdeveloped nations face substantial trade obstacles. As a result, these nations' exports are heavily centred on raw materials and semi-manufactured goods. Countries having export concentration are more sensitive to external shocks. Aware of the negative consequences, ASEAN and SAARC nations have prioritised export product diversification to increase exports and per capita income to globalise their economies. This study examines the trends and factors affecting export diversification in ASEAN and SAARC regions by employing the normalised Hirschman index covering the data from 2018 to 2021. The findings suggest that structural transformation was aimed at shifting the production line from basic and intermediate goods to exporting finished products. Except for the fuel-intensity variable, which demonstrates the dependence on natural resource exports minimises motives for broadening exports, the statistical results exhibit that all variables, such as competitiveness, industrial sector growth rate, institutional endurance, domestic capital growth, financial growth and macroeconomic situation efficiency, are positively and significantly associated with export diversification. The study's main finding is that institutional strength enables countries to diversify their exports.

Chapter 5 discusses Afghanistan's trade costs, primarily focusing on determinants and measurement. The trading expenses encountered domestically and across borders have a detrimental influence on global trade. Higher trade costs hamper trade and limit the benefits of trade liberalisation. The present study employs Novy's (2013) micro-founded trade cost measure to estimate the relative bilateral trade costs of Afghanistan's (agricultural and non-agricultural) trade with its significant trading partners. The advantage of employing this model is that trade costs may be determined purely from observable trade data. The data show that agricultural trade costs are much higher than in the non-agricultural industry.

Consequently, focusing on agricultural trade facilitation would be advantageous. The research also investigates the elements that determine trade costs. It reveals that two sectors, trade infrastructure and free trade zones with trading partners, are ideal for governmental intervention to mitigate trade costs. Better shipment communication with trade partners increases transportation routes efficiently, cutting time and other expenses. Similarly, free trade agreements reduce trade costs by lowering non-tariff and behind-the-border regulatory measures. The study suggests successfully executing the WTO's trade facilitation agreement, decreasing red tape at border crossings, simplifying and harmonising non-tariff barriers (NTBs) and establishing soft infrastructures using current technologies.

Chapter 6 highlights the occurrence of the reverse capital flight to Afghanistan by analysing the incidence of evidence. Afghanistan has seen capital flight, which has long perplexed policymakers and planners, and concerns have been expressed about the 'paradoxical' nature of capital outflows (capital), which jeopardises national welfare. A craving for foreign exchange due to portfolio reasons, excessive taxation, the expectation of a significant exchange rate realignment, macroeconomic (large fiscal deficit and current account deficit), political instability and other external pull factors are the driving forces behind capital flight from a country. The illegal outflow of money is often supported by remittances routed via the Hawala (correspondence) system, under-invoicing of exports, over-invoicing of imports and capital transfer through smuggled precious metals, antiquities and other items. This study aims to investigate the nature and prevalence of reverse capital flight in Afghanistan. The results state four critical reasons for reverse capital. It aids in whitening black money (money laundering), which was previously unlawfully flown out of the nation; secondly, it allows import tax evasion and the realisation of unnecessary export rebates and refunds; thirdly, it facilitates the avoidance of non-tariff measures (NTMs) on imports; and lastly, it provides for the concealment of investment in the underground economy. The analysis recommends maintaining a detailed record of illegal cash flows in Afghanistan since the nature of trade in Afghanistan is arduous due to the simultaneous flow of illicit capital. Adjusting unrecorded private capital flows (from short-term capital movements or payment flows that do not show up immediately in recorded statistics) with illicit flows of capital arising from trade mis-invoicing becomes crucial.

Chapter 7 depicts the debate on trade creation vs trade diversion and general equilibrium effects in Afghanistan's regional and bilateral free trade agreements. This article emphasises welfare as a severe concern produced by free-trade zones and corresponding preferential tariff reductions as economies increasingly participate in regional and bilateral free-trade agreements. The impact of regional and bilateral free-trade agreements on Afghan imports is ascertained. As such, the technique isolates the effects of tariff changes due to free-trade agreements from the general equilibrium effects due to unobserved factors impacting the country's imports (historical ties, common language and culture, landlocked). This method evaluates whether preferential tariff reductions favouring partner countries would benefit or harm member countries. The findings show that the impact of trade creation is much more significant in scale than the impact of trade diversion. Surprisingly, trade creation produced by general equilibrium effects outperforms trade creation caused by tariff preferences offered to member countries. Afghanistan's free trade agreements are not harmful but enhance living conditions. The report recognises South Asian Free Trade Area (SAFTA's) trade growth potential. Of course, SAFTA requires members to demonstrate a solid commitment to regional integration and increased liberalisation via a more readily improved tariff structure and procedures, a trade facilitation system and simplified financial services. The findings are significant since WTO members are often wary of

Regional Trade Agreements (RTAs) or Bilateral Free Trade Agreements (BFTAs) because trade diversification harms welfare. However, trade diversion is only sometimes damaging since the consumer advantage from trade outweighs the trade losses implied by moving imports to the higher cost partner country. Consumption advantages accrue in trade because consumers may now consume imports at a lower price, closer to the true (distortion-free) global price determined by the least-cost non-member countries.

In contrast, simple average tariff imposition bilaterally harms the trade volume of the reporting country. Statistically, a 1% tariff rate change will decrease by 0.3% in Afghanistan's total trade. Moreover, a 1% increase in the GDP of the partner countries will increase Afghanistan's total trade by 0.5%. Furthermore, common language, landlocked and distance significantly impact Afghanistan's total trade. The results suggest that Afghanistan needs to explore the ways and means to improve its trade relations with the countries further and improve its market share. The study proposed that Afghanistan should use trade as an economic development tool to flourish in the region and capture the markets to realise its maximum trade potential. This research recommends that South Asian and EU countries revise the tariff rates and other non-tariff barriers to boost trade and connectivity for a better trade future.

Chapter 8 offers a conducive understanding of the impact of NTMs on trade within the SAARC region, primarily targeting Afghanistan. The benefits of global trade are attributed principally to reducing trade distortions between trading partners. The anticipated promise of a progressive diminution in tariffs throughout the globe was, regrettably, steadily superseded by NTMs. However, the impact of these NTMs is only sometimes evident since it occurs in various disguises. NTMs significantly influence trade in the SAARC, mandating prompt attention. The question is how much internal trade will expand if NTMs are repealed. Based on statistics from 2015 to 2020, the study endeavours to quantify the impact of NTMs on Afghanistan's trade volume within the SAARC region, primarily targeting four export destinations (Bangladesh, India, Pakistan and Sri Lanka). Using trade freedom scores as a proxy for trade distortions, it has been determined that Afghanistan's magnitude of export earnings is significantly lower due to NTMs imposed by its importing trading partners. According to the findings, a 1% rise in tariffs and NTMs applied by importing countries diminishes Afghanistan's exports by 1.23%. In contrast, the impact of tariffs alone lowers Afghanistan's exports by 1.13%. The incidence of NTMs also devoid actual Afghanistan exports by US$ 5.70 million, equal to a 0.029% loss of Afghanistan's GDP. The calculations also reveal that lowering or eliminating non-tariff barriers has diverse trade-growth effects in different trade groupings. The study recommends a serious NTM-oriented trade policy dialogue that is liberal and guarantees regional integration, thereby promoting and ensuring the future of Afghanistan's economic laurels and stability.

Hence, this book delivers an extensive and eclectic compilation of articles aimed at designing policies to reinvigorate exports from Afghanistan thoughtfully. The book encompasses insights based on current advances in international trade theory. The book argues to focus on the issues and challenges highlighted in the book. Afghanistan must establish a competitive edge in sectors to increase the capacity for the production of export-oriented sectors by tapping into their innate capabilities. Trade policy changes that are implemented effectively will promote an export growth drive based on advantageous foundations.

The chapters in this book complement to incentivise restoring exports to traditional markets where exporters have become prevalent and established. There is a need to ramify medium-term measures to improve competitiveness and explore new vibrant markets. The involvement in long-term mega connectivity projects, integration of trade policies and domestic adjustment measures with international standards and penetration in international and regional markets by evolving into a member of regional and international trade organisations is highly recommended and appreciated. Implementing governance changes to combat systemic corruption in the nation, which severely undermines legitimate trade activity, may also aid in achieving trade policy objectives.

Part II

# Nexus Between Trade and Development

Chapter 1

# Afghanistan's Regional Integration With Central Asia: Identifying Trade Linkages, Economic Recital and Future Latency

## Abstract

Using different trade indices spanning 2018–2021, this chapter investigates Afghanistan's current patterns, prospects and barriers for intra- and inter-regional trade perspectives, emphasising the different pathways by which Afghanistan trades with Central Asian economies. The empirical findings demonstrate that the anticipated significance of trade between Afghanistan and Central Asia is double compared to the existing levels of trade. Furthermore, the analysis encompasses the categorisation of sectors based on the intensity of usage of production factors like resource, labour and technology. The analysis further elaborates on Afghanistan's trade potential with Central Asia and vice versa by highlighting the comparative advantage, diversification, complementarity and similarity in trade. The findings suggest that larger economies are rated higher than smaller ones as size and development level are essential factors in regional trade development. The most effective channels of regional trade development are price competitiveness measures, intra-industry trade and trade complementarities. These findings have a substantial influence on the development of different trade policy efforts to stimulate investment and trade within and among the two regions.

*Keywords*: Afghanistan; Central Asia; latency; recital; performance

*JEL Codes*: F01; F12; F14

## 1. Introduction

Historically, the Central Asia Region (CAR) and South Asia (SA) have long trade relations. Movements of goods and people have almost always occurred between the regions, strengthening cultural and religious ties and influencing

Policy Solutions for Economic Growth in a Developing Country, 13–39
Copyright © 2024 Nassir Ul Haq Wani
Published under exclusive licence by Emerald Publishing Limited
doi:10.1108/978-1-83753-430-220241002

economic relations (Andaya & Andaya, 2015). CAR and Afghanistan trade, investment and economic cooperation are critical to economic growth for the region. CAR is a resource-rich region that faces numerous development challenges. Natural resources, a skilled labour force, a diverse population and a strategic location close to China provide a solid foundation for the region's economies to grow (Abdih & Medina, 2013). In contrast, Afghanistan is land-locked and has a small market and population, poor infrastructure and political instability and insecurity that pose risks to human development – the dynamic interaction between the various variables influencing growth and threats (Abuseitova, 2007; Mogilevskii, 2012). Consistent observation and detailed, evidence-based analysis of the region's most crucial development determinants are required to understand these dynamics.

The trade between countries remains limited even within regions (Rahman, 2022). The cross-trade between CAR and SA equates to less than 5.5% and 1.7% of overall trade, respectively. Afghanistan's trade relations with its northern neighbours are becoming increasingly important, with the potential to grow significantly (Starr, 2005). Afghanistan and the Central Asian Republics are landlocked countries that depend on land and air connectivity to access global and regional markets (Akbari, 2021; Ali & Mujahid, 2015). Although there is enormous potential for greater investment and trade, both regions are among the least economically linked globally, with less than 1% of overall trade involving Central Asian nations and Afghanistan (ADB, 2006; Ando, 2006).

In this context, the study investigates Afghanistan's current trends and trade potential with Central Asian countries and examines intra- and inter-regional trade through trade competitiveness and complementarities. The research, in particular, evaluates present and projected trade pathways at the product layer quantitatively. Against this backdrop, this study explains the concept underlying increasing international trade fragmentation and why applying it to Afghanistan and the CARs could significantly escalate intra- and inter-trade. Furthermore, the study examines regional trade at the product level to identify prospects associated with comparative and competitive trade differences and assess whether these distinctions might result in regional production fragmentation. The analysis begins by determining the extent to which regions have geographical and product diversification and ascertaining how focused their exports are towards competitive or sluggish geographic markets. It then evaluates trade compliance in trade-promoting sectors (both intra and inter), as well as the quantity of trade between industries linked to differentiated products and their access to international and regional markets.

## 2. Regional Trade Patterns: Analysing Intra- and Inter-Trade

Afghanistan's size in comparison to Central Asian countries varies greatly. Afghanistan is in the middle, with the same population as Uzbekistan but half the economy. Afghanistan is the least developed country (as classified by the UN) in both regions, trailing only Tajikistan and Kyrgyzstan. Kazakhstan, on the other hand, has 16 times the per capita GDP of Afghanistan. The growth stories are mixed as specified from the evidence of Central and SA economies, Kazakhstan and Turkmenistan have experienced substantially greater growth rates than the lowest-income countries (Batsaikhan & Dabrowski, 2017). The remaining six countries are coming together. Except for Kazakhstan and Turkmenistan, Afghanistan and Tajikistan have feeble per capita incomes, surpassing others in the two regions' growth rates (Kawai & Wignaraja, 2014).

Similarly, Kyrgyzstan's economy has expanded faster than Afghanistan's. As a result, as predicted by neoclassical growth theory, per capita GNP and economic growth have an inverse relationship – however, size matters. Turkmenistan, Kyrgyzstan and Tajikistan, for example, are primarily classified as raw material input sources as well as processing centres for component industries and other industrial processes (Hausmann et al., 2007); however, the dynamism in these markets is least appealing compared to larger economies in the region. Land-lockedness further adds to the misery as these countries face higher trading costs (Hiebert & Lamberg-Karlovsky, 2003). However, some countries are double-landlocked and encounter additional challenges in accessing sea freight services for trade expansion. Trade expansion has long been recognised as reducing global inequality by bringing closer per capita incomes. Generally, trade encourages economic growth by increasing accessibility to goods, services, information and technological advances. According to the World Trade Organisation (WTO), this growth is attributed to higher private sector entrepreneurial activity, capital investments (private and foreign), job creation, lower price distortions, growth of competitive businesses and reinvesting foreign exchange gains.

As a result, greater trade openness guarantees the significant contribution of these factors to growth. It provides a fantastic opportunity for less developed economies to trade with developed economies. CAR is three times more open than Afghanistan with Kyrgyzstan as the most open economy (Three times more open than Afghanistan). In terms of openness, Central Europe (123%) tops the list followed by Central Asia (74%), Baltics (86%) and SA (37%) (Laruelle, 2015).

Regardless, SA has evolved over time and grown more inclusive (Lord, 2015), while CAR continues to remain merely steady; yet, the overall tendency obscures regional distinctions (Zekria & Wani, 2019). Central Asia's openness has increased significantly in Kyrgyzstan and Kazakhstan while decreasing in others. Tajikistan and Turkmenistan are now more open than they once were. The relatively small openness of the Uzbek economy has been gradually increasing. It has, however, fallen precipitously since the global recession of 2007/08, and it is now back to pre-recession levels. Diverging trends have emerged among SA countries as well.

Afghanistan is now half the size it was in the early 2000s. In general, a country's level of development has nothing to do with its openness. However, it is related to economic growth. Central Asia has an average trade openness of 74%, while Afghanistan has a trade openness of 24.49% (Ramay & Abbas, 2013). A large body of empirical literature investigates the relationship, with frequently contradictory results due to measurement and methodology issues. The available evidence, on the other hand, generally supports the positive relationship between openness and economic growth. Studies focusing on SA countries support this conclusion, demonstrating that openness significantly influences regional economic growth (Arif et al., 2022; Rahman et al., 2020; Wani, 2019). Recent evidence indicates that the mass trade performance in Kazakhstan and Kyrgyzstan is explained by bilateral networking goals (Lord, 2015). Trade performance in Tajikistan, Turkmenistan and Uzbekistan, on the other hand, is well understood via specific national features like stringent economic policies and fiscal emoluments (Mazhikeyev et al., 2015).

## 2.1 Intra-Regional Trade

The literature suggests that regional trade is frequently cited as an instrument to mitigate disparities in income within countries on overall trade development strategy as evidenced by the Association of South-East Asian Nations (ASEAN) economies. ASEAN has benefitted from significant trade openness, liberalisation and regional integration, allowing lower income nations to escalate economic growth at rates greater than the region's developed ones.

CAR and Afghanistan have significantly lower intra-regional trade than ASEAN and other adjoining countries. The average intra-trade within the CAR is 4.7%, with Afghanistan accounting for 86% of the overall trade in SA (Fjaestad & Overland, 2013). However, SA's regional trade disparity is less pronounced than Central Asia's (Mogilevskii, 2012). Central and South Asian intra-regional trade appears last among other regions, with the EU at the top. For example, the EU's intra-regional trade share (IRTS) is 18 times that of the two regions combined (Chaturvedi et al., 2015).

The IRTS of SA has grown over time. Between 1995 and 2021, it increased from 0.5% to 2.6%. This modest gain is primarily due to India's experience as the region's trade dominator. Afghanistan's IRTS increased from 11.2% in 2008 to 37.2% in 2021. Intra-regional trade in Central Asia plummeted between the middle of the 1990s and the beginning of the 2000s. This was the time when the CAR region switched from trade dependency with Russia to intra-regional (1991–1996) after independence and then onto global blending (1997–2005).

CAR reduced IRTSs and implemented faster transitional reforms as highlighted in Kazakhstan and Kyrgyzstan. These two economies were quite reactive compared to Tajikistan, Turkmenistan and Uzbekistan and thus experienced a fall in intra-regional trade (Mustafa, 2014). The intra-regional patterns in the mid-2000s for Kazakhstan, Turkmenistan and Uzbekistan were reversed. In contrast, Kyrgyzstan and Tajikistan's intra-regional shares have gradually increased. The 2007 global financial crisis had a larger impact on these two countries, shifting their priority to trade with neighbours (Batsaikhan & Dabrowski, 2017; Burns, 2014).

## 2.2 Inter-Regional Trade (IRT)

The current trading pace between the CAR and South Asian Association for Regional Cooperation (SAARC) is modest, accounting for about 0.2% of overall trade. A significant dispersion is noticeable in the specific country's IRT shares in CAR and Afghanistan. The tendency is either more or less than the average. Afghanistan has a 10% IRT share, compared to a 1.4% average. Tajikistan (3.2%) and Turkmenistan (1.9%) have above-average IRT shares. Uzbekistan (0.1%) has the lowest IRT shares (0.2%). However, there are calculation discrepancies, as inter-regional unweighted mean average trade is 3.7% greater instead of 1.4%. This discrepancy emerges as a result of considerable differences in reported trade across trading partners. Afghanistan's overall trade with Kazakhstan and vice versa in 2020 was US$1.54 million and $622.2 million (IMF, 2021). However, there was a 10% variation from the reported trade values by Afghanistan. Consequently, Central Asian nations' IRT shares primarily fluctuate substantially.

Afghanistan's proportion of CAR trade, on the other hand, has changed significantly, increasing in the 1990s, declining in the early 2000s, increasing significantly in the later part of the 2000s and steady and stable following 2010. Afghanistan's proportion of CAR trade, on the other hand, has changed significantly, increasing in the 1990s, declining in the early 2000s, increasing significantly in the later part of the 2000s and remaining fairly stable following 2010. This trend continued till 2019 and is anticipated to continue and persist. Several tendencies have emerged for CAR. Kazakhstan and Tajikistan have increased their IRT shares, while the rest have remained flat or slightly declined (Cochrane & O'Regan, 2016; Kang & Liu, 2020).

## 3. Research Methodology

The key indices employed in this study are depicted as follows:

### 3.1 Intra-Regional Trade Share (IRTS)

*The* IRTS is the percentage of intra-regional trade to total trade in the region calculated using total trade data. It is determined as the ratio of intra-regional trade to total regional trade.

$$\text{IRTS} = T_{ij} / T_i$$

where $T_{ii}$ represents the region $i$'s exports and imports to/from the partner region $j$, and $T_i$ represents the region $i$'s total exports and imports to/from the world.

### 3.2 Intra-Regional Trade Intensity Index (IARTII)

It is the proportion of intra-regional trade to total global trade. Based on the region's role in global trade reveals whether regional trade is more or lower than projected. Given the area's importance in international commerce, an index greater than one suggests that regional trade flows are more than expected.

$$IARTII = (T_{iiii}/T_{ii})/(T_{ii}/T_{ww})$$

where $T_{ii}$ represents the region $i$'s exports to region $i$ plus the region $i$'s imports from region $i$, $T_i$ represents the region $i$'s total exports to the world plus the region $i$'s total imports from the world and $T_w$ represents total trade.

### 3.3 Inter-Regional Trade Intensity Index (IERTII)

It is the proportion of the nation's overall trade involving a partner nation to its global trade with the exact same partner nation. A value larger than one implies that global trade volumes are significantly greater than predicted, regardless of their significance in global trade.

$$IERTII = (T_{iiii}/)/(T_{wwii}/T_{wwww})$$

where $T_{ij}$ represents '$i$' country's/region's total trade with country/region '$j$', $T_{iw}$ represents the dollar value of the country's total global trade, $T_{wj}$ presents the country's regional trade with $j$ (region) and $T_{ww}$ is the global trade (dollar value).

### 3.4 Export Diversification (ED)

It reflects trade development illustrating a country's capacity to produce diverse goods (Varela, 2013). In general, advanced economies' production structures are highly diverse, whereas developing economies are mono-exporters. This index displays each country's top 10 items exported to the world and Central Asian and Afghan markets (combined).

### 3.5 Herfindahl-Hirschman Product Concentration Index (HHI)

The HHI index helps us to assess a country's export product concentration or diversification.

$$HHI = \frac{\sum_{K=1}^{nj}\left(\frac{x_{ik}}{X_i}\right) - \frac{1}{n_i}}{\frac{1}{n_i}}$$

where $X$ represents the overall export value of country I, $x$ represents the value of the exports item $k$ by country I and $n$ indicates the number of items provided by nation $i$. A higher index (near 1) indicates more concentration in fewer industries, while an index nearing 0 indicates that a country's portfolio is completely diverse.

## 3.6 Export Survival Rates

This index evaluates and summarises the survival rate of new product-market linkages valued at least $10,000 in Central Asia and Afghanistan over successive years.

$$\text{EDit} = \frac{n_{ijt}}{n_{ijt} \text{ start}}$$

where $n$ is the total volume of items delivered by nation I to partner country $j$ in year $t$ and start is the year chosen.

## 3.7 Export Sophistication (ES)

Sophistication encompasses beyond just technological features; it also covers differentiated products, manufacturing disintegration, availability of resources and other elements. It does, however, provide unique continuous ratings for each item at any degree of detail. We provide sophistication ratings for chosen nations, technological groupings and sectors' exports. Thus, this index categorises all CAR and Afghanistan products into five categories and is defined as follows:

$$\text{ESI} = 100 * \sum k \in \Omega \text{tec} \frac{x_{ijk}}{X_{ij}} \ \forall \text{ for all } \Omega \text{tec}[\text{HT}, \text{MT}, \text{LT}, \text{PP}, \text{RB}]$$

Here, $x$ represents the value in dollars of the commodity $k$ from partner $i$ to partner $j$, and $X$ represents the aggregate value of all $i$ to $j$ exports. Based on the nature of the commodities, $\Omega$tec refers to all mutually exclusive items that could be high, medium or low tech, primary or resource-based items.

## 3.8 Revealed Comparative Advantage (RCA)

As used by other scholars (Mogilevskii, 2012; Sadiqi & Wani, 2018; Wani & Dhami, 2014), RCA is defined as follows:

$$\text{RCA} = \frac{\frac{x_i}{\sum_{i} x_i}}{\frac{x_{iw}}{\sum_{i} x_{iw}}}$$

where $x_i$ denotes the nation's exports of products $i$, and $X_{iw}$ denotes the total exportation of product $i$.

## 3.9 Trade Complementarity Index (TCI)

The TCI formally defines how a country's exports align with its trading partners' imports.

$$\text{TCI} = 100 * \left[ 1 - \sum_k \frac{\left| \frac{m_{jk}}{M_k} - \frac{x_{ik}}{X_i} \right|}{2} \right]$$

Here, $X$ denotes the value of commodity $k$ exports from reporting nation $i$, and $X$ represents the country's overall exports. Imports ($m$) signify the value of the partner nation $j$'s imports of product $k$, and $M$ denotes the overall value of its imports. An index value of 100 shows exported items as consistent with trading countries, while an index value close to 0 suggests the reverse.

# 4. Analysis, Findings and Discussion

The indicators of regional trade expansion opportunities of Afghanistan with Central Asia and vice versa are explained in light of ED, product concentration, comparative advantages, trade complementarity and country similarity and two-way trade.

## 4.1 Export Diversification (ED)

Table 1 shows the significant exports of Central Asia and Afghanistan. The commodities are all displayed at the 6-digit Harmonised System (HS) level, representing the annual average US dollar value of exports from 2018 to 2021. Observations regarding export to all destinations indicate products aimed for intra- and inter-regional trade, which is needed in market regions in the near future. Furthermore, Table 1 also depicts the most significant exports to the Central and Afghanistan marketplaces, and the subsequent findings about product trade patterns are notable.

Afghanistan's exports (top 5) are primarily aimed at Central Asian markets, and edible fruits and vegetables comprise half of the country's top 10 exports. Cotton, iron scrap, coal, gums and resin are all important industrial or agricultural raw materials. Vegetables and fruit, on the other hand, are practically exported to every nation in the CAR. Mineral-based fuels and other items are Central Asia's most important regional exportable. Tajikistan, Turkmenistan and Uzbekistan are significant regional exporters of petroleum and bituminous mineral oils (not crude). Crude petroleum, on the other hand, is Kazakhstan's most important regional and global export. The main export of Kyrgyzstan is electricity.

## 4.2 Product Concentration

### 4.2.1 Regional Products Traded at Intra- and Inter-Level

Central Asia's trade with Afghanistan is more diverse than its IRT. From 2018 to 2021, the number of product exports worth more than $10,000 in each region is presented in Table 2. On average, Afghanistan's trading capacity is more severe than Central Asian countries accounting for 2.5 times, whereas the inter-Central Asian trade is almost four times with each other. However, significant variations in trade patterns exist between countries. Afghanistan exports are oriented towards SA countries like Pakistan and India compared to Central Asian countries. Afghanistan exports are almost twice as much to Kazakhstan; however, the

Table 1. Top 10 Global and Regional Exports of Central Asian Countries and Afghanistan, 2018–2021 (Average).

### AFG

| Top 10 Exports Globally | | Top 10 Inter-Regional Exports | |
|---|---|---|---|
| HS Code | AVG 2018–2021 | HS Code | AVG 2018–2021 |
| 520100 | 7,19,72,532 | 520100 | 7,14,14,941 |
| 720449 | 4,53,16,969 | 720449 | 4,53,16,969 |
| 999999 | 4,47,34,118 | 80420 | 3,99,87,808 |
| 80420 | 4,00,43,780 | 270119 | 3,80,36,531 |
| 80620 | 3,82,82,764 | 130190 | 3,53,20,878 |
| 270119 | 3,80,37,566 | 80620 | 1,56,80,502 |
| 130190 | 3,54,16,664 | 80610 | 1,26,04,132 |
| 80250 | 1,53,39,074 | 70310 | 1,25,62,491 |
| 430130 | 1,31,03,149 | 252610 | 96,42,132 |
| 840734 | 1,27,89,418 | 80250 | 86,03,925 |

### KZN

| Top 10 Exports Globally | | Top 10 Inter-Regional Exports | |
|---|---|---|---|
| HS Code | AVG 2018–2021 | HS Code | AVG 2018–2021 |
| 270900 | 68,34,38,70,432 | 270900 | 2,70,900 |
| 270119 | 27,03,78,00,667 | 110100 | 1,10,100 |
| 271121 | 15,02,89,56,692 | 100190 | 1,00,190 |
| 260111 | 8,92,33,17,062 | 271000 | 2,71,000 |
| 260112 | 8,56,19,49,798 | 271112 | 2,71,112 |
| 100190 | 4,93,69,50,103 | 260800 | 2,60,800 |
| 271000 | 4,86,39,91,378 | 252400 | 2,52,400 |
| 250310 | 4,01,64,33,314 | 730511 | 7,30,511 |
| 760110 | 2,67,51,93,648 | 720449 | 7,20,449 |
| 110100 | 2,07,55,23,542 | 270119 | 2,70,119 |

### KYN

| Top 10 Exports Globally | | Top 10 Inter-Regional Exports | |
|---|---|---|---|
| HS Code | AVG 2018–2021 | HS Code | AVG 2018–2021 |
| 710812 | 68,34,38,70,432 | 271600 | 5,13,81,421 |
| 271000 | 27,03,78,00,667 | 870423 | 2,77,26,342 |
| 999999 | 15,02,89,56,692 | 271000 | 2,57,87,215 |
| 71333 | 8,92,33,17,062 | 261690 | 1,24,36,246 |
| 271600 | 8,56,19,49,798 | 40120 | 1,20,64,182 |
| 870423 | 4,93,69,50,103 | 70190 | 1,18,05,057 |

### TKN

| Top 10 Exports Globally | | Top 10 Inter-Regional Exports | |
|---|---|---|---|
| HS Code | AVG 2018–2021 | HS Code | AVG 2018–2021 |
| 760110 | 46,15,71,520 | 271000 | 2,13,02,658 |
| 520100 | 12,57,60,787 | 760110 | 1,47,93,711 |
| 999999 | 5,39,68,010 | 81310 | 97,59,264 |
| 760120 | 4,91,54,341 | 260800 | 90,46,206 |
| 260700 | 3,55,98,220 | 260700 | 82,91,932 |
| 70310 | 2,37,41,956 | 520100 | 78,45,632 |

Table 1. (*Continued*)

|  | AFG | | | | KZN | | |
|---|---|---|---|---|---|---|---|
|  | Top 10 Exports Globally | | Top 10 Inter-Regional Exports | | Top 10 Exports Globally | | Top 10 Inter-Regional Exports | |
| | HS Code | AVG 2018–2021 | HS Code | AVG 2018–2021 | HS Code | AVG 2018–2021 | HS Code | AVG 2018–2021 |
| | **520100** | 4,86,39,91,378 | 700529 | 99,98,425 | **261710** | 2,34,65,954 | 81350 | 76,79,121 |
| | **261690** | 4,01,64,33,314 | 401199 | 97,98,884 | **81310** | 2,32,16,715 | 70310 | 66,79,041 |
| | **620640** | 2,67,51,93,648 | 80810 | 94,92,343 | **271000** | 2,13,02,658 | 110100 | 55,66,643 |
| | **620443** | 2,07,55,23,542 | 252329 | 91,32,212 | **81350** | 1,84,38,645 | 640320 | 22,99,771 |

|  | TMN | | | | UZB | | |
|---|---|---|---|---|---|---|---|
|  | Top 10 Exports Globally | | Top 10 Inter-Regional Exports | | Top 10 Exports Globally | | Top 10 Inter-Regional Exports | |
| | HS Code | AVG 2018–2021 | HS Code | AVG 2018–2021 | HS Code | AVG 2018–2021 | HS Code | AVG 2018–2021 |
| | **271121** | 6,01,56,56,543 | 271000 | 19,94,81,306 | **520100** | 85,69,54,012 | 271000 | 47,57,04,738 |
| | **271000** | 1,04,37,65,221 | 271121 | 17,40,93,615 | **271121** | 61,99,83,059 | 271121 | 24,58,63,083 |
| | **710813** | 26,30,17,586 | 520100 | 2,29,80,088 | **271000** | 48,01,35,201 | 870322 | 4,76,64,267 |
| | **520100** | 21,92,32,504 | 280120 | 75,68,809 | **740311** | 47,57,04,738 | 310230 | 4,57,27,566 |
| | **520512** | 13,98,18,958 | 390210 | 27,31,398 | **284410** | 41,99,51,836 | 80610 | 4,34,92,204 |
| | **390210** | 10,38,26,206 | 520819 | 15,16,870 | **870322** | 29,55,57,693 | 81090 | 2,86,86,238 |
| | **520812** | 3,53,71,333 | 870590 | 13,93,345 | **870321** | 20,15,92,243 | 252329 | 2,36,89,772 |
| | **999999** | 2,21,02,704 | 410210 | 10,60,965 | **710812** | 17,10,40,538 | 71331 | 2,13,04,359 |
| | **520942** | 2,08,74,783 | 70200 | 9,63,028 | **520512** | 15,88,36,714 | 70200 | 1,90,19,960 |
| | **270900** | 10,79,81,745 | 180690 | 8,65,187 | **870323** | 13,85,66,425 | 70700 | 1,55,24,792 |

*Source:* Authors' preparation based on the statistics retrieved from the UN's COMTRADE.

*Note: AFG* is Afghanistan, *KZN* is Kazakhstan, *KYN* is Kyrgyzstan, *TKN* is Tajikistan, *TMN* is Turkmenistan and *UZB* is Uzbekistan.

Table 2. Average Volume of Product Exports Valued at More Than $10,000 to Each Trading Partner, 2018–2021.

| | Import | | | | | |
|---|---|---|---|---|---|---|
| **Exporter** | **AFN** | **KZN** | **KYN** | **TKN** | **TMN** | **UZB** |
| AFN | | 17 | 32 | 3 | 4 | 1 |
| KZN | 231 | | 477 | 409 | 398 | 503 |
| KYN | 66 | 441 | | 219 | 41 | 349 |
| TKN | 28 | 98 | 66 | | 0 | 0 |
| TMN | 15 | 45 | 7 | 0 | | 0 |
| UZB | 30 | 538 | 221 | 0 | 0 | |

*Source:* Authors' preparation based on the statistics retrieved from the UN's COMTRADE.

trade escalation is less skewed with Tajikistan, Turkmenistan, Kyrgyzstan and Uzbekistan. Kazakhstan and Kyrgyzstan trade considerably more products in Central Asia than the rest of the region combined. Tajikistan, Turkmenistan and Uzbekistan export the most goods to Kazakhstan and Kyrgyzstan.

### 4.2.2 Herfindahl-Hirschman (HH) Product Concentration Index

The HH product concentration index is a sophisticated indicator of export concentration that determines how much a country's earnings from exports are centred on a few products or broadened across several goods. The extent of export concentration or diversification in Central and SA is assessed through each country's exports to every destination, intra-regional markets and inter-regional markets. Generally, a country's product concentration level demonstrates its susceptibility to trade fluctuations.

Table 3 demonstrates how Central Asian and Afghan exports are diverse or centred on a few products. Kazakhstan and Kyrgyzstan have the most varied exports, whereas Turkmenistan, Tajikistan and Afghanistan export a limited pool of commodities. The export latency of Uzbekistan is close to the region's average. The trading experiences could be more stable. For example, Afghanistan's export flows to Turkmenistan and Tajikistan are strongly centred on certain commodities but those to Kyrgyzstan are more varied. Central Asian countries' product exports to one another are reasonably various, but their exports to Afghanistan are concentrated in fewer products.

### 4.2.3 Export Survival Rates (ESR)

Due to transaction-level export data availability, ESR analysis is a unique and quickly evolving trade research domain. In the case of CAR–Afghanistan trade, despite a few products' dominance in total export earnings, regional trade

Table 3. Average HHI to Each Trading Partner, 2018–2021.

| Exporter | AFN | KZN | KYN | TKN | TMN | UZB | World |
|---|---|---|---|---|---|---|---|
| AFN | | 0.29 | 0.1 | 0.54 | 0.97 | None | 0.04 |
| KZN | 0.23 | | 0.05 | 0.15 | 0.03 | 0.12 | 0.41 |
| KYN | 0.42 | 0.04 | | 0.1 | 0.12 | 0.04 | 0.19 |
| TKN | 0.47 | 0.1 | 0.08 | | None | None | 0.22 |
| TMN | 0.7 | 0.84 | 0.21 | None | | None | 0.54 |
| UZB | 0.57 | 0.07 | 0.14 | None | None | | 0.05 |
| World | 0.03 | 0.01 | 0.04 | 0.01 | 0.01 | 0.01 | |

*Source:* Authors' preparation based on the statistics retrieved from the UN's COMTRADE.

includes a slightly diverse range of products. The broad spectrum of exported products shows that additional diversification is possible if innovative entries are able to gain access to the market. On the other hand, survival beyond the first years of entry into regional and global export markets is required for successful entry. However, the literature from the developing world signifies short-term success for new exports and elevated 'death' rates in developing countries. These new export spells are typically brief, lasting 2–3 years on average. Empirical evidence suggests that the number of firms exporting the same product to the same destinations within the same nation boosts the possibility of survival success. The findings suggest the existence of cross-firm externalities and information spillovers. According to the observation, a country's export performance frequently occurs as 'big hits', with one narrow export item unexpectedly proliferating. Our research results indicate that when several exporters concentrate on the same market simultaneously, their likelihood of success increases, potentially triggering a process of entry, survival and growth. Bridging and supporting such efforts may result in insignificant results if enough commodities and markets survive. Data on survival rates can aid in identifying solid and policy-driven determinants of export growth, specifically those associated with export sustainability. Fig. 1 summarises the findings for CAR and Afghanistan.

Fig. 1 depicts some stylised facts about survival rates. After introducing new export products, Kazakhstan has a 4-year survival rate greater than 50%. Survival rates in Kyrgyzstan, Uzbekistan and Tajikistan range from 30–40%. After 4 years of creating new export goods, Turkmenistan and Afghanistan had 22% and 17% survival rates, respectively. Economic shocks or new policy regulations, laws and procedures can be attributed to the widespread collapse of trade ties. To increase trade's long-term viability, it is necessary to strengthen current knowledge of

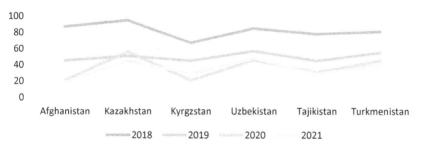

Fig. 1.    Rates of Survival in Central Asia and Afghanistan
(2018–2021). *Source:* Data output based on (WITS) trade outcomes. *Note:* These projections are centred on trade between countries at 6-digit HS-level products valued at least $10,000 at the start of 2018, as well as the number and percentage of the ones that endure every single year through the year's end (2021).

export items and domains, accelerate connections with trading nations and capitalise on neighbouring countries as release platforms for developing exports.

### 4.3 Comparative Advantages

#### 4.3.1 Product Sophistication

The distribution of exports based on technical ability demonstrates information about the country's development and its position in the global manufacturing chains. Specialisation in certain goods may result in enormous latency for both backward and forward interactions along the value chain and a likelihood to enhance networks through technological ripple effects. For gauging the intra- and inter-regional trade opportunities, the commodities are identified based on their nature and classified into five mutually exclusive categories based on technology (high-, medium- and low-tech) and products classified as primary or resource-based. Table 4 categorises all Central Asian and Afghan exports by the level of complexity. According to the statistics, primary or resource-intensive items account for more than 70–80% of total Afghan and CAR exports, excluding Uzbekistan and Turkmenistan. Over half of Uzbekistan's exports are techno-centric with the remainder being medium- and low-tech.

#### 4.3.2 Revealed Comparative Advantages

RCA is employed to investigate the country's export vitality and its concentration in commodities trade. It juxtaposes a nation's export capacity in a specific product to that of other nations. It is helpful for categorising a country's exports based on their factor intensity level (like human capital (skilled or unskilled), natural resource and technology-intensive). Furthermore, RCA analysis helps determine prospective cross-border production disintegration in regional value chain evaluation. The calculations are based on the data from 2018 to 2021 at the

Table 4. Classification of Central Asian and Afghanistan Exports Based on Degree of Sophistication (in per cent).

| Country | Primary Products | Resource-Based | Low-Tech | Medium-Tech | High-Tech |
|---|---|---|---|---|---|
| AFN | 82 | 10 | 5 | 2 | 2 |
| KZN | 84 | 11 | 3 | 3 | 1 |
| KYN | 72 | 17 | 10 | 9 | 3 |
| TKN | 78 | 15 | 5 | 1 | 1 |
| TMN | 23 | 67 | 13 | 0 | 0 |
| UZB | 44 | 13 | 15 | 23 | 1 |

*Source:* World Bank, 'World Integrated Trade Solution (WITS)'.

Table 5. RCA of CAR and Afghanistan.

| Section | AFN | KZN | KYN | TKN | TMN | UZB |
|---|---|---|---|---|---|---|
| I | 1 | 0.1 | 3.26 | 1.59 | 0.01 | 1.3 |
| II | 8.47 | 1.1 | 5.71 | 17.8 | 3.04 | 11.51 |
| III | 0.92 | 7.24 | 0.37 | 0.51 | 13.09 | 0.28 |
| IV | 0.25 | 0.23 | 1.68 | 0.66 | 7.2 | 1.05 |
| V | 6.75 | 2.16 | 7.28 | 12.45 | 1.78 | 4.2 |
| VI | 0.92 | 0.99 | 0.79 | 0.5 | 0.43 | 2.55 |
| VII | 0.44 | 0.05 | 0.42 | 0.37 | 0.12 | 0.25 |
| VIII | 13.96 | 0.11 | 7.16 | 3.14 | 0.44 | 2.98 |
| IX | 0.42 | 0.02 | 0.16 | 0.02 | 0 | 0.09 |
| X | 0.65 | 0.15 | 0.38 | 0.16 | 0.01 | 0.99 |
| XI | 7.92 | 0.13 | 2.96 | 5.4 | 2.68 | 7.07 |
| XII | 0.72 | 0.02 | 0.3 | 2.68 | 0.01 | 1.67 |
| XIII | 0.68 | 0.17 | 4.59 | 0.86 | 0.02 | 1.05 |
| XIV | 3.98 | 2.67 | 2.26 | 0.68 | 1.18 | 1.55 |
| XV | 0.93 | 2.38 | 0.85 | 2.3 | 0.02 | 1.85 |
| XVI | 0.92 | 0.05 | 0.59 | 0.18 | 0.05 | 0.23 |
| XVII | 1.27 | 0.18 | 1.17 | 0.14 | 0.11 | 1.05 |
| XVIII | 0.38 | 0.03 | 0.3 | 1.15 | 0.07 | 0.08 |
| XIX | 1.36 | na | na | 0.13 | na | 0.05 |
| XX | 0.21 | 0.01 | 0.45 | 0.28 | 0.01 | 1.17 |
| XXI | 4.35 | 0 | 0.24 | 0.48 | 0.07 | 0.22 |

*Source:* Authors' preparation based on the statistics retrieved from the UN's COMTRADE.

disaggregated HS 6-digit level and are summarised in Table 5. Table 6, on the other hand, categorises each country's comparative advantages into seven major domains.

In terms of RCA values, the primary agricultural products have the highest RCA values followed by textiles and footwear in the second place, minerals and mineral products in the third place and processed agricultural commodities in the fourth place. The highest RCA ratings are held by Afghanistan and Kyrgyzstan. Uzbekistan has a competitive leverage in the export of chemicals, plastics and rubber. Afghanistan has a comparative advantage in miscellaneous manufacturing, which has the sixth-highest average RCA. In terms of producing and exporting wood and wood products, neither of the countries possesses a comparative advantage. Based on traditional RCA analysis, the calculated values above provide a method for determining intra- and inter-regional opportunities. The technique follows standard practices and premises employed in earlier

Table 6. RCA Based on Broad Product Categories.

| AFG | Value | KYN | Value |
|---|---|---|---|
| (I to III, VIII) | 6.1 | (V, XIII–XIV) | 4.7 |
| (IV) | 4.3 | (I to III, VIII) | 4.2 |
| (V, XIII–XIV) | 3.8 | (IV) | 1.7 |
| (VI–VII) | 1.3 | (XI–XII) | 3.9 |
| (IX–X) | 0.7 | (VI–VII) | 0.7 |
| (XI–XII) | 0.3 | (XVI–XXI) | 0.6 |
| (XVI–XXI) | 0.2 | (IX–X) | 0.3 |
| **KZN** | | **TKN** | |
| (I to III, VIII) | 2.1 | (I to III, VIII) | 5.8 |
| (V, XIII–XIV) | 1.8 | (V, XIII–XIV) | 4.8 |
| (VI–VII) | 0.5 | (XI–XII) | 4.0 |
| (IV) | 0.3 | (IV) | 1.3 |
| (IX–X) | 0.2 | (VI–VII) | 0.7 |
| (XI–XII) | 0.1 | (XVI–XXI) | 0.5 |
| (XVI–XXI) | 0.1 | (IX–X) | 0.2 |
| **TMN** | | **UZB** | |
| (XI–XII) | 2.1 | (XI–XII) | 4.2 |
| (I to III, VIII) | 2.7 | (I to III, VIII) | 3.9 |
| (V, XIII–XIV) | 1.3 | (V, XIII–XIV) | 2.3 |
| (VI–VII) | 0.6 | (VI–VII) | 0.9 |
| (IV) | 0.3 | (IV) | 0.9 |
| (IX–X) | 0.2 | (IX–X) | 0.4 |
| (XVI–XXI) | 0.2 | (XVI–XXI) | 0.4 |

*Source:* Authors' preparation based on the statistics retrieved from the UN's COMTRADE.

research to determine trade opportunities. It is assumed that identical items are exchanged in and between CAR and Afghanistan under perfect competition, with no trade restrictions or other obstacles. The analysis contrasts product exports based on comparative advantage with respect to the level of imports from partner countries. Although the approach's assumptions are seldom right, they do indicate the possible direction of regional trade flows if they were widened. Only products that provide a country with a competitive edge over its trade partners are more likely to be exported. RCAs identify commodities or goods that have a greater probability to be shipped over borders considering comparative prices and non-price disparities depending on real trade with partner countries.

The regional trade possibilities for each CAR and Afghanistan are examined at the HS 6-digit level, and all product exports were found to have a comparative advantage in 2018–2021. Table 6 compares each nation's major exports with its foreign demand from other nations. The findings state that the overall inter- and intra-regional trade might have been 25% greater in 2018–2021, if trade had been conducted based on each country's RCA analysis in product exports. Actual and prospective trade differentials vary greatly among countries. Trade between nations (Turkmenistan) surpasses the value indicated by their stated comparative advantages across all exporting items. Turkmenistan would have contributed between 70% and 80% of the overall exports during 2018 and 2021.

In contrast, the potential exports predicted through RCAs for Kazakhstan and Afghanistan would have been significantly higher than the actual volume. The potential trade for Afghanistan and Kazakhstan would have been 74 times and 47 times greater compared to their actual trade. Afghanistan's significant missed opportunities were coal exports, ferrous scrap, logs, dry beans, semi-precious stones and fresh fruits and vegetables. In the case of Kyrgyzstan, crude oil, copper ores, liquid propane, and other liquefied fuels, unwrought silver casings, tubing and oil drilling pipes comprise the significant missed trade opportunities. The anticipated significance of regional trade for Kazakhstan, Tajikistan and Uzbekistan was less extensive than that of Afghanistan and Kazakhstan. The potential earnings are immense, with Tajikistan having potential four times, whereas Uzbekistan and Kazakhstan have 4.5 and 2.5 times greater potential than their actual exports. The top 40 products comprise all of a country's potential regional revenues. The top 40 products exported by Kazakhstan and Turkmenistan account for 90%–95% of their possible regional revenues, whereas in Afghanistan, Kyrgyzstan and Tajikistan, it accounts for more than 75% of total potential revenues.

## 4.4 Trade Complementarities

### 4.4.1 Complementarities in Global and Bilateral Trade

An alternative method for examining potential trade possibilities in an environment with greater volatility is to presuppose that nations have scant natural resources and visible technological deficiencies. In general, economies have become more concentrated as a result of the operations of global corporations, which consolidate economic activity in certain environments, enabling some countries to progress faster. It is now obvious that regional trading agreements may assist nations in achieving agglomeration. Agglomeration economies are strongly tied to efficiencies of production, network impacts of comparable enterprises collaborating to profit by accessibility to both downstream and upstream operations and the technical consequences of data transfers happening wherever industrial operations are grouped.

The latency of trade integration between a country's export structure and trade partners significantly measures its capacity to shift its comparative advantage, thus helping in gauging regional export prospects using the TCI. Following the

Table 7. Trade Complementarity of CAR and Afghanistan Exports (Bilateral).

| Exports | Imports | | | | | |
|---|---|---|---|---|---|---|
| | AFG | KZN | KYN | TJN | TKN | UZB |
| AFG | | 9 | 9 | 8 | 14 | 11 |
| KZN | 8 | | 12 | 13 | 5 | 13 |
| KYN | 22 | 18 | | 19 | 18 | 18 |
| TJN | 11 | 8 | 7 | | 11 | 11 |
| TKN | 14 | 8 | 16 | 11 | | 7 |
| UZB | 15 | 15 | 19 | 16 | 10 | |

*Source:* Authors' preparation based on the statistics retrieved from the UN's COMTRADE.

determination of product compatibility, performance indicators could be utilised to assess how each nation might compete successfully in those markets. Export success, measured by quickly evolving exports and rising market shares, demonstrates how economies can shift their competitive edge in the global marketplace.

The trade compatibility analysis for CAR and Afghanistan includes each country's exports. It demonstrates how an exporting country's export identity complements the trading partners' import identities. The compatibility index for trade between developed countries typically ranges between 50 and 60, while it hovers around 20 for trade between developing countries. The overall bilateral trade complementarity indices for CAR and Afghan exports are shown in Table 7.

In CAR, Kazakhstan has significant possibilities to expand its exports to Afghanistan. In contrast, Kyrgyzstan has an opportunity to broaden its trade with all of its trading partners. Turkmenistan has prospects for expanding its trade with Afghanistan, and Uzbekistan's exports are compatible with Kyrgyzstan's. In general, Afghanistan's export opportunities with Turkmenistan are limited. At the second level, each country's goods for export are classified based on four categories including large, medium, small and emerging exports. Since the CAR region and Afghanistan sizes differ significantly, the export values in monetary terms vary by country, as presented in Table 8.

As reflected in Table 8, the trade complementarity is diverse. The trade complementarity ranges from medium-to large-size exports in the case of Afghanistan, while Kazakhstan, Kyrgyzstan and Tajikistan enjoy benefits in small- and medium-sized exports, and Turkmenistan and Uzbekistan enjoy leverages in medium-sized exports. On a bilateral trade basis, complementarities are frequently significantly greater than the entire level of each country's export adherence to imports from the two regions. The bilateral trade between the two

Table 8. TCI of CAR and Afghanistan.

| | | AFG | KZN | KYN | TJN | TKN | UZB |
|---|---|---|---|---|---|---|---|
| | Large-size exports | | 26 | 19 | 19 | 13 | 20 |
| | Medium-size exports | | 28 | 29 | 20 | 5 | 23 |
| **AFN** | Small-size exports | | **44** | **53** | 26 | **44** | **35** |
| | Emerging exports | | 20 | 28 | 17 | 21 | 25 |
| | Large-size exports | 9 | | 11 | 23 | 8 | 34 |
| | Medium-size exports | **35** | | **35** | 30 | 17 | 31 |
| **KZN** | Small-size exports | 25 | | 29 | 26 | 22 | **37** |
| | Emerging exports | 25 | | 32 | 31 | **36** | **42** |
| | Large-size exports | 20 | 27 | | 21 | 26 | 23 |
| | Medium-size exports | 19 | **41** | | **38** | 32 | 20 |
| **KYN** | Small-size exports | **41** | **49** | | **54** | **45** | 29 |
| | Emerging exports | 26 | **62** | | **44** | **38** | **39** |
| | Large-size exports | 9 | 18 | 8 | | 11 | 17 |
| | Medium-size exports | 20 | 30 | 20 | | 23 | 16 |
| **TJN** | Small-size exports | **35** | **35** | 24 | | 31 | 27 |
| | Emerging exports | 37 | **43** | 34 | | 34 | 33 |
| | Large-size exports | 14 | 25 | 21 | 16 | | 17 |
| | Medium-size exports | 27 | 33 | 24 | 19 | | 27 |
| **TKN** | Small-size exports | 20 | 32 | 15 | 14 | | 12 |
| | Emerging exports | 8 | 31 | 29 | 28 | | **36** |
| | Large-size exports | 17 | **39** | 26 | 18 | 19 | |
| | Medium-size exports | 15 | **48** | **42** | 20 | 23 | |
| **UZB** | Small-size exports | 21 | **40** | 23 | 12 | 29 | |
| | Emerging exports | 20 | **46** | 25 | 30 | 13 | |

*Source:* Authors' preparation based on the statistics retrieved from the UN's COMTRADE.
*Note:* The highlighted bold numbers reflect the number of the highest occurrences of the commodity's trade within each country.

regions has a trade complementarity index greater than 35 and is thus impressive. While Afghanistan's overall export figures showed minimal trade compatibility with the CAR, its small-size exports to Kazakhstan, Kyrgyzstan and Turkmenistan provide fewer bilateral trade opportunities. Kyrgyzstan enjoys significant bilateral trade latency in the CAR, and the export orientation of Uzbekistan to Kazakhstan is also significant. Commodities including manufacturers, minerals, agro-foods and raw materials comprise the small and emerging trade basket from Kazakhstan, Kyrgyzstan and Tajikistan, whereas agricultural and mineral raw materials, fruits and vegetables are the medium-sized exports of Turkmenistan and Uzbekistan.

*4.4.2 Matching Top Regional Imports With Top Product Exports*

Another approach to evaluate possibilities for export is to look at whether countries export the products demanded by the countries. Table 9 depicts an arrangement of each country's top 1,000 imports and exports at 6-digit HS-classified products. In the case of Afghanistan, 434 products are among the top 1,000 exports, while 434 are among the top 1,000 Central Asian imports. The region's countries, on average, have 485 products that correspond to the top 1,000 imports.

With an average of 114 export items, the region's trade compatibility matches the requirements of each country. Textiles, basic metals, chemical commodities and animal and vegetable products are among the products that correlate to each of the nation's key geographical demands. Prepared meals and different measuring instruments for optical, time-keeping and medicinal purposes

Table 9. Top 1,000 Import of CAR and Afghanistan (Number of Matches).

|    | Commodity Description | AFG | KZN | KYN | TJN | TKN | UZB |
|----|----------------------|-----|-----|-----|-----|-----|-----|
| 1  | Animal and vegetable | 38 | 35 | 32 | 39 | 19 | 33 |
| 2  | Fats and oils | 4 | 6 | 2 | 2 | 3 | 1 |
| 3  | Prepared foods | 14 | 24 | 25 | 16 | 11 | 17 |
| 4  | Mineral products | 12 | 26 | 10 | 12 | 18 | 12 |
| 5  | Chemical products | 33 | 37 | 25 | 33 | 19 | 40 |
| 6  | Plastics and rubber | 28 | 27 | 32 | 34 | 20 | 26 |
| 7  | Leather and its products | 4 | 5 | 3 | 5 | 7 | 4 |
| 8  | Wood and its products | 4 | 1 | 4 | 1 | 2 | 6 |
| 9  | Pulp and paper | 9 | 7 | 9 | 7 | 7 | 9 |
| 10 | Textiles | 39 | 24 | 62 | 77 | 95 | 72 |
| 11 | Footwear | 2 | 8 | 9 | 12 | 6 | 8 |
| 12 | Cement and similar prod. | 8 | 5 | 8 | 4 | 7 | 8 |
| 13 | Semi-precious stones | 7 | 4 | 5 | 8 | 7 | 5 |
| 14 | Base metals | 44 | 78 | 45 | 34 | 39 | 37 |
| 15 | Machinery and equip. | 130 | 131 | 110 | 117 | 111 | 103 |
| 16 | Transport equipment | 35 | 42 | 40 | 30 | 33 | 33 |
| 17 | Measuring instruments | 13 | 12 | 9 | 13 | 12 | 13 |
| 18 | Arms and ammunition | 0 | 0 | 0 | 0 | 0 | 0 |
| 19 | Misc. manufactures | 6 | 6 | 10 | 9 | 12 | 10 |
| 20 | Work of Art | 4 | 2 | 1 | 1 | 4 | 3 |
|    | **Total** | **434** | **480** | **441** | **454** | **432** | **440** |

*Source:* Authors' preparation based on the statistics retrieved from the UN's COMTRADE.

transportation equipment, plastics and rubber, photographic and cinemato-graphic constitute some of the additional items reflected in the export basket. These exports are comparable to the top regional imports.

### 4.4.3 Product Exports and Dynamic Regional Markets

The third technique for analysing the dynamism of CAR and Afghan exports is to look at the pattern of trade. This dynamism accrues whether exports from the region have focused on competitive markets and validate if exporters are expanding their activity in these areas. The prospective expansion of the CAR and Afghan industries is reflected in high export growth rates and expanding market shares. This research reveals the region's exporters' actual or projected penetration into developing markets. The overall upward trajectory of product exports is gauged on the basis of their size and market penetration ranging from large, medium, small and emerging exports. Furthermore, the analysis also incorporates the ratio analysis of product exports to capture the market dynamism. Considering potential markets, each nation's export accomplishment has been divided into four distinct groups. These include exploited market opportunities (EMA) (those with a growing market share and increasing imports from CAR and Afghanistan), increased penetration in stagnant markets (IPSM) (those with a growing market share but decreasing imports from CAR and Afghanistan), ignored market opportunities (IMA) (those with a falling market share despite rising imports from CAR and Afghanistan) and missed market opportunities (MMA) (those with a falling market share regardless of increased imports from CAR and Afghanistan).

Based on the analysis, the ideal scenario for trade escalation is to engage in either exploited or IMA. EMA offers a conducive entry of products that have advanced into dynamic sectors, whereas IMA allows substantial export perspective if competitiveness and market access requirements are improved. For all countries and products, Table 10 presents the annual growth rates (average) of CAR and Afghanistan imports based on the HS 6-Digit classification from 2018 to 2021. Some of the most important findings are as follows:

Commodities such as works of art, oils and fats, prepared meals and food, footwear and animals and vegetables in their natural condition are among the fastest-growing import categories. Leather and its derivatives, cement, chemical goods, pulp and paper are all witnessing slower-than-average growth rates. Agricultural and mineral products surpassed processed goods and manufacturers.

Machinery parts are the most common product type for matching exports to dynamic markets, with rapidly expanding Central Asian and Afghan markets in which the region's producers are expanding their access. The rapidly developing markets include fresh and processed seafood and consumables, footwear, jewellery, bicycle and motorcycle components and bicycle and motorcycle parts. Due to slow exports, the region's exporters have lost market share. On the other hand, exports of fresh animal goods, rubber items, low-tech equipment and electrical products have increased slowly or stagnantly in CAR. Finally, slow-growing

Table 10. Annual Growth Rate of CAR and Afghanistan Imports (Average), 2018–2021.

| HS Section | | Percent | HS Section | | Percent |
|---|---|---|---|---|---|
| 1 + 2 | Animal and vegetable | 0.245 | 12 | Footwear | 0.289 |
| 3 | Fats and oils | 0.295 | 13 | Cement and similar prod. | 0.075 |
| 4 | Prepared foods | 0.291 | 14 | Semi-precious stones | 0.082 |
| 5 | Mineral products | 0.174 | 15 | Base metals | 0.106 |
| 6 | Chemical products | 0.071 | 16 | Machinery and equip. | 0.102 |
| 7 | Plastics and rubber | 0.088 | 17 | Transport equipment | 0.16 |
| 8 | Leather and its products | 0.08 | 18 | Measuring instruments | 0.093 |
| 9 | Wood and its products | 0.148 | 19 | Arms and ammunition | 0.206 |
| 10 | Pulp and paper | 0.047 | 20 | Miscellaneous manufactures | 0.066 |
| 11 | Textiles | 0.171 | 21 | Work of art | 0.397 |
| **Average** | | **0.159** | | | |

*Source:* Authors' preparation based on the statistics retrieved from the UN's COMTRADE.

regional exports from CAR and Afghanistan include fresh and chilled seafood, cement, plastics and paper. Processed foods, chemicals, textiles, machinery and electronic equipment are among the medium-sized exports experiencing rapid growth. Among other fast-growing industries, products include cocoa goods (processed foods), soaps, amino compounds (chemicals), acyclic alcohols, plastic containers, t-shirts, electronic items (motors, generators, television and radio components) and chairs (furniture). While exporters have failed to expand their market share in fast-growing industries, thus evidence of increased penetration in sluggish or stagnant markets is reflected. Exporters in the region have reduced their share of the region's stagnant markets, which include finished clothing, batteries, low-tech audio equipment and plastics.

The trade basket aimed for large-scale exports to fast-growing markets, including auto components, processed alloys (copper and nickel), automobile tyres, accumulates and palm oil. The region's exports have increased in the region's rapidly developing markets for crustaceans (raw), furniture, coffee, motorcars, plywood, and leather-upper (footwear). Certain industries, such as foods (prepared), machinery (high-tech) and electronics and vehicle parts, have significant growth markets, while others have a mixed outlook. Solid options for market penetration exist for furniture, various types of footwear, certain chemical products and jewellery in markets with no clear sector-wide growth pattern.

Unprocessed fruits and vegetables have less dynamic markets than processed food products. The same is seen in the case of unprocessed metals, minerals and chemicals with metals, wood products and furniture.

## 5. Conclusion and Policy Recommendations

### 5.1 Conclusion

The six regional trade-enhancing mechanisms investigated in this study suggest the essence of the policy mechanisms and frameworks. The analysis bases its discussions on overall indices across countries. Large nations outperformed smaller and less advanced economies, suggesting that a nation's size and degree of economic advancement are important predictors of global trade growth. Overall, Kazakhstan has higher ratings than the average, whereas Afghanistan and Turkmenistan have lower ratings. The five most effective trade enhancement channels are trade complementarities, price competitiveness, intra-industry trade and comparative advantages.

The main barriers to regional trade have been ineffective trade facilitation measures, high trade costs, low survival rates, exports concentrated in low value-added products and the absence of ED. Intra-industry trade, price competitiveness, comparative advantages, ED and exporter survival rates have all benefited Kazakhstan the most. Kyrgyzstan has benefited significantly from its competitive advantages, trade within its industries and diversified exports. In the case of Uzbekistan, intra-industry trade and ES have benefited the economy; while in the case of Afghanistan, trade potential is realised on the basis of competitive benefits. Tajikistan and Turkmenistan have gained the most through price competition. Due to Kazakhstan's high ratings, trade complementarities are the third most crucial mechanism. Afghanistan, Kyrgyzstan and Kazakhstan have significant intra- and inter-regional trade potential, contributing significantly to comparative advantages. ED and sophistication are highly valued, whereas structural factors are critical for Uzbekistan, Kyrgyzstan and Tajikistan exports. Kyrgyzstan places high importance on regional value chains (both current and potential). Kazakhstan has the greatest survival rate, while Afghanistan and Tajikistan have the lowest. Trade costs are a problem in the CAR and Afghanistan, and trade facilitation should be improved. According to the study's empirical findings, the prospective significance of intra- and inter-regional trade in CAR and Afghanistan is around twice as great as the current level determined by current trade patterns. Relevant trade growth assumes that countries may export to regional trading nations based on current competitive leverages, with no price, non-price or structural obstacles.

### 5.2 Policy Recommendations

The study offers policy recommendations to increase trade and investment in Central Asia and Afghanistan, highlighted below.

*Interdependence of Regional Policies:* Regional trade can only be intensified by elevating other trade-improving areas as these mechanisms are frequently highly interconnected. Regional value chain expansion, for example, is inextricably linked to trade-enhancing channels.

*Hinge the Trade as per Comparative Trade Analysis:* The CAR and Afghanistan possess an advantageous position in the export of raw materials and labour-intensive commodities. These commonalities imply the potential for trade between countries in the two areas. Governments can shift the environment by integrating new technology internally via research and development (R&D) or externally through foreign direct investment (FDI). It is also suggested that cross-border manufacturing facilities with value chains be established, thereby expediting a country's ability to change its comparative advantages and, as a result, improve its economic structures and income levels.

*Interdependence of Policies:* When linking regional policies and programmes, the association between and among trade-enhancing mechanisms does not imply causation. Implementing ED policies, for example, only results in regional expansion of value chains, increased ES in exports or higher survival rates. Adequate attention must be paid to all steps required to protect the interests of traders and other key stakeholders, as these trade-enhancing channels are interdependent.

*ED Policies:* There is significant room to expand regional trade. Diversification is critical for both regions' growth, stability and export performance. Countries with export-oriented growth strategies diversify export collections along product and destination lines to hedge against development- or market-specific external shocks. Central Asian countries lack export-oriented growth strategies because their exports primarily concentrate on natural resource-rich products. Diversification of export policies is more likely to enhance export shares. Focusing on a few product exports, on the other hand, will discourage new ones.

*Strategies for Regional Export Growth Must Address Low ESR:* Understanding the reasons and implications of export survival is crucial for understanding the dynamics of Central and Afghanistan exports. It also helps policymakers focus export promotion initiatives more efficiently. At the same time, strategies aimed exclusively at stimulating new exports overlook an important part of export dynamics: exporters' survivability after they reach the tradable market. Given their past experience with learning by doing, incumbents have a natural advantage, and that knowledge may be a crucial contribution to share with rivals.

*Reduction in Trade Costs and Other Impediments:* These economies continue to face high trade costs, both in and out of the country. Non-tariff trade barriers constitute up to 90% of trade expenses, with most indirect costs connected with national and international standards. IRT costs are greater in CAR and Afghanistan compared to intra-trade costs. The increase in licences, permits and documents alters the global viability of trade in both domains along with the inability of small businesses to comprehend the complexities of such measures.

Furthermore, sensitive lists and restricted commodities that safeguard local manufacturers compete with possible intra-industry trade possibilities that might otherwise exist among regional trading partners. Not surprisingly, CAR and Afghanistan are among the bottom 3% of countries worldwide regarding cross-border trade ease. If comprehensive reforms address these trade costs, intra- and inter-regional trade development will improve.

*Revisit Regional Trade Agreements (RTAs):* RTAs have proliferated both within and across regions, but execution is critical to their success. Regional trade agreements include FTAs, trade facilitation and transportation agreements and transit agreements. Their trade influence, however, is confined to fully executing these agreements. So far, they have had little impact. For traders, bureaucratic delays and 'red tape' are a burden when it comes to moving goods across borders. As a result, trade facilitation – the simplification, modernisation and harmonisation of export and import processes – has emerged as a critical issue for the global trading system. Measures recently proposed under the WTO's Agreement on Trade Facilitating Agreement (TFA) should be incorporated into regional trade facilitation efforts. The new TFA regulations have the potential to improve trade facilitation measures dramatically. Steps such as better information availability and document simplicity, automated operations, simplifying border procedures and strong governance should be prioritised. While trade facilitation efforts are of greater significance for manufactured products than agricultural commodities due to the involvement of input imports and processed goods exports, agriculture is crucial for poverty reduction and inclusive development in these regions.

# References

Abdih, Y., & Medina, L. (2013). *Measuring the informal economy in the Caucasus and Central Asia*. International Monetary Fund. IMF Working Paper WP/13/137.

Abuseitova, M. K. (2007). Historical and cultural relations between Kazakhstan, Central Asia, and India from ancient times to the beginning of the 20th century. In J. N. Roy & B. B. Kumāra (Eds.), *India and Central Asia: Classical to contemporary periods*. Concept Publishing Company.

Akbari, S. (2021). *The WTO transit regime for landlocked countries and its impacts on members' regional transit agreements: The case of Afghanistan's transit trade with Pakistan* (Vol. 17). Springer Nature.

Ali, M., & Mujahid, N. (2015). An analytical study of economic cooperation organization (ECO): Challenges and perspectives. *European Academic Research, 2*(2), 14031–14045.

Andaya, B. W., & Andaya, L. Y. (2015). *A history of early modern Southeast Asia* (pp. 1400–1830). Cambridge University Press.

Ando, M. (2006). Fragmentation and vertical intra-industry trade in East Asia. *The North American Journal of Economics and Finance, 17*, 257–281.

Arif, A., Sadiq, M., Shabbir, M. S., Yahya, G., Zamir, A., & Bares Lopez, L. (2022). The role of globalization in financial development, trade openness and sustainable environmental-economic growth: Evidence from selected South Asian economies. *Journal of Sustainable Finance & Investment, 12*(4), 1027–1044.

Asia Development Bank (ADB). (2006). *Central Asia: Increasing gains from trade through regional cooperation.*

Batsaikhan, U., & Dabrowski, M. (2017). Central Asia—Twenty-five years after the breakup of the USSR. *Russian Journal of Economics, 3*(3), 296–320.

Burns, W. J. (2014, September 23). *Remarks by deputy secretary of state on 'expanding economic connectivity in greater central Asia'.* Delivered to the Asia Society.

Chaturvedi, P., Hussain, Z., & Nag, B. (2015). SAARC geopolitics and trade: Missing intra-regional connectivity a hindrance to further economic integration. *South Asian Survey, 22*(1), 78–106.

Cochrane, L., & O'Regan, D. (2016). Legal harvest and illegal trade: Trends, challenges, and options in khat production in Ethiopia. *International Journal of Drug Policy, 30*, 27–34.

Fjaestad, K., & Overland, I. (2013). Tariffs and formal and informal trade barriers in Central Asia. *Central Asia Regional Data Review*, (10), 1–9.

Hausmann, R., Hwang, J., & Rodrik, D. (2007). What you export matters. *Journal of Economic Growth, 12*(1), 1–25.

Hiebert, F. T., & Lamberg-Karlovsky, C. C. (2003). Central Asia and the Indo-Iranian Borderlands. *Iran, 30*, 1–15.

IMF. (2021, April). *World Economic Outlook: Managing divergent recoveries.* International Monetary Fund.

Kang, L., & Liu, Y. (2020). Characteristics of industrial structure evolution and isomorphism in Central Asia. *Journal of Geographical Sciences, 30*, 1781–1801.

Kawai, M., & Wignaraja, G. (2014). *Trade policy and growth in Asia.* ADBI Working Paper Series No. 495. Asian Development Bank Institute.

Laruelle, M. (2015). The US silk road: Geopolitical imaginary or the repackaging of strategic interests? *Eurasian Geography and Economics, 56*(4), 360–375.

Lord, M. (2015). *Regional economic integration in Central Asia and South Asia.* https://mpra.ub.uni-muenchen.de/66436/1/MPRA_paper_66436.pdf

Mazhikeyev, A., Edwards, T. H., & Rizov, M. (2015). Openness and isolation: The trade performance of the former Soviet Central Asian countries. *International Business Review, 24*(6), 935–947.

Mogilevskii, R. (2012). *Trends and patterns in foreign trade of Central Asian countries.* Working Paper No. 1. University of Central Asia, Graduate School of Development, Institute of Public Policy and Administration.

Mustafa, G. (2014). *Openness, economic growth, and human development: Evidence from South Asian countries from 1990–2007.* Middlesex University, Department of Economics and Statistics.

Rahman, N. (2022). *RIS, World Trade and Development Report 2021: Trade, technology and institutions WTO@ 25: The way forward.* https://doi.org/10.1177/26316846211073632

Rahman, M. M., Saidi, K., & Mbarek, M. B. (2020). Economic growth in South Asia: The role of CO2 emissions, population density and trade openness. *Heliyon, 6*(5).

Ramay, S. A., & Abbas, M. H. (2013). *South Asian Free Trade Agreement (SAFTA) and implications for Pakistan.* Working Paper 138. Islamabad, Sustainable Development Policy Institute (SDPI).

Sadiqi, M. K., & Wani, N. U. H. (2018). Latency of Afghanistan-SAARC merchandise trade relation: An economic evaluation. *Kardan Journal of Economics and Management Sciences*, *1*(2), 101–120.

Starr, S. F. (2005). *Greater Central Asia partnership for Afghanistan and its neighbors.* Central Asia-Caucasus Institute & Silk Road Studies Program.

Varela, G. J. (2013). *Export diversification in twelve European and Central Asian countries and the role of the commodity boom.* World Bank, Poverty Reduction and Economic Management Network.

Wani, N. U. H. (2019). Nexus between openness to trade and economic growth: An empirical investigation of Afghanistan. *South Asia Economic Journal*, *20*(2), 205–223.

Wani, N. U. H., & Dhami, J. K. (2014). Economic concert, collaboration and prospective of trade between India and Brazil. *Foreign Trade Review*, *49*(4), 359–372.

Zekria, T., & Wani, N. U. H. (2019). Evaluation of Afghanistan export performance: A constant market share analysis approach. *Kardan Journal of Economics and Management Sciences*, *2*(2), 16–40.

# Chapter 2

# Trade Potential of Afghanistan With SAARC Region and European Union: A Gravity Model Approach

## Abstract

This study investigates the trade potential of Afghanistan with the South Asian Association for Regional Cooperation (SAARC) and European Union (EU) by employing an augmented gravity model approach. The model used the latest Economic and Social Commission for Asia and the Pacific (ESCAP) dataset with the base year 2016, covering data from 2015 to 2021. The results of the study satiate that out of the chosen 15 countries of the EU, the magnitude of Afghanistan's trade potential is high with three EU countries (Germany, France and Spain), whereas in the case of SAARC, Afghanistan's trade potential is the highest with Pakistan, followed by India and Bangladesh. Results show that simple average tariff imposition and partner countries' GDP positively impact Afghanistan's trade value.

In contrast, simple average tariff imposition bilaterally harms the trade volume of the reporting country. Statistically, a 1% tariff rate change decreases Afghanistan's total trade by 0.3%. Moreover, a 1% increase in the GDP of the partner countries will increase Afghanistan's total trade by 0.5%. Furthermore, common language, landlocked and distance significantly impact Afghanistan's total trade. The results suggest that Afghanistan needs to explore the ways and means to improve its trade relations with the countries further and improve its market share. The study proposed that Afghanistan should use trade as an economic development tool to flourish in the region and capture the markets to realise its maximum trade potential. This research recommends that South Asian and EU countries revise the tariff rates and other non-tariff barriers to boost trade and connectivity for a better trade future.

Policy Solutions for Economic Growth in a Developing Country, 41–57
Copyright © 2024 Nassir Ul Haq Wani
Published under exclusive licence by Emerald Publishing Limited
doi:10.1108/978-1-83753-430-220241003

*Keywords*: Afghanistan; trade potential; gravity model; South Asian Association for Regional Cooperation; European Union

*JEL Codes*: F19; 016

# 1. Introduction

The political-economic aspect of globalisation stimulates global trade and mass production. Countries engage in different economic and trade agreements to increase and bolster economic and trade interactions (Ahmed et al., 2021; Anderson, 1979; Anderson & Van Wincoop, 2003; Anderson et al., 2017; Bergstrand, 1989; Bergstrand, 1990; Deardorff, 2007; Helpman, 1984; Khan et al., 2018; Bergeijk & Brakman, 2010). On the other hand, trade liberalisation and trading both benefit growth regionally (Evenett & Keller, 2002; Helpman, 1987; Helpman & Krugman, 1985). However, studies demonstrate an uneven effect on income distribution (Khan et al., 2021), particularly in Afghanistan (Ahmad & Wani, 2019; Muram & Wani, 2020).

For an economy to flourish globally, trade plays a vital role in a country's development and growth (Wani et al., 2016). Over the last few decades, trade has significantly changed by easing trade barriers. This trade liberalisation was the consequence of two distinct approaches. The first is derived from multilateral treaties such as the General Agreement on Tariffs and Trade (GATT). The second is the adoption of regional trade agreements or trade blocs by some nations (Carbaugh, 2007; Yotov et al., 2016). South Asian region has continuously worked together to improve trade and regional cooperation; in December 1985, seven South Asian countries formed the South Asian Association for Regional Cooperation (SAARC). As shown by the European Union (EU), the situation of regional trade blocs has resulted in economic laurels. The EU, the world's most important trade and strategic bloc (excluding the United Kingdom), is made up of 27 nations that have boosted the living standards and economic well-being of the people in the incumbent countries via considerable cooperation in trade and political issues (Iqbal et al., 2017; Khan, 2017).

Furthermore, the North American Free Trade Agreement (NAFTA) is a major RTA between the United States, Canada and Mexico, resulting in high economic integration and trade growth. Similarly, various RTAs, such as South Asian Free Trade Agreement (SAFTA), have been signed across Asia. However, because of numerous political and ideological impediments, the member states needed help to realise the benefits detailed in the early drafts and signed pledges. The South Asia Preferential Trade Agreement (SAPTA) was formed in 1993 among South Asian states to increase trade (Wani & Rasa, 2023). Sahoo and Bhunia (2014) investigated trade proportions across key worldwide areas. They discovered that South Asian trade with each other is about 5%. Trade within NAFTA accounts for 52% of total trade, while trade within the Association of Southeast Asian Nations (ASEAN) accounts for 26%.

While doing so, nations must consider the availability of trade potential within the trading partner to escalate the trade further or shift the trade's direction, as Afghanistan experienced four decades of conflict, resulting in mass deterioration of the economic system, thereby increasing the state's economic fragility. Afghanistan's exports were paltry in 2001, at \$166.24 million, reflecting the country's limited economy (WITS, 2021a, 2021b). Afghanistan emerged from obscurity despite foreign involvement, and economic activity flourished. Trade diversification was recognised as a required policy action to enhance regional trade. On 3 April 2007, Afghanistan became the eighth member state of SAARC, regarded as a historic occasion since it completed the South Asian sphere and its regional identity. Since then, the trade flow has rapidly increased. According to the statistics, Afghanistan's exports to SAARC (Bangladesh, India, Pakistan and Sri Lanka [BIPS]) grew from USD 374 million in 2010 to USD 991.33 million in 2020 (WITS, 2021a, 2021b). Since Afghanistan is seen as a natural and important part of the SAARC community, the export orientation is focused towards surrounding nations such as Pakistan, India and Iran, owing to a need for more resources and adequate transit and transportation infrastructure. Afghanistan's trade has grown since the foundation of the new government in 2001, with the country's trade slope increasing, with exports reaching 1.76 billion USD in 2020, up from 73 million USD in 2001 (World Bank, 2020a, 2020b). Meanwhile, imports have risen from \$368 million in 2001 to \$6.9 billion in 2020 (WITS, 2021a, 2021b). However, the composition of Afghan trade has shifted more towards SAARC than the EU. Imports from Afghanistan to the EU climbed from USD 58 million in 2011 to USD 95 million in 2021 (WITS, 2021a, 2021b).

The EU's export flow to Afghanistan in 2021 was USD 360.74 million, compared to USD 856 million in 2011 (United Nations COMTRADE, 2021). Afghan goods have infiltrated worldwide markets such as South Asia, the Gulf area, the EU, Central Asia and North and South America (OEC, 2023). Furthermore, the diversification of Afghanistan's exports to the EU has revitalised the country's export base. The top export and import destinations are studied based on their percentage share of exports and imports to provide a picture of Afghanistan's trade relationships.

As a result, the current research has significance in terms of their general economic relationship and trade interaction. Despite a vast and growing body of material on the economies of the SAARC and EU, orderly and relative experiential studies on the nature of economic performance in Afghanistan's trade structure with SAARC and EU economies have yet to be permitted. This research aims to investigate Afghanistan-SAARC and Afghanistan-EU commerce, focusing on nations with significant trade potential for Afghanistan. As a result, identifying and determining the nations or locations where Afghanistan has trade potential (versus the EU and the SAARC region) is critical. As a result, the present research was done to determine Afghanistan's genuine trade potential with South Asian nations and the EU area. This research aims to scientifically examine Afghanistan's trading prospects with South Asian nations and the EU. Afghanistan's geostrategic position completes the South Asian region's sphere. However, promoting regional commerce in South Asia is critical, owing to several strategic, demographic and consumer advantages. After the African area, the South Asian region is the hardest afflicted by high poverty.

Similarly, water security and climate change threaten the region's breadbasket. As a result, if the incumbent nations eliminated trade diversion barriers, poverty and unemployment would be alleviated. This research is distinct in two ways. First, we employed the comprehensive gravity trading model. The dataset is intended to help academics and policymakers assess the influence of different factors on total commerce, exports and imports.

On the other hand, other gravity trade models use fewer variables and measure the effect of exports or imports as a dependent variable, but not overall trade. Second, the comprehensive gravity trade model incorporates additional policy indicators and bilateral trade variables that assess the potential trade market by comparing present and anticipated values of exports and imports among trading partners. Similarly, we chose the most current data for the criteria under consideration.

## 2. An Overview of the Trade Relations of Afghanistan With SAARC and the EU

Afghanistan has a geostrategic location in South Asia. It is strategically vital since it links other South Asian nations with Central Asian ones. Afghanistan enjoys favourable trade relations with both regions; however, the trade latency with the EU is yet to reap the actual trade dividends. Pakistan, Bangladesh, Bhutan, India, the Maldives, Nepal and Sri Lanka are the South Asian nations. Developing a regional economic bloc has become crucial for countries' economic prosperity. South Asia has a population of 1.94 billion people. Pakistan, India and Bangladesh have larger economies than the rest of South Asia. Afghanistan's exports to other South Asian nations, such as Nepal, Maldives and Bhutan, are negligible. Austria, Belgium, Bulgaria, Croatia, Cyprus, the Czech Republic, Denmark, Estonia, Finland, France, Germany, Greece, Hungary, Ireland, Italy, Latvia, Lithuania, Luxembourg, Malta, the Netherlands, Poland, Portugal, Romania, the Slovak Republic, Slovenia, Spain and Sweden comprise the EU region.

Table 1 additionally reveals Afghanistan's total exports to South Asian nations and the EU. In 2021, Afghanistan's total exports to South Asia accounted for 81.46% of total exports, with India accounting for 47.12% of total exports, followed by Pakistan (34.31%) and Sri Lanka (0.04%). Similarly, in 2021, Afghanistan's total imports from South Asia were 18.27%. Pakistan was its major South Asian import partner, accounting for 12.87%, followed by India (5.30%) and Bangladesh (0.09%). Regarding Afghan exports to the EU, the trade flow between Afghanistan and the EU has also been accelerated. The EU is made up of 27 nations. They are recognised as having one of the world's biggest single marketplaces. According to data, Afghanistan's overall products and services exports to the EU increased from $46.4.9 million in 2010 to $60.6 million in 2020. Simultaneously, its overall imports of products and services from the EU fell precipitously from $775.8 million in 2010 to $324.8 million in 2020; nevertheless, the volume and variety of partners rose from 17 to 27 nations in 2019. In 2020,

Table 1. Afghanistan's Exports and Imports From SAARC and EU, 2021 (in 000's USD).

| Partner Name | No of Exported HS6 Digit Products | No of Imported HS6 Digit Products | Export Share in Total Products (%) | Import Share in Total Products (%) | Trade Balance | Export | Import | Import Partner Share (%) | Export Partner Share (%) |
|---|---|---|---|---|---|---|---|---|---|
| Bangladesh | 2 | 13 | 0.98 | 1.75 | −7304.64 | 312.76 | 7617.4 | 0.09 | 0.04 |
| India | 56 | 279 | 27.45 | 37.65 | −43560.03 | 410135.57 | 453695.6 | 5.3 | 47.12 |
| Sri Lanka | | 10 | | 1.35 | | | 767.79 | 0.01 | |
| Pakistan | 79 | 326 | 38.73 | 43.99 | −804354 | 298635.06 | 1102989.06 | 12.87 | 34.31 |
| Austria | 17 | 26 | 8.33 | 3.51 | −951.27 | 380.04 | 1331.31 | 0.02 | 0.04 |
| Belgium | 17 | 33 | 8.33 | 4.45 | −6981.1 | 61.45 | 7042.55 | 0.08 | 0.01 |
| Bulgaria | | 8 | | 1.08 | | | 121.46 | 0 | |
| Cyprus | | 2 | | 0.27 | | | 165.21 | 0 | |
| Czech Republic | 1 | 18 | 0.49 | 2.43 | −1399.65 | 1.15 | 1400.79 | 0.02 | 0 |
| Germany | 46 | 118 | 22.55 | 15.92 | −77997.46 | 11704.68 | 89702.14 | 1.05 | 1.34 |
| Denmark | 5 | 34 | 2.45 | 4.59 | −15737.33 | 5.42 | 15742.75 | 0.18 | 0 |
| Spain | 4 | 30 | 1.96 | 4.05 | −2898.37 | 388.57 | 3286.94 | 0.04 | 0.04 |
| Estonia | | 4 | | 0.54 | | | 718.08 | 0.01 | |
| Finland | 3 | 15 | 1.47 | 2.02 | 415.68 | 920.82 | 505.14 | 0.01 | 0.11 |
| France | 32 | 54 | 15.69 | 7.29 | −11390.69 | 338.66 | 11729.35 | 0.14 | 0.04 |

*(Continued)*

Table 1. (*Continued*)

| Partner Name | No of Exported HS6 Digit Products | No of Imported HS6 Digit Products | Export Share in Total Products (%) | Import Share in Total Products (%) | Trade Balance | Export | Import | Import Partner Share (%) | Export Partner Share (%) |
|---|---|---|---|---|---|---|---|---|---|
| Greece | | 5 | | 0.67 | | | 5930.18 | 0.07 | |
| Croatia | | 1 | | 0.14 | | | 490.59 | 0.01 | |
| Hungary | | 17 | | 2.29 | | | 1102.01 | 0.01 | |
| Ireland | | 17 | | 2.29 | | | 11188.09 | 0.13 | |
| Italy | 4 | 80 | 1.96 | 10.8 | −14264.88 | 491.21 | 14756.1 | 0.17 | 0.06 |
| Lithuania | 1 | 10 | 0.49 | 1.35 | −5581.32 | 5.78 | 5587.1 | 0.07 | 0 |
| Luxembourg | | 4 | | 0.54 | | | 203.26 | 0 | |
| Latvia | 1 | 3 | 0.49 | 0.4 | −98.74 | 16.28 | 115.02 | 0 | 0 |
| Malta | | 3 | | 0.4 | | | 0.17 | 0 | |
| Netherlands | 15 | 48 | 7.35 | 6.48 | −13652.84 | 283.03 | 13935.88 | 0.16 | 0.03 |
| Poland | 4 | 31 | 1.96 | 4.18 | −4970.66 | 124.52 | 5095.18 | 0.06 | 0.01 |
| Portugal | 1 | 8 | 0.49 | 1.08 | −410.94 | 8.44 | 419.39 | 0 | 0 |
| Romania | 1 | 5 | 0.49 | 0.67 | 266.12 | 306.08 | 39.96 | 0 | 0.04 |
| Slovak Republic | | 16 | | 2.16 | | | 300.73 | 0 | |
| Slovenia | | 1 | | 0.14 | | | 3.03 | 0 | |
| Sweden | 30 | 26 | 14.71 | 3.51 | −4892.54 | 307.09 | 5199.63 | 0.06 | 0.04 |

*Source:* World Integrated Trade Solution (WITS) country profile.

Afghanistan's total exports to the EU accounted for 1.76% of total exports, with Germany accounting for 1.34% of total exports, followed by Finland (0.11%) and Italy (0.06%), respectively. Similarly, in 2020, Afghanistan's total imports from the EU were 2.29%. Germany was its top import partner in the EU, accounting for 1.05%, followed by Denmark (0.18%) and Italy (0.17%).

Fruits and vegetables, textiles and cotton are Afghanistan's principal exports to the EU (European Commission, 2019). According to 2019 statistics, Germany is the only EU country that ranks among Afghanistan's top 10 export destinations, accounting for 0.63% of total exports. It should be noted that Afghanistan's exports to the EU are minor on the list, valued at less than $100,000. According to Table 1, Afghanistan's export pattern to the EU began with 12 countries in 2010, increased to 21 EU countries in 2015, decreased to 16 countries in 2018 and continued to 16 countries in 2021. Statistics show that Afghanistan imported from 17 EU nations in 2010. In 2015, the import trend reached 20 nations, 26 in 2018 and 27 in 2019. Afghanistan's market diversification has progressively risen as the country's export volume into EU countries has increased over the previous decade. In contrast, while imports from Afghanistan have declined from the EU, EU exports have lost market share in Afghanistan. In 2014, the withdrawal may have resulted in a fall in the EU's export volume to Afghanistan and a decrease in the number of international and military alliances and allies of Afghanistan, such as the North Atlantic Treaty Organization (NATO), the International Security Assistance Force (ISAF) and other nations.

## 3. Research Methodology

The investigation focuses on Afghanistan's trading prospects with South Asian nations and the EU. This study used the gravity model of commerce to analyse trade potential. The gravity model considers GDP, distance, RTA, imports and exports of reporting and partner countries, common language, tariffs and non-tariff measures and other trade considerations. Trade worth is directly related to the economy's mass (GDP) and indirectly to the distance between them. To summarise, trade is directly related to the product of the GDPs of economies and indirectly proportional to the distance between them.

### 3.1 Gravity Model

Tinbergen (1962) asserts that the gravity equation obtained from Newton's theory of gravitation may be used to compute the size of any two-nation bilateral trade pattern. Economists use the gravity model to study trade-related issues. The gravity model of commerce calculates the volume of bilateral trade. The size and proximity of the economies determine it. The GDP of the two countries affects trade volume, country proximity and various other factors. The gravity model is based on empirical and theoretical data (the observed strong relationship between the size of an economy and the quantity of commerce it generates). Trade volume is directly connected to the product of the GDP sizes of the two nations and indirectly to the distance between them. Trade will benefit and trade volume will increase if both nations' GDPs are high. When a wider distance separates two economies, commerce suffers, and their trade value falls. For nations with variable GDPs, the gravity model may be more applicable. Afghanistan's economic potential with SAARC countries is restricted due to geographical and political concerns. On the other hand, Afghanistan has enormous trade potential with Pakistan and India in the SAARC region and future trade potential with Bangladesh (Ahmad & Wani, 2018; Muram & Wani, 2018).

Policymakers and researchers have often used the gravity model of trade to assess the impact of various variables on total trade flow, net export and net import discrepancies. This dataset differs from the standard gravity model, including additional factors such as infrastructure, behind-the-border trade cost, doing business index, etc. The World Bank data spans more than 200 countries from 1995 to 2016. It is the most current data version, and we base our study on 2018. This gravity model also includes traditional tariffs, trade facilitation behind the border, GDP of partner and reporting countries, GDP per capita and GDP growth.

Similarly, in this model, the independent variables might include exports, imports and total commerce, while the dependent variables in the simple gravity model are merely imports and exports. Consequently, this model is more comprehensive than the basic gravity model. The equation below lists the dependent and independent variables for this study. Similarly, the variables demonstrated are outlined in Table 2.

$$\text{Ln}\left(Y_{ijt}\right) = \beta_1 + \beta_2 \ln\left(\text{GDP}_j\right) + \beta_3 \ln(\text{Dist}) + \beta_4 \ln(\text{Tariff})_{ji} + \beta_5 \ln(\text{RTA})$$
$$+ \beta_6 \ln(\text{Comlang})_{\text{ethno}} + \beta_7 \ln(\text{landlockedness})_j \ldots \ldots + \varepsilon_{it} \tag{1}$$

In the gravity model, we typically incorporate the GDP of both countries (reporting and trading partners). Suppose the GDP of the reporting country is considered, in that case, we must take the product of the GDP of reporting and

Table 2.  Description of Variables.

| S# | Variables | Description |
|---|---|---|
| 1 | $\text{Ln}(\text{GDP}_{nb})$ | Natural log GDP (current GDP) US$ of $j$ |
| 2 | $\text{Ln}(\text{dist})$ | Log of distance simple distance (most populated cities, km) |
| 3 | $\text{Comlang}_{\text{ethno}}$ | 1 if a language is spoken by at least 9% of the population in both countries |
| 4 | Landlocked | 1 if $j$ is landlocked |
| 5 | $\text{Ln}(\text{Tariffs}_{ji})$ | Simple tariff of $j$ charging partner $i$ |
| 6 | RTA | 1 if a regional trade agreement is in force |

*Source:* Authors Compilation.

partner countries, which could result in unreliable outcomes and issues with endogeneity due to substantial disparities in the GDPs of South Asian and EU countries regarding Afghanistan.

### 3.2 Policy Simulation

Table 3 describes the policy simulation employed in the current investigation. In the first simulation, the model automatically examined the effects of trade capability with existing tariffs and GDP level without adjusting the policy shock. The study altered the tariffs and GDP growth rate in the second simulation. The reporting country's rationale for decreasing the tariff rate to 5% is that the average tariff rate among EU states is 8.38%. South Asian tariff rates, on the other hand, are 5.9% (WITS, 2021a, 2021b). Similarly, typical GDP growth in South Asian and EU countries is 5%; hence, the study supplied a 5% shock to the GDP variable.

## 4. Results and Discussions

The relevant dependent and independent factors are examined using gravity regression using the ESCAP Trade Analytics Portal. The findings reflect that all independent variables demonstrated significant outcomes. Table 3 summarised the findings of regression analyses, which demonstrated the influence of independent factors on the dependent variable.

According to the findings, raising the GDP of the partner countries by 1% has a significant impact on Afghanistan's total trade, which will grow by 0.58%. As partner nations' income levels grow, so will demand for imported items. In the case of distance, evidence shows that increasing the distance between partner countries by 1% decreases Afghanistan's total trade by 4.757%. It implies that countries with which Afghanistan has a short border have a greater potential for trade than countries with whom Afghanistan shares a long border. Surprisingly, the common language has a negative coefficient value and has a 5.71% negative effect on Afghanistan's total trade.

Table 3. Regression Results.

| Variable | Coefficient | Std. Error | t-Statistic | p Value |
| --- | --- | --- | --- | --- |
| Comlang$_{ethno}$ | 5.71 | 0.317 | 17.94 | <0.001*** |
| Landlocked | 5.936 | 0.260 | 22.815 | <0.001*** |
| Ln(dist) | 4.757 | 0.196 | 24.263 | <0.001*** |
| Ln(GDP$_j$) | 0.586 | 0.055 | 10.629 | <0.001*** |
| Ln(tariff$_{ji}$) | 0.344 | 0.154 | −2.238 | 0.029*** |
| RTA | 1.531 | 0.252 | 6.069 | <0.001*** |

*Source:* Author's simulation.

Similarly, if the trading partner is a landlocked country that requires access to seawater, Afghanistan's trade is reduced by 5.93%. Furthermore, the landlocked country would like to trade with a bordering country with a border and water access. Afghanistan has one of the most affordable marine routes in South Asia, through Pakistan, to the Arabian Sea. Furthermore, Central Asian states wealthy in natural resources may be able to link their business to the rest of the world through Afghanistan and Pakistan's land connections.

Similarly, the primary variable in our research is that unilaterally cutting tariff rates to at least ASEAN levels would greatly impact overall commerce. If the partner countries increase tariffs by 1%, Afghanistan's total trade will fall by 0.34%. Tariffs function as a trade diversion, boosting the price of imported goods and causing the consumer to lessen his demand. More RTAs between South Asian states, such as SAFTA, will improve Afghanistan's total trade. If South Asian countries sign another RTA, Afghanistan's trade will grow by 15.3%. Because the RTA's coefficient value is 1.15 or 15%, the new RTA will be beneficial and act as business diplomacy to reduce political tensions, particularly between India and Pakistan. Another free trade agreement (FTA) between South Asian countries will increase commerce by 15%. Similarly, the World Trade Organisation prioritises RTAs above bilateral FTAs.

Furthermore, existing states may create cooperative customs unions to enhance regional trade. Language, distance and landlocked status are all key factors in trading. The values of the incumbent variables are somewhat higher than projected.

Consequently, the language, distance and landlocked coefficient values are high. The standard error represents the dispersion of data points around the fitted line. Table 3 shows the distance between the fitted line and the data points for the variables indicated above as comlang$_{ethno}$ (0.317%), landlocked (0.260%), distance (0.196%), GDP$_j$ 0.0552%, tariff$_{ji}$ 0.154% and RTA 0.252%. The *p*-value demonstrates that the common language, landlockedness, percentage of distance variable, ln GDP, and RTA variable are all significant at the 1% level when analysing the significance of the coefficients. In comparison, the ln (tariff imposed by Afghanistan on South Asian countries) is substantial at 5%.

### *4.1 Trade Simulation and Trade Potential of Afghanistan With South Asian and EU Countries*

One of the essential aspects of the ESCAP Trade Analytics Portal is assessing trade potential after the post-estimation procedure. Trade potential is the ratio of expected to actual trade between reporting (Afghanistan) and partner states (South Asia and EU). This trade simulation demonstrates how trade deficits, improvements and growth persist between the nations involved. The trade simulation equation is as follows:

$$TP_i = \frac{\text{Estimated Trade}_{ij}}{\text{Actual Trade}_i}$$

TP represents trade potential between Afghanistan ($i$) and nations in South Asia and Europe ($j$). If the value of $TP_{ij}$ is more than one, the potential for trade expansion is greater, but if the value of $TP_{ij}$ is less than one, the potential for trade growth is greater.

### 4.2 Pre-Shock Trade Potential Results (Simulation 1)

The study displayed Afghanistan's trade capability with South Asian and EU states based on the results in Table 4. It helps us estimate the actual trade ratio by comparing real and expected trade values. The result is shown in Table 4, where [Ln(trade)] embodies the actual value of trade, [Ln(trade)] represents the projected value of trade and the last column represents the estimated actual trading ratio. It has been demonstrated that the potential for trading between Afghanistan and South Asian states exceeds one, suggesting the enormous potential for trade expansion.

Table 4. Existing Trade Potential of Afghanistan With South Asian and European Union Countries Before Giving Shock (Simulation 1).

| Partner | Ln(trade$_{ij}$) | Ln(trade$_{ij}$)$^\wedge$ | Estimated Trade to the Actual Ratio |
|---|---|---|---|
| Bangladesh | 17.416 | 17.217 | 0.988573725 |
| India | 21.445 | 21.813 | 1.017160177 |
| Sri Lanka | 16.902 | 16.865 | 0.99781091 |
| Pakistan | 21.808 | 21.887 | 1.003622524 |
| Austria | 12.804 | 12.313 | 0.961652609 |
| Belgium | 11.615 | 11.243 | 0.967972449 |
| Czech Republic | 11.416 | 11.451 | 1.003065872 |
| Germany | 15.315 | 15.392 | 1.005027751 |
| Denmark | 12.902 | 12.371 | 0.95884359 |
| Spain | 12.868 | 12.163 | 0.945212931 |
| Estonia | 9.611 | 9.67 | 1.006138799 |
| Finland | 12.318 | 12.41 | 1.007468745 |
| France | 13.416 | 13.543 | 1.009466309 |
| Italy | 14.415 | 14.651 | 1.016371835 |
| Lithuania | 10.902 | 10.302 | 0.944964227 |
| Netherlands | 11.818 | 11.831 | 1.001100017 |
| Poland | 9.704 | 9.183 | 0.9463108 |
| Sweden | 10.615 | 10.671 | 1.005275553 |

*Source:* Author's simulation.

### 4.3 Trade Potential After Calibrating Trade Simulation (Simulation 2)

Table 5 is based on the regression findings after evaluating the trading potential. Similarly, the research calibrated trade simulation in which the current study reduced tariff rates by 50% and raised partner nations' GDP by 5%; we receive the result for prospective trade among the various economies. The reporting country's reason for lowering the tariff rate to 50% is that the average tariff rate of EU nations is 8.38%. The tariff rate between South Asian nations, on the other hand, is 5.9% (WITS, 2021a, 2021b). Similarly, GDP growth in South Asian and EU nations is about 5% on average. As a result, the research shocked the GDP variable by 5%. The outcome for trade potential is displayed in Table 5, where Afghanistan has a lot of opportunities for development and trade with South Asia and the EU.

Except for the Maldives and Sri Lanka, Afghanistan has substantial trade potential with all trading partners, showing that there is still tremendous trade

Table 5. Afghanistan's Trade Simulation and Potential With South Asian and European Union Countries.

| Simulations Partner | Simulation 1 Results ln(trade$_{ij}$) | Simulation 2 Results ln(trade$_{ij}$)$^\wedge$ | % Change $\Delta$ln(trade$_{ij}$)$^\wedge$ |
|---|---|---|---|
| Bangladesh | 17.217 | 18.229 | 1.012 |
| India | 21.813 | 22.859 | 1.046 |
| Sri Lanka | 16.865 | 17.188 | 0.323 |
| Pakistan | 21.887 | 23.789 | 1.902 |
| Austria | 12.313 | 13.325 | 1.012 |
| Belgium | 11.243 | 12.389 | 1.146 |
| Czech Republic | 11.451 | 11.574 | 0.123 |
| Germany | 15.392 | 16.518 | 1.126 |
| Denmark | 12.371 | 13.403 | 1.032 |
| Spain | 12.163 | 13.309 | 1.146 |
| Estonia | 9.67 | 9.971 | 0.301 |
| Finland | 12.41 | 13.426 | 1.016 |
| France | 13.543 | 14.145 | 0.602 |
| Italy | 14.651 | 15.454 | 0.803 |
| Lithuania | 10.302 | 10.723 | 0.421 |
| Netherlands | 11.831 | 12.407 | 0.576 |
| Poland | 9.183 | 10.295 | 1.112 |
| Sweden | 10.671 | 11.817 | 1.146 |

*Source:* Author's simulation.

opportunity. However, the trading potential of the Maldives and Sri Lanka is less than one (0.88% and 0.90%, respectively) because Afghanistan has yet to have an FTA with Sri Lanka, and we have already exhausted our economic potential. In contrast, the Maldives, whose economy strongly relies on the blue economy, must learn more about Pakistan's economy. Furthermore, current shocks to tariff rates and partner countries' GDP will create trade. India has the most potential for commerce (1.280%), followed by Bangladesh and Nepal (1.16%). Afghanistan, another landlocked country, mainly relies on Pakistan and has a 1% trade potential.

Table 5 demonstrates that simulation outperforms Simulation 1 because Simulation 2 provided an exceptional trade volume outcome. If Simulation 2 is used, all South Asian countries have the highest potential for increased trade volume, according to the table. It is a bit percentage change, but it is similar to millions when translated to monetary value. Because the export and import baskets of the incumbent countries are similar, the 16.8% and 28% trade creation are nevertheless considerable. Pakistan, India and Bangladesh compete fiercely in textiles and other exporting goods. Simultaneously, oil, which they all buy from the Middle East, accounts for a significant share of their imports.

According to the data, Afghanistan might increase trade with Germany, Italy, Sweden, the Netherlands, Belgium, Austria, France, Spain, Poland and Ireland. Furthermore, in the case of Finland and Denmark, the P/A ratio is closer to unity, indicating that potential has been realised. Afghanistan's commerce with Latvia, Romania and Greece has also outpaced its potential. The coefficient for trade with Germany is 2.31, followed by France at 2.37 and Spain at 2.16, with additional nations including Italy, Sweden, the Netherlands, Belgium, Austria and Poland. Afghanistan has the lowest commercial potential in Ireland compared to the rest of the EU nations. Table 5 shows EU countries with whom Afghanistan has exceeded its trading potential. These nations have a coefficient (P1), including Greece, Romania and Latvia.

## 5. Conclusion and Recommendations

This study uses a partial general equilibrium model to examine Afghanistan's trading possibilities with South Asian and EU nations. Globalisation and political economics principles are also covered, with detailed examples demonstrating how commerce affects the general view and strengthens its international links. The gravity model is the foundation for the research technique used in this work. This model integrates Afghanistan's economic agreements with other nations, particularly with South Asian neighbours. It not only assists in comprehending the facts and figures of trade and economic development, but it also gives insight into the GDP growth of each nation. Only a few gravity model elements include size, GDP growth and distance between countries. The ESCAP analytics software provided us with a precise gravity model. Afghanistan's economic standing and financial potential in South Asia are shown in this model. The model's findings show that Afghanistan and South Asian countries have huge trade potential, with Pakistan equalling (1.011%), Bangladesh (1.618%), India (1.280%) and Sri Lanka (0.909%). The largest chance is with India, with which we have a Preferential trade arrangement (PTA), whereas the least significant prospect is with Sri Lanka. We have already achieved trade potential because Pakistan has an FTA with Sri Lanka.

To summarise, a multilateral trade agreement (MTA) among South Asian states is critical for the economic well-being of billions of people. We propose that the appropriate authorities construct a MTA or RTA among South Asian states to enhance trade and production based on the present study findings. Another RTA, like the SAFTA, would boost Afghan trade by 1.5%.

Furthermore, since South Asian countries' average GDP growth rate is 5%, it will benefit Afghanistan's trade flows. Afghanistan should negotiate FTAs with individual states in addition to RTAs since there is enormous economic potential between Afghanistan and other South Asian countries. In particular, the trade potential value with India is 1.2, which is more than the value with other countries reported in the previous study. There are several reasons for an FTA with India. It boasts the fastest-growing economy in Asia and the world's second-largest economy. Second, the air corridor lowers business costs between Afghanistan and India.

This research fully depicts Afghanistan's economic ties with South Asian and European countries, considering previously available literature and new facts and figures. Globalisation and political economics ideas are addressed in depth, with examples illustrating how commerce influences a country's overall outlook and deepens its international relations.

### *5.1 Policy Recommendations*

The study has policy suggestions to develop further economic and trade ties with the South Asian region and the EU.

- There is no single trade agreement between Afghanistan and the EU; to ease the trade relations, Afghanistan and the EU must sign a preferential trade agreement.
- Afghanistan has to reduce tariffs on EU exports to maximise the trade volume between Afghanistan and the EU.
- Based on the European Asylum Support Office, most Afghan refugees in the EU live in Germany, followed by France, Austria and Sweden. Correspondingly, Afghanistan has maximum trade potential with Germany, followed by France, though it is understood that Afghanistan has more trade potential where the Afghan diaspora lives. Therefore, the Afghan government has to focus on exporting those domestic products used by most of the Afghan diaspora in EU countries.
- Data reveal that Afghanistan can expand trade with 10 EU countries, while the trade reaches its potential with two countries and the trade potential is exceeded with other three countries. Hence, Afghanistan has to channel its exports from those five countries where Afghanistan has exceeded trade

potential or reached the potential towards those 10 EU countries where the potential exists for maximising the trade.

- To compete in international markets, especially the EU, Afghanistan has to pay more attention to the quality of products and packaging and labelling. This policy will help Afghanistan to flourish in the existing markets and to explore new markets as well.
- The Afghan government has to support local businesses inside the country through financing and subsidies so the businesses can develop and upgrade themselves according to international standards. This policy helps the country in two dimensions: the country grows economically and the exports boom.
- The study reveals that the highest trade potential for Afghanistan exists with Pakistan, followed by India and Bangladesh, and they represent the primary sources of export and import. The trade sector needs to be revitalised, prioritising the markets, especially in markets where the country enjoys a comparative advantage.
- Reducing the trade barriers is a need for the Afghanistan economy to flourish globally, which is directly related to the stability in the political and security conditions.
- Afghanistan should have access to better market opportunities for sustainable export growth instead of diversifying.
- There is a need for updating the technologies and upgrading the qualities and quantities of Afghani products that should be based on the demands and country-specific needs.

### 5.2 Future Scope

Future researchers interested in trade relations between Afghanistan, SAARC and the EU can use the updated data for analysis. In addition, this study only considers the merchandise data regarding products and commodities traded between Afghanistan, SARC and the EU. The trade relations of Afghanistan with the SAARC and EU could be further explored by considering services and commodities. However, the data used in this study are taken from a globally authentic source, World Integrated Trade Solution (WITS); nevertheless, future researchers could use the UN COMTRADE data on HS 12 classification. Subsequently, future researchers can examine the trade potential of the EU with Afghanistan and vice versa to understand the complete trade scenario in terms of explaining the trade feasibility and potential.

# References

Ahmad, S. S., & Wani, N. U. H. (2018). Trade potential of Afghanistan against SAARC: An application of gravity model approach. *Kardan Journal of Economics and Management Sciences, 1*(4), 1–19.

Ahmed, S., Khan, M. A., & Mustafa, U. (2021). Agricultural trade and ultra-poor in Pakistan: An application of CGE model. *Millennial Asia.* https://doi.org/10.1177/09763996211010607

Anderson, J. E. (1979). *A theoretical foundation for the gravity equation.* American Economic Review.

Anderson, J. E., Larch, M., & Yotov, Y. V. (2017). *Trade and investment in the global economy* (No. w23757). National Bureau of Economic Research. https://doi.org/10.1016/j.jinteco.2020.103341

Anderson, J. E., & Van Wincoop, E. (2003). Gravity with gravitas: A solution to the border puzzle. *The American Economic Review, 93*(1), 170e192. https://doi.org/10.1257/000282803321455214

Bergeijk, P. A., & Brakman, S. (2010). *The Gravity Model in International Trade: Advances and Applications.* Cambridge University Press.

Bergstrand, J. H. (1990). The Heckscher-Ohlin-Samuelson model, the Linder hypothesis, and the determinants of bilateral intra-industry trade. *The Economic Journal, 100*(403), 1216e1229. https://doi.org/10.2307/2233969

Bergstrand, J. H. (1989). The generalized gravity equation, monopolistic competition, and the factor-proportions theory in international trade. *The Review of Economics and Statistics, 67*(3), 143e153. https://doi.org/10.2307/1928061

Carbaugh, R. J. (2007). Is international trade a substitute for migration? *Global Economy Journal, 7*(3). https://doi.org/10.2202/1524-5861.1297

Deardorff, A. V. (2007). *Determinants of bilateral trade: Does gravity work in a neo-classical world?* University of Chicago Press. https://doi.org/10.7208/9780226260228-005

European Commission. (2019, March 30). https://commission.europa.eu/index_en/; https://international-partnerships.ec.europa.eu/policies/programming/projects/boosting-afghan-trade-eu-trade-assistance-afghanistan_en

Evenett, S. J., & Keller, W. (2002). On theories explaining the success of the gravity equation. *Journal of Political Economy, 110*(2), 281e316. https://doi.org/10.1086/338746

Helpman, E. (1984). A simple theory of international trade with multinational corporations. *Journal of Political Economy, 92*(3), 451e471.

Helpman, E. (1987). Imperfect competition and international trade: Evidence from fourteen industrial countries. *Journal of the Japanese and International Economies, 1*(1), 62e81. https://doi.org/10.1016/0889-1583(87)90027-X

Helpman, E., & Krugman, P. (1985). *Market structure and foreign trade: Increasing returns, imperfect competition, and the international economy.* MIT Press.

Iqbal, M. S., Anwar, S., Mukhopadhay, K., & Khan, M. A. (2017). GSP plus status and income distribution: A CGE model for Pakistan. *Journal of Management Sciences, 4*(1), 27e53.

Khan, M. A. (2017). *Regional trade and economic development: Options for Pakistan.* https://ageconsearch.umn.edu/record/332899

Khan, M. A., Mehmood, Q., Zakaria, M., & Husnain, M. I. U. (2018). A household level analysis of the Pakistan–Malaysia free trade agreement. *Journal of Asian and African Studies, 53*(7), 1062–1085.

Khan, M. A., Walmsley, T., & Mukhopadhyay, K. (2021). Trade liberalization and income inequality: The case for Pakistan. *Journal of Asian Economics, 74,* 101310.

Muram, S., & Wani, N. U. H. (2020). Linkage between international political relations and foreign direct investment: A case study of Afghanistan. *Kardan Journal of Social Sciences and Humanities, 3*(1), 1–32.

OEC. (2023, March 24). https://oec.world/en. https://oec.world/en/profile/country/afg

Sahoo, P., & Bhunia, A. (2014). BCIM Corridor is a game changer for South Asian trade. *East Asia Forum, 18*.

Tinbergen, J. (1962). An analysis of world trade flows. In *Shaping the world economy: Suggestions for an international economic policy*. The Twentieth Century Fund.

UNCOMTRADE. (2021). European Union | Imports and Exports | Afghanistan | Total COMMODITIES | Value (US$) and Value Growth, | 2008 – 2019. https:// comtrade.un.org/data/. Accessed on February 17, 2022.

Wani, N. U. H., Dhami, J. K., & Rehman, A. U. (2016). The determinants of India's imports: A gravity model approach. Munich Personel RePEc Archive.

Wani, N. U. H., & Rasa, M. M. (2023). Dynamics of trade specialization and performance of SAFTA: A case study of Afghanistan. *South Asia Economic Journal, 24*(2), 153–179.

WITS. (2021a). Afghanistan | Imports and Exports | SAARC, European Union | ALL COMMODITIES. https://wits.worldbank.org/countrysnapshot/AFG/textview

WITS. (2021b, March 25). https://wits.worldbank.org/; https://wits.worldbank.org/ countrysnapshot/AFG/textview

World Bank. (2020a). *Afghanistan development update, January 2020: Navigating a sea of uncertainty*. https://doi.org/10.1596/33210

World Bank. (2020b). *The human capital index 2020 update: Human capital in the time of COVID-19*. https://openknowledge.worldbank.org/handle/10986/34432

Yotov, Y. V., Piermartini, R., & Larch, M. (2016). *An advanced guide to trade policy analysis: The structural gravity model*. WTO iLibrary.

Part III

# Determinants of Trade Costs, Export Supply, Diversification and Growth

# Chapter 3

# Drivers of Export Supply in SAARC: Investigating the Cross Evidence From Afghanistan

## Abstract

Recognising the significance of international trade in economic growth, this research explores the drivers of exports in South Asian Association for Regional Cooperation countries from 2008 to 2021. The study employs the export demand model and the augmented exports supply model and utilises pooled time-series data. This study questions whether export supply decisions are based on traditional trade model factors, emerging trading realities or macroeconomic variables. The model based on fixed effects evaluates the connection between exports and their possible drivers. Traditional export supply models suggest determinants like production capacity, variable cost and relative pricing influencing South Asian export supply performance substantially. Changes in trade, for example, have a substantial impact on export supply, demonstrating that the trade liberalisation procedure promotes growth in exports, compression in imports and technological advancement. The worsening state of the energy industry and growing levels of corruption have proved to be significant deterrents to export supply decisions. The results verify foreign direct investment's positive and medium influence on the expansion of exports. Other variables, however, such as GDP and its growth, Official Development Assistance (ODA), development expenditure, indirect taxation, labour supply and the exchange rate of currencies, have a positive impact on the flow of exports. Furthermore, the data corroborate the notion that increased savings have a significant beneficial influence on the flow of exports. The study proposes that concerned governments examine their export policies and adopt new policies adapted in accordance with changing circumstances with the goal of increasing and enhancing the performance of exports.

*Keywords*: Exports; South Asian Association for Regional Cooperation; export supply; drivers; economic growth

*JEL Codes*: F11; F13; F33; F40

Policy Solutions for Economic Growth in a Developing Country, 61–82
Copyright © 2024 Nassir Ul Haq Wani
Published under exclusive licence by Emerald Publishing Limited
doi:10.1108/978-1-83753-430-220241004

## 1. Introduction

In most countries' experiences, a robust and functioning external sector has been deemed the companion of a rising economy. The experience of the East Asian nation is the most dramatic and well-known example. Identifying the factors that substantially impact export performance could aid in developing policies to increase performance and overall economic growth. Such rules also limit the negative impacts on trade balances that often emerge shortly after trade liberalisation. Export performance determinants may be divided into internal and external components. External variables include market access constraints and other factors that influence import demand (Bhagwati, 1982; Dunning, 1993; Fugazza, 2008; Goldstein & Khan, 1978; Greenaway & Sapsford, 1997; Jana et al., 2020). Aside from trade obstacles and competition, transportation costs, which include location and physical infrastructure, influence international market access. Supply-side circumstances are referred to as internal factors. Location-related factors, such as the availability of raw materials and other resources, can impact supply capacity. It is also affected by cost factors like workforce and capital. Besides resource endowment, factor costs result from economic policy, the institutional environment, and technological access, which also impact external sector productivity.

In line with classical economists and contemporary liberals' perspectives on trade, is akin to an economic growth engine. The nation thrusts its concentration on producing competitive items, and thus the export tendency is often based on its comparative advantage (Kersan-Skabic & Zubin, 2009; Khan et al., 2019; Kmenta, 1986; Levin et al., 2002; Mahmood & Azhar, 2001; Mahmood & Nazli, 1999; Nath, 2009). The products become more affordable globally, resulting in increased market share. Emphasising and encouraging exports will kickstart the efficient use of global resources, resulting in export recital. The exports of goods and services as demonstrated by various studies (Arif et al., 2022; Awokuse, 2003; Srinivasan, 1998) encourage a more effective distribution of resources, a productive managerial pattern, and manufacturing effectiveness, thereby benefiting the country's economic growth.

In addition, exports allow for the procurement of critical supplies and capital equipment, which boosts industrial investment as well as output (Rana & Dowling, 1990). In response to the rationale for export-specific growth, several emerging economies, particularly South Asian Association for Regional Cooperation (SAARC), switched their approach from import substitution to export promotion in the 1990s. Consequently, SAARC economies, especially Bangladesh, India and Pakistan, have enjoyed sustained gains in trade and economic growth during the previous three decades. Several studies have demonstrated that export promotion strategies may help Asian nations improve their economic development (Bhavan, 2016; Dornbusch, 1992; Feldstein & Krugman, 1990).

Achieving sustained export growth demands identifying the factors affecting a country's export performance, and policies must be designed and executed appropriately.

Tracing the drivers of the export supply, it is believed that latency to produce, competitive export pricing and the fluctuating costs of output have a deep impact on the flow of exports (Algieri, 2015). Initially, during the previous two decades, these conventional parameters were enough to understand export success.

However, as global economic conditions have changed, the variables influencing export choices have transformed during the previous two decades. Post-1980s, SAARC countries began to liberalise their economic systems, which accelerated in the 1990s. Reducing trade obstacles and boosting openness was meant to boost trade and, as a consequence, expedited the export performance in each country.

Furthermore, a country requires critical imports and technological improvements in order to create affordable products and grow exports; the liberalisation method was meant to decrease restrictions on particular import flows, and thus encourage exports. Despite trade reform (TR) initiatives intended to aid the export growth process, South Asian countries' export performance has been inconsistent throughout the years, hampering the developing economies' expanding resilience. Changes in export supply for specific South Asian countries could be further due to internal problems like deteriorating safety and security, an escalating energy shortage and malfeasance. A number of investigations have been undertaken using traditional factors to determine the drivers affecting export decisions (Barbosa et al., 2023; Chantruprakakul et al., 2023; Filatotchev et al., 2009; Greenaway et al., 2007; Haleem et al., 2005; Kang & Jiang, 2012; Zhang et al., 2023). Recent research, on the other hand, has focused on traditional factors such as trade liberalisation, import contraction and advances in technology affecting export supply functions (Ali, 1991; Khan & Knight, 1988; Le et al., 2023; Liu et al., 2023; Sajjad et al., 2014; Utkulu et al., 2004; Yang & Ma, 2022).

Similarly, Prasad (2000) demonstrated that exports are affected by relative export prices, trading partners' income and agricultural supply shocks. Muñoz (2006) stated that corruption and an unfriendly business environment negatively impact firm export growth. Although exports remain one of the most significant economic indicators internationally, their significance for South Asian nations cannot be overstated since they suffer chronic balance of payments (BoP) deficit and economic growth challenges.

This study hinges on the approach proposed by Utkulu et al. (2004). This model has been evaluated using datasets that represent the global market access and supply-chain capabilities of five countries. Thus, the performance of exports may be decomposed to determine the degree to which its constituents have limited it. It, therefore, contributes to the current research by investigating corruption and the energy crises as new variables influencing the export supply choices of Afghanistan, Bangladesh, India, Sri Lanka and Pakistan from 2008 to 2021. Less seminal work exists on panel data estimates on export drivers for many developing countries. The current research employs a panel data estimation approach and provides cross-evidence for Afghanistan in order to identify the determinants of encouraging exports in the SAARC region.

## 2. Literature Review

Exports steer the economic development process and are thus assumed as driving force of economic expansion. A country could establish allies if it has economic relationships that allow for the optimal use of available resources. Trading across borders is centred on the concept of comparative advantage, stating that each nation produces and distributes items that are relatively inexpensive to produce. Trade gains are contingent on boosting exports and discovering new markets; consequently, the nation's export effectiveness is influenced by various factors. These variables may be classed as demand or supply-side determinants. Demand-side elements involve trading partners' capacity, which GDP generally assesses, the income level of the country, the prices of exportable commodities and competing items, global pricing and the exchange rate (ER). On the other hand, supply-side aspects include legal, political or regulatory difficulties, the country's manufacturing capacity at the domestic level, currency ERs, comparative pricing, wage rate and input imports.

Certain studies have underlined the importance of demand-side factors including worldwide demand and global price in affecting export behaviour (Liu et al., 2020; Muscatelli et al., 1995). Other studies have placed a stronger focus on changes in major export supply factors that have a significant long-term influence on essential export groups (Hussain et al., 2020; Khan & Knight, 1988). Roy (2020) explored the commodity-level determinants influencing agricultural exports. The outcomes of the export determination models show that variables such as delayed export, output and global income predominate in determining agricultural exports. The studies involving the understanding of export drivers concentrate primarily on nation-specific variables including export growth programmes and incentives. Classical and modern economics have both emphasised the importance of exports, as export growth and economic growth are inextricably linked (Marshall, 1890; Nurkse, 1961). The trade between nations is the driving force behind economic advancement. Assuming that exports develop faster than imports, the country's purchasing power improves as a result of better economic growth, a stronger BoP and stronger foreign currency reserves, boosting export revenue (Azam, 2010).

Several studies have been conducted to investigate the nexus between economic growth and export recital, thereby confirming the positive effect of GDP on exports (Ahdi et al., 2013; Fugazza, 2004; Kumar, 1998). On the TR side, implications can potentially be utilised to determine if liberalisation of trade results in deterioration of export performance or not (Bader, 2006; Mohanan, 2007). The ER on the other hand exerts a favourable and statistically significant effect on export performance. The undervaluation or depreciation of the currency enhances tradable sector profitability, resulting in an escalation of the domestic value added. Some investigations have highlighted the role of infrastructures in boosting exports and foreign direct investment in certain Southeast Asian countries (Rehman & Noman, 2020; Wani & Rasa, 2023). Real appreciation or overvaluation, on the other hand, stifles exports and inhibits economic expansion, as various other variables like foreign assistance inflows degrade emerging nations' competitiveness in exports. Studies of the link between a country's export performance and foreign aid are dependent on several variables, including investment and improvements in trade-facilitating infrastructure (Arvin, 1999; Azam & Feng, 2021; Edwards, 2015; Kamguia et al., 2022; Munemo, 2011; Stanikzai & Wani, 2023). Studies have revealed that governments with strong policies and institutions benefit the most from aid. To improve export capacity, governments must adopt suitable policies and methods addressing supply-side constraints. However, cross-national research yields inconsistent findings that need further generalisability. This research tries to address a methodological gap noted in previous studies.

## 3. Methodology

In our export equation, we analyse all aspects that might have an impact on exports in developing nations as presented in Table 1 presenting the outline of variables under study. The study hinges on the assumption that the role of export promotion procedures under the trade liberalisation regime is significant as well. Table 1 presents a comprehensive overview of the variables as follows.

Table 1. Operationalisation of the Variables.

| Variable | Abbreviated as | Proxied as | Data Source |
|---|---|---|---|
| Export supply | Xs | Exports of goods and services | WDI, World Bank |
| Productive capacity | $K$ | The potential output of GDP | |
| Relative prices | Px/Pd | The ratio of the unit value of exports to the domestic price | |
| Variable cost | VC | Average monthly wage rate per worker annually | |
| Exchange rate | ER | Yearly average of official exchange rate | |
| Trade reform | TR | Measured on two variables like trade openness and trade reform dummy | |
| Import compression | IC | Import of raw materials and capital goods | |
| Technological innovation | TI | FDI inflows | |
| Corruption | Cor | Corruption index (0–6) | |
| Energy crisis | EN | Usage of energy and the discrepancy between prospective and actual utilisation | |
| National savings | $SAV$ | National savings | |

*(Continued)*

Table 1. *(Continued)*

| Variable | Abbreviated as | Proxied as | Data Source |
|---|---|---|---|
| Labour force | *LF* | Total labour force | |
| Indirect taxes | IT | Indirect taxes | |
| Official development assistance | *OD* | Official development assistance | |

*Source:* Authors' compilation.

### 3.1 Data and Procedures for Assessment

The data have been collected from World Development Indicators (WDI) 2022. The study utilises pooled data to estimate parameters using an extensive set of data. The variations in variables related to institutional, political and structural aspects differ within countries, and thus, enforcing sole connection within the variables limits the information paradigms. This problem is addressed using the uniform shifts technique. The literature suggests employing fixed and random effects models for gauging persistent changes (Bell & Jones, 2015; Filipe Lages & Montgomery, 2004; Sousa et al., 2008; Zou & Stan, 1998).

Furthermore, the empirical treatment suggests the usage of the export demand model and supply function model. The 'imperfect substitute model (ISM)' is the usual way of assessing the supply-related drivers of exports. In accordance with this premise, the ISM predicts that a country's export supply is determined in the long run by its ability for production, input costs and competitive export price. As a consequence, the following equation represents the long-run generalised export supply function:

$$X^s = f\left(\frac{P^x}{P_d}, \text{VC}, K\right) \tag{1}$$

The framework in Eq. (1) is the export supply function (standard in nature), which has been used in numerous previous studies, where $X^s$ denotes the export supply volume, which is affected by relative prices for export, the potential to produce ($K$) and the price of inputs (VC) in both positive and negative relationships (Goldstein & Khan, 1985). In addition to the typical variables contained in Eq. (1), some scholars have introduced additional aspects to the classic export supply model, including trade liberalisation by Utkulu et al. (2004). This enhanced export supply model incorporated the import compression (IC) factor through highly restrictive quotas and technical innovation (TI).

$$X^s = f\left(\frac{P^x}{P_d}, \text{VC}, K, \text{TR}, \text{IC}, \text{TI}\right) \tag{2}$$

Greater openness, an affinity for the liberalisation of trade, and a decrease in the export restricting policies in regulations and tariffs all contribute to increased exports. Trade liberalisation (as represented by TR) and openness to trade are anticipated to boost exporting capacity. Government action is expected to remove tariff and non-tariff obstacles such as quotas and licencing, as well as to prevent operations such as deflation and currency depreciation, which deter importing and lead to import constriction. Import contraction diminishes if the liberalisation of trade eliminates tariff and non-tariff restrictions. Since export supply is reliant on import input availability, import compression can exert a detrimental effect on a country's export earnings (Babatunde, 2009; Hussain et al., 2020; Islam et al., 2023; Rattsø, 1994). Reduced import compression will result in a considerable rise in export supply due to increased export supply. Technological innovation (TI), on the other hand, is critical in trade. International trade and supplies for export are stimulated by enhanced technological advancement (Azar & Ciabuschi, 2017; Leonidou et al., 2007; Márquez-Ramos & Martínez-Zarzoso, 2010).

### 3.2 Empirical Model

The factors influencing trade are constantly changing due to the constantly changing domestic and international trade environment. Aside from trade liberalisation, South Asian countries confront internal challenges such as depreciating currencies, a deepening energy crisis (EN) and corruption (Cor). As a consequence, for the instance of South Asia, the expanded model in Eq. (2) is augmented as follows:

$$X^s = f\left(\frac{P^x}{P_d}, \text{VC}, K, \text{TR}, \text{IC}, \text{TI}, \text{ER}, \text{Cor}, \text{EN}\right) \tag{3}$$

Considering a country's trade relies on international markets, the currency ER is critical in influencing trade. As the globe has progressed towards free trade and product movement has been increasingly impacted by fluctuating global demand and currency fluctuations, this dependency has expanded enormously. Accounting for currency swings, an ER was implemented, and the annual average of the official ER gauges it. Corrupt activities hamper a nation's export performance, and its widespread presence impedes the efficiency of the customs assessment and finance sectors, as well as discourages exporters, causing a reduced supply of exports by the nation at large. Apart from corrupt government practices, exporters engage in illegal activities like misinvoicing of exports through the assistance of government officials with the goal of collecting enormous duty deductions and transferring illegal cash out of the country (Forstater, 2018; Garg, 2022; Herkenrath, 2014; Jancsics, 2019; Kar & Spanjers, 2014; Ndikumana et al., 2020; Qureshi & Mahmood, 2015). For gauging the intensity of corruption, the insights are drawn from the Corruption indicator (Cor), which defines a nation's median level of corruption from 0 to 6, with a lower number indicating higher levels of corruption. Thus, the incidence of corruption in a country is expected to hamper the export performance of a nation. The same is true for the energy crisis, with a pervasive energy crisis when companies shut down, and energy supplies are redirected from this to fulfil residential demands. Energy or power is a critical aspect of every industry's output. Energy consumption is rising at both the consumer and production levels as the economy and population develop. Consequently, energy supply must increase at the same pace, which has not happened in South Asian nations. Since accessible energy sources are expensive, the efficiency of the goods produced, in addition to the poorer attractiveness of exports as a result of these limits in domestic facilities, hinder export supply. Additional energy needs to be delivered to the areas that are crucial to generate sufficient exportable surpluses. As a consequence, an energy deficit, defined as the gap between prospective and current consumption of energy, would harm exporting supplies.

As a result, the augmented exports supply model incorporating all of the variables is presented as follows:

$$X^s = \beta_0 + \beta_1 \left(\frac{P^x}{P_d}\right) + \beta_2 \, VC + \beta_3 \, K + \beta_4 \, TR + \beta_5 \, IC + \beta_6 \, TI + \beta_7 \, ER + \beta_8 Cor$$
$$+ \beta_9 \, EN + \beta_{10} \, SAV + \beta_{11} \, OD + \beta_{12} \, IT + \beta_{13} \, LF + \varepsilon_t \quad (4)$$

Estimating this expanded model in Eq. (4) helps in assessing the impact of the aforementioned factors on South Asian nations' supply of exports in considering their current state of affairs. It will therefore have significant policy implications since it will assist policymakers in determining whether the massive trade changes implemented had the intended effect on the trade flows.

## 4. Results and Analysis

The analysis encompasses the evaluation of the export supply drivers in selected five SAARC economies by employing datasets from 2008 to 2021. To determine a long-term connection involving supply for export and explicating factors, the time serial properties of these components are analysed. Based on the cointegration tests for evaluating the non-stationary panels, Levin's test for panel unit root test is employed. Based on the insights from Table 2, it is concluded that all variables accepted the null hypothesis of the standard unit process at the level. Nonetheless, we disregarded it at the first difference, indicating that all variables were stationary at I(1).

The usage of Kao's (1999) panel cointegration examination was applied with a null hypothesis of no cointegration to assess if the I(1) parameters produce spurious regression and ascertain whether an extended association exists. The null assumption of not having cointegration has been ruled out by Table 3, confirming the long-run association of the variables.

The usage of Kao's (1999) panel cointegration examination was applied with a null hypothesis of no cointegration to assess if the I(1) parameters produce spurious regression and ascertain whether an extended association exists. The null assumption of not having cointegration has been ruled out by Table 3, confirming the long-run association of the variables.

The Kao cointegration test findings revealed a linear combination with a long-term connection among the variables. Thus, the ordinary least squares

Table 2. Test for Stationarity.

| Variable | Level | | First Difference | | Order of Integration |
|---|---|---|---|---|---|
| | **Stat.** | **Prob.** | **Stat.** | **Prob.1** | |
| EXP | 4.876 | 1.0000 | −3.836 | 0.001*** | I(1) |
| K | 2.86 | 0.9966 | −9.604 | 0.000*** | I(1) |
| Px/Pd | −0.108 | 0.5473 | −4.419 | 0.000*** | I(1) |
| VC | 0.457 | 0.6727 | −5.989 | 0.000*** | I(1) |
| TI | −0.713 | 0.2189 | −2.498 | 0.005*** | I(1) |
| IC | 0.067 | 0.5285 | −6.210 | 0.000*** | I(1) |
| ER | 0.804 | 0.7829 | −4.223 | 0.000*** | I(1) |
| COR | −0.790 | 0.2280 | −6.212 | 0.000*** | I(1) |
| EN | −0.048 | 0.4746 | −6.823 | 0.000*** | I(1) |
| Say | −0.712 | 0.2890 | −2.329 | 0.005*** | I(1) |
| OD | 0.067 | 0.5176 | −6.270 | 0.000*** | I(1) |
| IT | 0.805 | 0.7761 | −4.130 | 0.000*** | I(1) |
| LF | −0.739 | 0.2218 | −6.186 | 0.000*** | I(1) |

*Source:* Authors' compilation of the data output from the EViews 8.0.
*Note:* *** shows statistical significance at 1%.

Table 3. Estimation of the Kao Cointegration Test.

| Var | t-stat | Prob. |
|---|---|---|
| Augmented Dickey–Fuller | −2.16418 | 0.0001*** |

Augmented Dickey–Fuller Test Equation (Dep. Variable: D(RESID))

| Variable | Coefficient | Std. Error | t-statistic | Prob. |
|---|---|---|---|---|
| RESID (−1) | −0.2714 | 0.047620 | −4.7204 | 0.0000*** |

*Source:* Authors' compilation of the data output from the Eviews 8.0.
*Note:* *** shows statistical significance at 1%.
Null Hypothesis: No cointegration.

(OLS) estimators on a co-integrated panel will be biased and inconsistent. As a consequence, a different technique (the Pedroni cointegration test in Table 4) is required.

Consequently, we have employed the fully modified OLS (FMOLS) panel as suggested by Pedroni (2000). Pedroni (1996) developed FMOLS, which applies a corrective technique for interacting with extraneous factors and provides long-run coefficients devoid of endogeneity and serial correlation. FMOLS can estimate common cointegration vectors while allowing for temporal and cross-sectional

Table 4. Pedroni Cointegration Test.

|  | Statistic | Prob. |
|---|---|---|
| Panel *v*-statistic | 1.86114 | 0.0414*** |
| Panel PP-statistic | −1.584217 | 0.0549** |
| Panel-ADF statistic | −1.762314 | 0.0231** |

*Source:* Data output from EViews 8.0.

*Note:* *** shows statistical significance at 1%.
Null hypothesis: No cointegration.

variability. As a result, we use FMOLS estimates to assess the long-run influence of variables with no serial correlation.

$$\beta_{FM} = \left[ \sum_{i=1}^{N} \sum_{t=1}^{T} \left( X_{it} - \overline{X_i} \right)' \right]^{-1} \left[ \sum_{i=1}^{N} \left( \sum_{t=1}^{T} \left( X_{it} - \overline{X_i} \right) \widehat{Y}_{it}^{+} + T \widehat{\Delta}_{\varepsilon\mu}^{+} \right) \right]$$

where $\widehat{\Delta}_{\varepsilon\mu}^{+}$ denotes serial correction, $\widehat{Y}_{it}^{+}$ accounts for endogeneity. These estimations provide consistent parameter estimates even in small samples and aid in controlling for possible endogeneity and serial correlation.

Table 5 displays the predictions for Goldstein and Khan's (1985) classical export supply model in Eq. (1), illustrating that all variables have a substantial influence on export supply in selected South Asian nations. In contrast, Table 6 represents the output as per the Utkulu et al. (2004) model as depicted in Eq. (2).

Table 5. FMOLS Estimation (Classical Export Supply Model).

| Variable | Co-efficient | Std. Error | *t*-stat | Prob. |
|---|---|---|---|---|
| *K* | 1.911911 | 0.027585 | 69.30907 | 0.0000*** |
| RP | 0.13053 | 0.015093 | 8.64826 | 0.0000*** |
| VC | −0.000624 | 0.000365 | −1.70767 | 0.0907* |
| *Cross-Section Dummy:* | | | | |
| AFG-C | −24.54473 | | | |
| PAK-C | −25.15324 | | | |
| IND-C | −26.03732 | | | |
| BANG-C | −22.56041 | | | |
| SRI-C | −21.02414 | | | |
| *R*-squared | 0.98104 | Mean Dep var | 21.32105 | |
| Adjusted *R*-squared | 0.959394 | SD. Dep var | 1.206521 | |
| SE of regression | 0.166124 | Sum sq. resid | 3.231657 | |
| Durbin–Watson stat | 0.244314 | Long-run var | 0.013218 | |

*Source:* Authors' compilation of the data output from the EViews 8.0.

Table 6. FMOLS Estimations (Extended Model).

| Variable | Co-efficient | Std. Error | *t*-stat | Prob. |
|---|---|---|---|---|
| K | 0.913319 | 0.001267 | 720.9147 | 0.0000*** |
| RP | 0.063194 | 0.007395 | 8.545798 | 0.0000*** |
| VC | 0.002367 | 0.000307 | 7.720391 | 0.0000*** |
| TR | 0.05164 | 0.014314 | 3.60773 | 0.0005*** |
| IC | −0.002331 | 0.000118 | −19.718 | 0.0000*** |
| TI | 0.007828 | 0.000298 | 26.25261 | 0.0000*** |
| SAV | 0.05164 | 0.014314 | 3.60773 | 0.0005*** |
| LF | −0.002331 | 0.000118 | −19.718 | 0.0000*** |
| IT | 0.05164 | 0.014314 | 3.60773 | 0.0005*** |
| OD | 0.007828 | 0.000298 | 26.25261 | 0.0000*** |
| AFG-C | −23.769 | | | |
| PAK-C | −22.602 | | | |
| IND-C | −24.391 | | | |
| BANG-C | −22.067 | | | |
| SRI-C | −20.638 | | | |
| *R*-squared | 0.98104 | Mean Dep var | 23.18015 | |
| Adjusted *R*-squared | 0.98949 | SD. Dep var | 1.266011 | |
| SE of regression | 0.17821 | Sum sq. resid | 3.373068 | |
| Durbin–Watson stat | 0.25409 | Long-run var | 0.015269 | |

*Source:* Authors' compilation of the data output from the EViews 8.0.

The adjusted *R*-squared suggested that the independent variables had strong explanatory power, explaining 98.89% of the supply of exports as shown in Table 7. The model ably provides an answer regarding the variation in South Asian exports as can be seen from the low values of residuals and standard deviation. The model adjusts for serial correlation issues and potential endogeneity problems in accordance with FMOLS estimations. Table 8 depicts the results of the FMOLS cross-sectional dependency test.

Table 7. Statistics of Model Fitness (Overall).

| | | | |
|---|---|---|---|
| *R*-squared | 0.984123 | Mean dependent var. | 21.43213 |
| Adjusted *R*-squared | 0.986314 | SD dependent var. | 1.432178 |
| SE of regression | 0.136131 | Sum squared resid. | 2.785314 |
| Durbin–Watson stat | 0.493218 | Long-run var. | 0.003124 |

*Source:* Authors' compilation of the data output from the EViews 8.0.

Table 8. Cross-Sectional Dependence Test for FMOLS Residuals.

| | Statistic | Prob. |
|---|---|---|
| Breusch–Pagan LM | 1.86114 | 0.0314* |
| Pesaran scaled LM | −1.685853 | 0.0459* |
| Bias-corrected scaled LM | −1.85146 | 0.0321* |
| Pesaran CD | 1.918788 | 0.0560* |

*Source:* Authors' compilation of the data output from the EViews 8.0.
*Note:* *** shows statistical significance at 1%.
Null hypothesis: no cross-section dependence (correlation).

In the long term, the estimations were created by taking into account various coefficients. The findings show that the export supply function is highly dependent on the model variables. A one-point increase in industrial capacity boosts export supply by 2.64% (Table 7). These results back up Dunlevy's (1980) findings in the United States and the United Kingdom, as well as Faini's (1994) findings in Turkey.

Relative pricing (RP) also shows a positive relationship, meaning that when relative export prices rise by 1%, South Asian export supply rises by 0.62%. As can be observed, a 1% rise in relative price resulted in a less than 1% increase in export supply, indicating the inelastic nature of export supply. The RP findings are comparable to those of Giordani et al. (2016).

The FMOLS findings are shown in Table 9. The data show that a one-unit reduction in variable cost enhances export supply by 0.1021 units since variable cost raises the cost of manufacturing exportable commodities, reducing competitiveness and decreasing export supply. ERs were shown to affect export supply, with a one-unit increase in ER resulting in a 0.0073 unit increase in export supply, confirming that ER depreciations boost export competitiveness because exports become less costly, so demand rises. TR is a step towards trade liberalisation, defined as a reduction in anti-export prejudice and policy tariff phases that contributes to increased export supply. The TR variable positively influences export supply, with 1% more TR improving export supply by 0.0162%. Tariff reductions and radical cuts in import licencing schemes are part of the TR process, as is the elimination of state enterprise control over critical goods imports, the reduction of quantitative restrictions, the exposition of tariff levels and the elimination of export levies and taxes. These policies will conclusively benefit trading partners, thereby improving performance (Pursell & Ahsan, 2011). These results back up Thirwall's (2000) findings, notably those of Utkulu et al. (2004).

Imports impact a country's exports since the production of commodities may depend on raw materials that are imported. Growing trade freedom and openness in the economy will culminate in reduced restrictions on imports and tariffs, as well as decreased import contraction implications and improved raw material accessibility, leading to a higher flow of exports. The impact is illustrated in Table 4, where the value of the IC variable had a significant positive effect,

Table 9. Estimations Results Based on FMOLS.

| Variable | Co-efficient | Elasticity | Std. Error | *t*-statistic | Prob.3 |
|---|---|---|---|---|---|
| K | 0.1021 | 2.673210 | 0.0143 | 118.3134 | 0.0000*** |
| Px/Pd | 0.0042 | 0.628213 | 0.0001 | 67.8908 | 0.0000*** |
| VC | −0.0034 | −0.159234 | 0.0001 | −12.54033 | 0.0000*** |
| TR | 0.0162 | 1.560461 | 0.0001 | 117.1765 | 0.0000*** |
| TI | 0.0002 | 0.070349 | 0.0002 | 23.37134 | 0.0000*** |
| IC | 0.0015 | 0.191323 | 5.8705 | −23.6701 | 0.0000** |
| ER | 0.0073 | 0.572813 | 0.0001 | 57.54761 | 0.0000*** |
| EN | −0.2675 | 0.309281 | 0.0058 | −45.60454 | 0.0000*** |
| COR | 0.1084 | 0.246590 | 0.0039 | 27.242461 | 0.0000*** |
| SAV | 0.0017 | 0.180233 | 6.37005 | −22.62911 | 0.0000** |
| OD | 0.0079 | 0.467823 | 0.0001 | 56.54661 | 0.0000*** |
| IT | −0.2610 | 0.309256 | 0.0058 | −44.61555 | 0.0000*** |
| LF | 0.1873 | 0.237598 | 0.0039 | 27.23217 | 0.0000*** |
| *Cross-Section Dummy:* | | | | | |
| AFG-C | | −19.55641 | | | |
| PAK-C | | −19.12535 | | | |
| IND-C | | −21.84038 | | | |
| BAN-C | | −19.219743 | | | |
| SRI-C | | −18.765315 | | | |

*Source:* Authors' compilation of the data output from the EViews 8.0.

revealing that a unit decrease in IC increases imports while decreasing the supply of exports by 0.016%, aligning with the findings of Bashir and Ibrahim (2022), Haveman et al. (2003), Svedberg (2002) and Utkulu et al. (2004). Therefore, South Asian exports are heavily reliant on natural resources, whereas imports play a tiny role; hence, the coefficient was determined to be large yet minuscule in predicting export provision.

Similarly, technological advancement in a country enhances its ability to manufacture new products that are in high demand, hence increasing export supply. Foreign direct investment is an avenue for technological disposal, leading to knowledge transmission. It increases export production, and as a result, export supply is a significant component that is positively associated with TI. A 1% increase in innovation in technology boosts South Asian export supply by 0.6%, corroborating the results of Kumar (2003), Márquez-Ramos and Martínez-Zarzoso (2010) and Razzaq et al. (2021).

Corruption and corrupt practices in a country restrict export performance. For example, corruption in the customs value and finance sectors deters exporters, decreasing the country's export supply. The corruption variable along with its incidence reflects that greater levels of corruption result in decreased export supply. As a consequence, every 1% reduction in corruption increases the supply of exports by 0.24%, corroborating the results of Dutt and Traca (2010), Tanzi (1998) and Thede and Gustafson (2012).

Similarly, some South Asian nations' energy crises are projected to crimp regional export supplies. Energy is expensive, resulting in higher manufacturing costs and increased export competitiveness – deficits in domestic infrastructure hurt export supplies. The energy crisis had a negative influence on export supply, with energy crises increasing by 1%, resulting in a 0.303 unit decline in export supply. These findings back up Amjad et al.'s (2012), Costantini et al.'s (2007) and Sajjad and Mahmood's (2014) survey-based findings.

## 4.1 Discussions

This article investigated the impact of country-specific variables that affect exports. We were especially driven by the fact that previous research had only given single-country analyses. There was a scarcity of a panel dataset of nations to uncover country-specific drivers influencing export fluctuations in the SAARC context. We looked specifically at the effects of output level, growth in production, ODA, savings, workforce, an inflow of foreign direct investment (FDI), indirect taxation and the currency ER on the performance of exports. According to the findings of the fixed effects model, all components are favourably and substantially connected with the economic recital and latency of exports and thus have an immense role in increasing export diversification. The study also satiates the cosmic importance of FDI's favourable but modest influence on export growth and thus aligns with the findings of Jawaid et al. (2016), Prasanna (2010) and Sun (2001). Governments may use FDI-led export growth methods to boost exports while benefiting from both inflows of FDI and expansion of exports. A surplus of output in a closed economy generates a reduction in prices, which prompts businesses to turn gloomy. Such surpluses generate foreign reserves in an open economy by exporting output. As predicted, the analysis discovered a positive influence of GDP on export growth, corroborating Kumar's (1998) empirical results. The increase in GDP is an indicator of production levels' potential for growth and resilience. Growth, rather than GDP, is a more reliable indicator of exports since it analyses the long-term viability of output patterns. The data indicate that expansion in GDP has a positive impact on the development of exports. The significant amount of government development aid envisaged will very certainly support infrastructure expansion, which will benefit the investment climate. The research discovered that ODA had a favourable influence on export growth, correlating with the findings of earlier studies (Munemo et al., 2007; Moyo, 2010; Naseri et al., 2018; Rangarajan & Kannan, 2017; Wani, 2019). In general, the share of savings utilised for non-productive purposes, such as acquiring jewellery and real estate, is higher in emerging countries. As a consequence, increased savings result in a greater amount of commodities accessible for export, thus benefiting the flow of exports. On the other hand, the labour force is a significant factor in determining the flow of exports, as optimal resource utilisation is dependent on the labour force, portraying the labour force positively influencing output levels. With the persistence of disguised unemployment in emerging nations, a considerable proportion of the agricultural workforce may be shifted to the industrial sector without impacting agricultural productivity. Such a workforce may be effectively used in the industrial sector, hence growing the export industry. Our study findings confirm the positive association between the labour force and the flow of exports, which supports the empirical research of Islam and Alhamad (2023).

The elements of indirect taxes have a favourable influence on export growth rates. The state (the government) gives tax incentives to exporting companies, resulting in an arrangement of growth in exported goods that demonstrates its beneficial effect on export intensity. Furthermore, the findings demonstrate that an increase in savings has a considerable impact on exports. Higher savings suggest lower interest rates, which encourage investment. Investment is the primary driver of export growth. The government of developing nations gives several incentives for export promotion initiatives. Domestic investment occurs in a variety of industries, although it is far more sensitive to government-provided incentives in the trade sector. Following the WTO's lead, developing countries are strengthening their focus on export strategies for investment. These constitute the justifications that support our presumptions regarding investment-led expansion of exports. Following the same trajectory, savings could assist emerging economies in their deficits. Based on the two-gap hypothesis, significant savings in emerging countries create an internal gap, which then fills the external gap by increasing growth in exports. The industrialisation factor is critical for comprehending the expansion of exports in the case of emerging nations. The agricultural output levels remain variable owing to weather and insect assaults. As a result, a country's export potential cannot be increased just via agricultural production. The findings highlight the significance of industrialisation as a strategy for sustaining export growth. The empirical data also imply that real currency depreciation is lucrative, increasing the competitiveness necessary for export diversification, and thus matching theoretical and empirical data from prior research (Bebczuk & Berrettoni, 2006; Noureen & Mahmood, 2016; Rashid & Waqar, 2017; Sharma, 2000).

## 5. Conclusion and Policy Enunciations

The study primarily focused on determining the drivers of exports in emerging economies based on a large sample of panel observations for five SAARC nations from 2008 to 2021, by employing the fixed effects model. The empirical evidence suggests that sustainable growth patterns encourage exporting. There is substantial empirical proof that the production potential, variable costs and relative price exert a considerable influence on South Asian nations' export supply expansion. Increases in manufacturing capacity, relative export prices and the ER all enhance export supply, but increases in variable costs lower export supply. The augmented model, which incorporates TR variables and other key variables like import compression, TI, corruption and energy accessibility, exerts a positive impact on the supply of exports. The degradation of the energy business, in addition to escalating instances of corruption, has been demonstrated to significantly impede factors affecting export supply decisions.

### 5.1 Policy Recommendations

The analysis suggests that South Asian countries should focus on capacity development to increase export supply and reduce anti-export bias in export policies. This can be achieved by simplifying tax systems, increasing labour market flexibility, building infrastructure, eradicating corruption and boosting security. This will attract FDI for TI and knowledge transfer.

To maintain a stable ER policy, domestic currencies must build competitive strength in overseas markets. Proper incentives and laws to simplify the tax system, provide flexible labour markets and improve infrastructure are essential.

South Asian countries must continue the TR process, as the current trade policies are anti-export. Addressing anti-export prejudice in export promotion campaigns is crucial. Tariff cuts and constraints on importation have culminated in imports outpacing exports of goods, causing the BoP crisis and harming industrial sector performance.

To foster a vibrant exporter-friendly environment, governments should accept a more restricted liberalisation of imports through designated export processing zones.

Corruption adversely impacts export latency, and it is necessary to defend trust and safety, reform anti-corruption legislation and create a good macroeconomic environment for exporters. Simplifying trade regulations and processes can reduce corruption and transaction costs, enhancing export competitiveness. Corrective steps by the government and the creation of suitable procedures can minimise discretionary powers, reduce corruption potential and restore exporters' trust, leading to fewer restrictions and more exports.

Addressing the energy problem impacting manufacturing processes requires importing energy from regional surplus nations or developing indigenous energy resources to reduce corporate load shedding and maintain a smooth production process.

### References

Ahdi, N. A., Aye, G. C., Balcilar, M., & Gupta, R. (2013). *Causality between exports and economic growth in South Africa: Evidence from linear and nonlinear tests.* The University of Pretoria, Department of Economics. Working Papers, No. 201339.

Algieri, B. (2015). Price and non-price competitiveness in export demand: Empirical evidence from Italy. *Empirica, 42,* 157–183.

Ali, I. (1991). Estimating the determinants of export supply in India. *Planning and Development of Key Sectors in India: Tertiary Sector Development, 5,* 441.

Amjad, R., Ghani, E., & Mahmood, T. (2012). Export barriers in Pakistan: Results of a firm-level survey. *The Lahore Journal of Economics*, 103–134.

Arif, A., Sadiq, M., Shabbir, M. S., Yahya, G., Zamir, A., & Bares Lopez, L. (2022). The role of globalization in financial development, trade openness and sustainable environmental-economic growth: Evidence from selected South Asian economies. *Journal of Sustainable Finance & Investment*, *12*(4), 1027–1044.

Arvin, M. (1999). Assessing aid: What works, what does not, and why. *Journal of Development Studies*, *35*(6), 162.

Awokuse, T. O. (2003). Is the export-led growth hypothesis valid for Canada? *Canadian Journal of Economics*, *36*(1), 126–136.

Azam, M. (2010). Exports and economic growth in Pakistan: An empirical analysis. *Journal of Managerial Sciences*, *5*(2), 159–166.

Azam, M., & Feng, Y. (2021). Does foreign aid stimulate economic growth in developing countries? Further evidence in both aggregate and disaggregated samples. *Quality and Quantity*, 1–24.

Azar, G., & Ciabuschi, F. (2017). Organizational innovation, technological innovation, and export performance: The effects of innovation radicalness and extensiveness. *International Business Review*, *26*(2), 324–336.

Babatunde, M. A. (2009). Can trade liberalization stimulate export performance in sub-Saharan Africa? *Journal of International and Global Economic Studies*, *2*(1), 68–92.

Bader, S. (2006). Determining import intensity of exports for Pakistan. *SBP Research Bulletin*, *II*(2).

Barbosa, D. E., Salas-Páramo, J., & Moreno-Charry, A. V. (2023). Drivers' analysis of trajectories (commercial, logistical, and financial) of China's export performance: A comparative analysis between eastern and south-eastern Asian countries. *Research in Globalization*, *6*, 100129.

Bashir, M. S., & Ibrahim, A. (2022). Examining the export-led growth hypothesis: Empirical evidence from Sudan. *Journal of Economics, Business, & Accountancy Ventura*, *25*(1), 77–92.

Bebczuk, R. N., & Berrettoni, D. (2006). *Explaining export diversification: An empirical analysis*. Documentos de Trabajo.

Bell, A., & Jones, K. (2015). Explaining fixed effects: Random effects modelling of time-series cross-sectional and panel data. *Political Science Research and Methods*, *3*(1), 133–153.

Bhagwati, J. N. (1982). Introduction to import competition and response. In *Import competition and response* (pp. 1–8). University of Chicago Press.

Bhavan, T. (2016). The determinants of export performance: The case of Sri Lanka. *International Research Journal of Social Sciences*, *5*(8), 8–13.

Chantruprakakul, A., Lata, P., & Silpcharu, T. (2023). Factors affecting the development of Thai auto parts manufacturing industry for export. *Journal of Namibian Studies: History Politics Culture*, *34*, 1853–1873.

Costantini, V., Gracceva, F., Markandya, A., & Vicini, G. (2007). Security of energy supply: Comparing scenarios from a European perspective. *Energy Policy*, *35*(1), 210–226.

Dornbusch, R. (1992). The case for trade liberalisation in developing countries. *The Journal of Economic Perspectives*, *6*(1), 69–85.

Dunlevy, J. A. (1980). A test of the capacity pressure hypothesis within a simultaneous equations model of export performance. *The Review of Economics and Statistics, 62*(1), 131–135.

Dunning, J. H. (1993). *Multinational enterprises and the global economy.* Addison-Wesley.

Dutt, P., & Traca, D. (2010). Corruption and bilateral trade flows: Extortion or evasion? *The Review of Economics and Statistics, 92*(4), 843–860.

Edwards, S. (2015). Economic development and the effectiveness of foreign aid: A historical perspective. *Kyklos, 68*(3), 277–316.

Faini, R. (1994). Export supply, capacity, and relative prices. *Journal of Development Economics, 45*(1), 81–100.

Feldstein, M. S., & Krugman, P. R. (1990). International trade effects of value-added taxation. In *Taxation in the global economy* (pp. 263–282). University of Chicago Press.

Filatotchev, I., Liu, X., Buck, T., & Wright, M. (2009). The export orientation and export performance of high-technology SMEs in emerging markets: The effects of knowledge transfer by returnee entrepreneurs. *Journal of International Business Studies, 40,* 1005–1021.

Filipe Lages, L., & Montgomery, D. B. (2004). Export performance as an antecedent of export commitment and marketing strategy adaptation: Evidence from small and medium-sized exporters. *European Journal of Marketing, 38*(9/10), 1186–1214.

Forstater, M. (2018). Illicit financial flows, trade misinvoicing, and multinational tax avoidance: The same or different. *CGD Policy Paper, 123*(29).

Fugazza, M. (2004). Export performance and its determinants: Supply and demand constraints. In *Policy issues in international trade and commodities study series, No. 26.* UNCTAD.

Fugazza, M. (2008). Export performance and its determinants: Supply and demand constraints. In *Policy issues in international trade and commodities study series, No. 26.* https://ssrn.com/abstract=1281486

Garg, M. (2022). *Money politics as a driver of trade misinvoicing: A comparative case study analysis of Philippines and India.* https://doi.org/10.6082/uchicago.4316

Giordani, P. E., Rocha, N., & Ruta, M. (2016). Food prices and the multiplier effect of trade policy. *Journal of International Economics, 101,* 102–122.

Goldstein, M., & Khan, M. S. (1978). The supply and demand for exports: A simultaneous approach. *The Review of Economics and Statistics, 60*(2), 275–286.

Goldstein, M., & Khan, M. S. (1985). Income and price effects in foreign trade. In *Handbook of international economics* (1st ed., Vol. 54, pp. 77–100). Elsevier.

Greenaway, D., Guariglia, A., & Kneller, R. (2007). Financial factors and exporting decisions. *Journal of International Economics, 73*(2), 377–395.

Greenaway, D., & Sapsford, D. (1997). Modelling growth (and liberalisation) using smooth transitions analysis. *Economic Enquiry, 35*(4), 798–814.

Haleem, U., Mushtaq, K., Abbas, A., Sheikh, A. D., & Farooq, U. (2005). Estimation of export supply function for citrus fruit in Pakistan [with comments]. *Pakistan Development Review,* 659–672.

Haveman, J. D., Nair-Reichert, U., & Thursby, J. G. (2003). How effective are trade barriers? An empirical analysis of trade reduction, diversion, and compression. *The Review of Economics and Statistics, 85*(2), 480–485.

Herkenrath, M. (2014). Illicit financial flows and their developmental impacts: An overview. *International Development Policy | Revue internationale de politique de développement*, (5.3).

Hussain, S. I., Hussain, A., & Alam, M. M. (2020). Determinants of export supply in Pakistan: A sector-wise disaggregated analysis. *Cogent Economics & Finance, 8*(1), 1732072.

Islam, M. S., & Alhamad, I. A. (2023). Do personal remittance outflows impede economic growth in Saudi Arabia? The role of trade, labor force, human, and physical capital. *Humanities and Social Sciences Communications, 10*(1), 1–9.

Islam, M. S., Hossain, M. E., Bekun, F. V., & Sujan, M. H. K. (2023). Impact of COVID-19 on Bangladesh's agriculture sector and the ways forward to recovery: An overview. *Journal of Public Affairs, 23*(2), e2862.

Jana, S. S., Sahu, T. N., & Pandey, K. D. (2020). How far is FDI relevant to India's foreign trade growth? An empirical investigation. *Journal of Economic Structures, 9*, 1–19.

Jancsics, D. (2019). Border corruption. *Public Integrity, 21*(4), 406–419.

Jawaid, S. T., Raza, S. A., Mustafa, K., & Karim, M. Z. A. (2016). Does inward foreign direct investment lead export performance in Pakistan? *Global Business Review, 17*(6), 1296–1313.

Kamguia, B., Tadadjeu, S., Miamo, C., & Njangang, H. (2022). Does foreign aid impede economic complexity in developing countries? *International Economics, 169*, 71–88.

Kang, Y., & Jiang, F. (2012). FDI location choice of Chinese multinationals in East and Southeast Asia: Traditional economic factors and institutional perspective. *Journal of World Business, 47*(1), 45–53.

Kao, C. (1999). Spurious regression and residual-based tests for cointegration in panel data. *Journal of Econometrics, 90*, 1–44.

Kar, D., & Spanjers, J. (2014). *Illicit financial flows from developing countries: 2003–2012* (Vol. 20). Global Financial Integrity.

Kersan-Skabic, I., & Zubin, C. (2009). The influence of foreign direct investment on GDP growth, employment, and export in Croatia. *Ekonomski Pregled, 60*, 119–151.

Khan, M., Andreoni, A., & Roy, P. (2019). *Illicit financial flows: Theory and measurement challenges.* https://ace.soas.ac.uk/publication/illicit-financial-flows/

Khan, M. S., & Knight, M. D. (1988). Import compression and export performance in developing countries. *The Review of Economics and Statistics, 70*, 315–321.

Kmenta, J. (1986). *Elements of econometrics* (2nd ed.). MacMillan.

Kumar, N. (1998). Multinational enterprises, regional economic integration, and export-platform production in the host countries: An empirical analysis for the US and Japanese corporations. *Weltwirtschaftliches Archiv, 134*, 450–483.

Kumar, N. (Ed.). (2003). *Globalization, foreign direct investment and technology transfers: Impacts on and prospects for developing countries.* Routledge.

Le, N., Huy, N., Minh, C., Tuan, V., & Diep, N. (2023). Factors affecting Vietnam's handicrafts export. *Uncertain Supply Chain Management, 11*(2), 811–822.

Leonidou, L. C., Katsikeas, C. S., Palihawadana, D., & Spyropoulou, S. (2007). An analytical review of the factors stimulating smaller firms to export: Implications for policy-makers. *International Marketing Review, 24*(6), 735–770.

Levin, A., Lin, F., & Chu, C. J. (2002). Unit root tests in panel data: Asymptotic and finite-sample properties. *Journal of Econometrics, 108*, 1–24.

Liu, J., Wang, M., Yang, L., Rahman, S., & Sriboonchitta, S. (2020). Agricultural productivity growth and its determinants in the South and Southeast Asian countries. *Sustainability, 12*(12), 4981.

Liu, H., Zhang, J., Huang, H., Wu, H., & Hao, Y. (2023). Environmental good exports and green total factor productivity: Lessons from China. *Sustainable Development, 31*(3), 1681–1703.

Mahmood, Z., & Azhar, M. (2001). On overinvoicing of exports in Pakistan. *Pakistan Development Review, 40*(3), 173–185.

Mahmood, Z., & Nazli, H. (1999). Estimates of unrecorded private capital movements. *Economia Internazionale, 52*(1), 79–90.

Márquez-Ramos, L., & Martínez-Zarzoso, I. (2010). The effect of technological innovation on international trade. *Economics: The Open-Access, Open-Assessment E-Journal, 4*, 11.

Marshall, A. (1890/1920). *Principles of economics* (8th ed.). Macmillan & Co.

Mohanan, K. (2007). *Determinants of the Indian machine tools exports.* Jawaharlal Nehru University.

Moyo, D. (2010). *Dead aid: Why aid makes things worse and how there is another way for Africa.* Penguin Books.

Munemo, J. (2011). Foreign aid and export diversification in developing countries. *Journal of International Trade & Economic Development, 20*(3), 339–355.

Munemo, J., Bandyopadhyay, S., & Basistha, A. (2007). Foreign aid and export performance: A panel data analysis of developing countries. Chapter 21. In S. Lahiri (Ed.), *Theory and practice of foreign aid* (Vol. 1, pp. 421–433). Elsevier.

Muñoz, S. (2006). Zimbabwe's export performance: The impact of the parallel market and governance factors. *IMF Working Paper, 28*(6).

Muscatelli, V. A., Stevenson, A. A., & Montagna, C. (1995). Modelling aggregate manufactured exports for some Asian newly industrialised economies. *The Review of Economics and Statistics,* 147–155.

Naseri, M. E., Wani, N. U. H., & Sidana, N. (2018). Determinants of exports in SAARC countries: An empirical evaluation. *Kardan Journal of Economics and Management Sciences, 4*(3), 38–57.

Nath, H. K. (2009). Trade, foreign direct investment, and growth: Evidence from transition economies. *Comparative Economic Studies, 51*, 20–50.

Ndikumana, L., Naidoo, K., & Aboobaker, A. (2020). *Capital flight from South Africa: A case study.* https://doi.org/10.7275/28043202

Noureen, S., & Mahmood, Z. (2016). Explaining trends and factors affecting export diversification in ASEAN and SAARC regions: An empirical analysis. *NUST Journal of Social Sciences and Humanities, 2*(1), 1–28.

Nurkse, R. (1961). Further comments on Professor Rosenstein-Rodan's paper. In H. S. Ellis, & assisted by H. C. Wallich (Eds.). *Economic development for Latin America. Proceedings of a Conference held by the International Economic Association.* Macmillan.

Pedroni, P. (1996). *Fully modified OLS for heterogeneous Co-integrated panels and the case of purchasing power parity.* Working Paper No. 96-020. Department of Economics, Indiana University.

Pedroni, P. (2000). Fully modified OLS for heterogeneous co-integrated panels. In *The review of economics and statistics* (Vol. 83, No. 4, pp. 727–731). MIT Press.

Prasad, S. (2000). *Determinants of exports in Fiji*. Reserves Bank of Fiji. Working Paper: 04.

Prasanna, N. (2010). Impact of foreign direct investment on export performance in India. *Journal of Social Sciences, 24*(1), 65–71.

Pursell, G., & Ahsan, F. M. Z. (2011). *Sri Lanka's trade policies: Back to protectionism*. Australia South Asia Research Center (ASARC). Working Paper, 03.

Qureshi, T. A., & Mahmood, Z. (2015). *The size of trade misinvoicing in Pakistan.* https://mpra.ub.uni-muenchen.de/65801/1/MPRA_paper_65801.pdf

Rana, P. B., & Dowling, J. M. (1990). Foreign capital and Asian economic growth. *Asian Development Review, 8*(2), 77–102.

Rangarajan, C., & Kannan, R. (2017). Determinants of India's exports. *Journal of Quantitative Economics, 15*(3), 629–646.

Rashid, A., & Waqar, S. M. (2017). Exchange rate fluctuations, firm size, and export behavior: An empirical investigation. *Small Business Economics, 49*, 609–625.

Rattsø, J. (1994). Medium-run adjustment under import compression: Macroeconomic analysis relevant for sub-Saharan Africa. *Journal of Development Economics, 45*(1), 35–54.

Razzaq, A., An, H., & Delpachitra, S. (2021). Does technology gap increase FDI spillovers on productivity growth? Evidence from Chinese outward FDI in Belt and Road host countries. *Technological Forecasting and Social Change, 172*, 121050.

Rehman, F. U., & Noman, A. A. (2020). Does infrastructure promote exports and foreign direct investment in selected Southeast Asian economies? An application of global infrastructure index. *Journal of Economic Studies, 48*(7), 1346–1370.

Roy, B. (2020). Determinants of agricultural exports of India: A commodity level analysis. Parikalpana. *KIIT Journal of Management, 16*.

Sajjad, A., & Mahmood, Z. (2014). An investigation into the export supply determinants of selected South Asian Economies. In Z. Mahmood (Ed.), *Perspectives on Pakistan's trade and development* (pp. 99–126). NUST University Press.

Sajjad, A., Mahmood, Z., & Sector, H. (2014). An investigation into the export supply determinants of selected South Asian Economies. *Perspectives on Pakistan's Trade and Development, 99*.

Sharma, K. (2000). *Export growth in India: Has FDI played a role?* https://doi.org/10.22004/ag.econ.28372

Sousa, C. M., Martínez-López, F. J., & Coelho, F. (2008). The determinants of export performance: A review of the research in the literature between 1998 and 2005. *International Journal of Management Reviews, 10*(4), 343–374.

Srinivasan, T. N. (1998). India's export performance: A comparative analysis. In I. J. Ahluwalia & I. M. D. Little (Eds.), *India's economic reforms and development essay for Manmohan Singh*. Oxford University Press.

Stanikzai, M., & Wani, N. U. H. (2023). Foreign aid and its impact on Afghanistan's economic setup: Purposes and implications. *Kardan Journal of Economics and Management Sciences, 6*(1), 35–55.

Sun, H. (2001). Foreign direct investment and regional export performance in China. *Journal of Regional Science, 41*(2), 317–336.

Svedberg, P. (2002). Trade compression and economic decline in sub-Saharan Africa. In *Economic crisis in Africa* (pp. 20–38). Routledge.

Tanzi, V. (1998). *Corruption around the world: Causes, consequences, scope and cures.* IMF Working Paper, 98/63.

Thede, S., & Gustafson, N. Å. (2012). The multifaceted impact of corruption on international trade. *The World Economy, 35*(5), 651–666.

Thirwall, A. P. (2000). *Trade, trade liberalization, and economic growth: Theory and evidence.* African Development Bank. Economic Research Paper, 63.

Utkulu, U., Seymen, D., & Ari, A. (2004). Export supply and trade reform: The Turkish evidence. In *International Conference on Policy Modelling*, Paris, June 30–July 2, 2004.

Wani, N. U. H. (2019). Nexus between openness to trade and economic growth: An empirical investigation of Afghanistan. *South Asia Economic Journal, 20*(2).

Wani, N. U. H., & Rasa, M. M. (2023). Dynamics of trade specialization and performance of SAFTA: A case study of Afghanistan. *South Asia Economic Journal, 24*(2), 153–179.

Yang, Y., & Ma, J. (2022). Analysis of factors affecting enterprise export product structure. *International Journal of Research in Engineering, Science and Management, 5*(12), 1–7.

Zhang, W., Saghaian, S., & Reed, M. (2023). Investigation of export-driving forces and trade potentials of the US bourbon whisky industry. *Applied Economics*, 1–21.

Zou, S., & Stan, S. (1998). The determinants of export performance: A review of the empirical literature between 1987 and 1997. *International Marketing Review, 15*(5), 333–356.

Chapter 4

# Export Diversification in ASEAN and SAARC Regions: Exploring Trends Patterns and Determinants Through Empirical Investigation

## Abstract

Export product concentration is common in developing nations, where raw materials and semi-manufactured commodities face rigid demand in international markets. This leads to the monopolisation of exports, particularly when targeting the developed world. Association of Southeast Asian Nations (ASEAN) and South Asian Association for Regional Cooperation (SAARC) nations have prioritised diversification to boost exports and per capita income, globalising their economies. The normalised Hirschman index is employed to analyse the determinants influencing the diversification of exports in ASEAN and SAARC countries from 2018 to 2021. Except for the fuel intensity variable, the results show that structural transformation, competitive advantages, industrial sector expansion, institutional capability, local investment development, financial stability and overall economic performance positively promote export diversification intensity. The key result is that institutional strength helps nations rapidly diversify their exports, highlighting the importance of structural transformation in boosting exports and globalising economies.

*Keywords*: Exports; determinants; export diversification; Association of Southeast Asian Nations; South Asian Association for Regional Cooperation

*JEL Codes*: C22; F10; F43

Policy Solutions for Economic Growth in a Developing Country, 83–103
Copyright © 2024 Nassir Ul Haq Wani
Published under exclusive licence by Emerald Publishing Limited
doi:10.1108/978-1-83753-430-220241005

## 1. Introduction

The realms of export promotion in developing nations hinge typically on unprocessed commodities and semi-finished exportable. Despite these product lines, there is always a rigid demand in international markets along with close alternates, thus facing market access concerns. In international markets, finished manufactured goods exported by poor nations suffer substantial trade obstacles. As a result, these nations' exports have the most significant proportion of raw materials and semi-manufactured goods. Globally, countries that have yet to diversify their exports have evolved more slowly than those implementing efficient export diversification strategies. As a consequence, countries with concentrated exports are more vulnerable to external economic fluctuations (Hausmann et al., 2007; Herzer & Nowak-Lehnmann, 2006; Lederman & Maloney, 2003; Matthee & Naudé, 2007; Ngassam et al., 2022; Saleem et al., 2022). Developing economies have prioritised export product diversification to increase exports and per capita income. Aside from globalisation, numerous economies have conducted structural shifts by transitioning export lines from basic and intermediate products to finished products.

As a result of the accessible sustained foreign currency profits, they had better economic growth. Income and export diversification have a non-linear connection because (at low-income levels) nations prefer to export a restricted number of items, exposing them to significant uncertainty in revenue from exports and negotiations for trade (Rath & Akram, 2017). Diversifying their exports minimises their exposure to volatility, allowing them to achieve economic stability. When a country achieves a particular level of prosperity via export diversification, it produces distinct goods by internalising economies of scale. With such a shift, these nations are re-focusing on export items. Such items often have significantly greater elastic demand worldwide, allowing nations to develop economies and achieve more robust long-term growth (Noureen & Mahmood, 2016; Yama & Wani, 2021; Yasmin et al., 2020).

Export diversification is often achieved by changing the export product mix (including novel goods or diverse goods) or boosting the worth (quality) of existing export products. Emerging economies have vigorously undertaken changes in this setting and have embraced economic laurels.

Numerous nations, on the other hand, have experienced little or no success, owing to an absence of awareness of the fundamental factors and trends in export diversification. The assessment of the underlying patterns and determinants of export market diversification should provide realistic study and policy insights for proactive intervention by the government. We were prompted to examine the pattern and causes of export product diversification in depth due to a paucity of regional studies in the South Asian Association for Regional Cooperation (SAARC) and Association of Southeast Asian Nations (ASEAN) nations. The majority of the globe's workforce lives in South Asia. Although this region is packed with opportunity, it is also beset by socio-economic challenges that affect the whole region. South Asian regional cooperation must be increased. When contrasted with other regional groups, including the ASEAN and the European Union, it lags behind.

While several countries in the surrounding region believe economic activity is a key element of regional prosperity, it is worth noting that South Asian trade just accounts for 5% of regional trade, whereas ASEAN accounts for 25%. As a result, Afghanistan's participation in SAARC was critical to the establishment of peace and prosperity in the region. Although Pakistan was earlier against it, with time realised the advantages of Afghanistan's inclusion. Following the spirit of escalating the trade intensity, an agreement was signed in 2010 between Pakistan and Afghanistan referred to as the 'Pakistan–Afghanistan Transit Trade Agreement'. This agreement aimed and expected to use each other's territory as a transit point for trade with other nations, like India (Wani & Rasa, 2023). Nonetheless, this has not occurred, and the agreement has not enhanced bilateral trade volume. The politicised nature of the inter-trade of Afghanistan, India and Pakistan is impeding economic collaboration in the region. Understanding how Afghanistan's unexpected entrance and lack of sufficient conditions have hampered SAARC is critical (Wani, 2019). The ratification of Afghanistan's participation by the founding members was driven more by geopolitical concerns than by a severe assessment of the benefits and downsides of this expansion (Ahmed & Zahoor, 2015).

According to the above debate, export diversification strategies have allowed SAARC and ASEAN nations to collaborate to boost exports and economies. Despite the two regions' success in export diversification, the current policy has room for improvement. A thorough examination of export diversification is required to determine the precise areas for future policy action. This chapter investigates the factors of export diversification in both areas to inform future policy design.

## 2. Literature Review

### 2.1 Diversification of Exports: Nature and Determinants

Understanding the underlying parameters of the diversification of exports is challenging since no complete theoretical or empirical framework, including all essential components, is available. Additionally, there are several explanations why export diversification and overall economic growth are desirable. The nation's GDP per capita, which includes the strength and quality of institutions, is one of the primary metrics for analysing the effect of diversification of exports. The growth theories (both the demand and supply side) project the vitality of GDP per capita. When a country's GDP per capita rises, so does its willingness to spend more (Aghion & Howitt, 1992). Other studies have stated that foreign direct investment (FDI) improves the macroeconomic situation efficiency by enhancing the country's business expansion rate (Hausmann et al., 2007). In theory, FDI (horizontal and vertical) has a positive impact on trade latency, principally contributing to the diversification of the export base (Alemu, 2008; Ndambendia, 2014; Yokota & Tomohara, 2009).

On the other hand, the depreciation of a country's real exchange rate increases overseas demand for its exportable products. It expands prospects for developing and shipping novel goods while also increasing the output of current exports (Felipe et al., 2010; Hlatshwayo & Saxegaard, 2016). The currency exchange rate and its volatility, on the other hand, have an impact on exports. Real exchange rate depreciation has been a significant driver of the diversification of export the supply chain (Kumeka et al., 2022; Nguse et al., 2021; Sekkat, 2016; Wondemu & Potts, 2016).

Literature also suggests other variables affecting the lineage of export growth like the gross fixed capital development (GFCD). The effects of GFCD are twofold; firstly, it helps in expanding the physical capital stock in the local economy, and secondly, helps in boosting technology. Many empirical studies have recently evaluated the favourable influence of GFC creation in export diversification (Duru & Ehidiamhen, 2018; Parteka & Tamberi, 2011; Rath & Akram, 2017). The most effective strategy for developing countries to boost their economic effectiveness is export diversification. The primary focus for economies is to lean towards the industrial sector by enhancing its foundations (Akbari, 2021; Lederman & Maloney, 2003). Noureen and Mahmood (2016) observed that macroeconomic variables have a significant connection with export diversification in the two regions (SAARC and ASEAN). In other words, depending too much on natural resource revenues lessens the need to diversify exports and thus results in a natural resource curse as elucidated in the case of ASEAN economies.

## 2.2 Theoretical Foundations

One of the oldest principles in economic growth theory is export diversification. The traditional international trade models suggested that nations should specialise and export based on their comparative advantages (Grimwade, 2003; Heckscher et al., 1991; Leamer & Levinsohn, 1995; Machado & Trigg, 2021; Ricardo, 1817; Smith, 1776). However, this principle was questioned by Prebisch (1950) and Singer (1950), later called as Prebisch–Singer hypothesis (PSH), who stated that specialisation in exporting items increases developing nations' reliance on exporting raw resources and agricultural products, consumer items and manufactured goods from advanced economies. They argued that the income sensitivity for purchasing essentials is lower than for manufactured products. As a result, emerging nations continue to need the possibility to expand quickly. Consequently, enterprises have to tailor their exported items to ensure continuity and expansion of their currency reserves as diversification reduces the likelihood of price swings and economic downturns. Several studies agreed with the PSH claiming that diversification of the export base improves a developing country's economic standing (Bonaglia & Fukasaku, 2003; Iqbal et al., 2021). Studies have also looked at the fluctuations in the exchange rate due to specialisation in natural resource exports in emerging economies. When such countries industrialise, capital-intensive products take precedence over knowledge-based ones. The human capital development and wage equity suffer as a consequence. Product-specific countries face export uncertainty as a result of substantial demand shocks in global markets (Matthee & Naudé, 2008).

Export diversification decreases the country's exposure to disruptions in such cases, resulting in stable exports.

## 3. Overview of the ASEAN and SAARC Regions

On 8 August 1967, Indonesia, Malaysia, the Philippines, Singapore and Thailand agreed to the Agreement of ASEAN (also known as the Bangkok Declaration), forming the Association of Southeast Asian Nations (ASEAN). On 7 January 1984, the ASEAN group was joined by Brunei Darussalam, followed by Vietnam on 28 July 1995, Lao PDR and Myanmar on 23 July 1997 and Cambodia on 30 April 1999 (Hong, 2021). SAARC, on the other hand, is one of the world's major economic groups, encompassing 23% of the global population, contributing to 6% of global GDP and 4.5% of globally traded goods, followed by trade among regions averaging roughly 6%. Mistrust and conflict are prevalent in South Asia (especially between India and Pakistan). To foster trust and collaboration in South Asia, India and Pakistan should learn valuable lessons from ASEAN's conflict resolution tactics and procedures (Jetly, 2003). South Asian nations may benefit from ASEAN's consultation and consensus-building tactics for addressing persistent strife without disturbing security, development and peace dynamics. Given the conditions in Afghanistan, SAARC may have adopted a staged approach, first offering temporary and later permanent membership. According to Kumari and Ocha (2016), SAARC is gaining a tighter relationship with ASEAN primarily via business collaboration and increased imports and exports. According to studies, ASEAN is critical to SAARC's business ties. ASEAN accounts for more than half of SAARC's trade. Because of its political stability, market size, infrastructure capability and economic openness, SAARC gravitates towards ASEAN.

Furthermore, bilateral and regional trade agreements have facilitated greater cooperation. Moreover, SAARC nations want to adopt new bilateral trade agreements with ASEAN to boost trade. Singla (2016) states that the 'ASEAN Way' of informal and low-key diplomacy has effectively managed conflict in Southeast Asia. However, tensions between ASEAN nations remain, as illustrated by bilateral disputes such as those between Singapore and Malaysia over water treaties and Singapore and Thailand over Temasek Holdings' investment. The success of ASEAN and the failure of SAARC may be connected to four key factors: mutual terror understanding, the significance of the crucial nation, extra-regional powers' engagement and a common standard. The SAARC economies experienced an annual growth rate hovering around 6.22%, and GDP per capita increased by 4.17%. Afghanistan and Bhutan had the most significant growth rates of 6.89 and 7.56% from 2008 to 2021, respectively, followed by India at 6.56%, Bangladesh at 5.30%, Sri Lanka at 5.19%, Nepal at 4.59% and Pakistan at 4.47% (Table 1).

Since SAARC's inception in 1985, trade openness has been relatively low (16.5%). It was primarily due to the SAARC's policy of an import substitution industrialisation approach while ignoring the promotion of exports.

Table 1. SAARC and ASEAN Countries' Economic Indicators.

| Country | GDP Growth (2008 and 2021) | Ratio of Exports with GDP (%) | | Ratio of Imports to GDP (%) | | GDP per Capita Growth (2008 and 2021) |
|---|---|---|---|---|---|---|
| | | 2008 | 2021 | 2008 | 2021 | |
| Afghanistan | 3.49 | 8.47 | 10.21 | 22.81 | 19.93 | 1.98 |
| Bangladesh | 5.30 | 5.55 | 19.54 | 13.23 | 26.76 | 3.34 |
| Bhutan | 7.89 | 15 | 40.08 | 51.1 | 62.9 | 6.01 |
| Nepal | 4.59 | 10.59 | 9.7 | 18.89 | 36.54 | 2.51 |
| India | 6.57 | 5.85 | 23.89 | 7.83 | 29.24 | 5.73 |
| Pakistan | 4.47 | 11.42 | 14.51 | 23.71 | 20.13 | 1.87 |
| Sri Lanka | 5.19 | 25.04 | 20.87 | 36.93 | 31.78 | 4.29 |
| **Total SAARC** | **5.35** | **11.7** | **19.82** | **24.92** | **32.46** | **3.67** |
| Indonesia | 3.49 | 8.47 | 10.21 | 22.81 | 19.93 | 1.98 |
| Malaysia | 5.3 | 5.55 | 19.54 | 13.23 | 26.76 | 3.34 |
| Philippines | 7.89 | 15 | 40.08 | 51.1 | 62.9 | 6.01 |
| Singapore | 4.59 | 11.57 | 10.7 | 19.97 | 37.51 | 2.5 |
| Thailand | 6.56 | 5.18 | 24.81 | 7.56 | 28.41 | 4.72 |
| **Total ASEAN** | **5.56** | **9.15** | **21.06** | **22.93** | **35.1** | **3.71** |

*Source:* Authors compilation based on the data from WITS database.

However, later in the 1980s, SAARC economies envisioned a new industrialisation strategy, concentrating on export promotion, trade liberalisation policies and efforts to diversify exports. These initiatives raised openness dramatically, from 16.5% in 1985 to 63.8% in 2021. Concurrently, there was a significant increase in export product diversification. SAARC nations have been able to stabilise their foreign currency revenues via both openness and export diversification. Afghanistan joined many significant international trade institutions in 2016, including the Trade Facilitation Agreement and the World Trade Organization. Afghanistan was given observer status under the Central Asia Trade and Investment Framework Agreement in 2014.

Tariff assurance, subsidies, subsidised export financing, technical assistance and skill and product development are all measures that contribute to the diversification of export products. Furthermore, the SAARC nations enacted more liberal labour regulations to aid export enterprises in sectors (non-traditional). Special incentives were put into place to increase local enterprises' engagement globally. To diversify trade, they all sought technical support from international organisations. With these policy efforts, SAARC nations experienced a structural shift in exports (essential commodities to manufactured products).

When the ASEAN countries changed their approach to development in the 1970s to focus on industrialisation that emphasised exports, countries witnessed unprecedented development. Countries likewise availed advantage of the liberalisation of trade for diversifying the economy. The measures taken included tax rebates and incentives for exporters, incentives to encourage FDI, improved trade facilitation and decreased bureaucratic inefficiencies, lower home expenses and greater investments in infrastructure. Furthermore, they gave global corporations industrial, financial and communication services to encourage exports. They also promoted labour-intensive enterprises and provided technical education to enhance labour skills.

With the implementation of the previously indicated policies, the industrial sector's proportion of GDP increased in the ASEAN nations between 2008 and 2021: from 29% to 56% in Indonesia, 27% to 54% in Thailand and 35% to 53% in Malaysia. Due to export diversification strategies, the ASEAN nations' export share of machinery and industrial items climbed from 20% in 1995 to 50% in 2010 and reached 59% in 2021 (Sabhasri et al., 2013).

According to Table 2, ASEAN nations' export diversification has risen since 2008. Export diversification was 0.374 from 2008 to 2012, 0.310 from 2013 to 2018 and 0.308 from 2019 to 2021. The decrease in the Herfindahl–Hirschman Index (HHI) indicates a growing proclivity for diversification of exports. Based on the data statistics, Malaysia has the most diverse export portfolio among ASEAN members, as the HHI dropped from 0.319 in 2008 to 0.267 between 2013 and 2018. Over the same time period, HHI in Thailand lowered from 0.353 to 0.321,

Table 2. Export Diversification of SAARC and ASEAN.

| Country | 2008–2012 | 2013–2018 | 2019–2021 |
|---|---|---|---|
| Afghanistan | 0.457 | 0.332 | 0.307 |
| Bangladesh | 0.371 | 0.277 | 0.267 |
| India | 0.375 | 0.322 | 0.338 |
| Pakistan | 0.457 | 0.332 | 0.307 |
| Sri Lanka | 0.353 | 0.31 | 0.321 |
| **SAARC (Average)** | **0.374** | **0.31** | **0.308** |
| Indonesia | 0.457 | 0.332 | 0.307 |
| Malaysia | 0.319 | 0.277 | 0.267 |
| The Philippines | 0.375 | 0.322 | 0.338 |
| Singapore | 0.457 | 0.332 | 0.307 |
| Thailand | 0.353 | 0.310 | 0.321 |
| **Total ASEAN** | **0.374** | **0.31** | **0.308** |

*Source:* The calculations are based on the data from the UNCOMTRADE.

while it fell from 0.375 to 0.338, 0.457 to 0.307 and 0.457 to 0.307 in the Philippines, Singapore and Indonesia, respectively. Surprisingly, after the 2010 economic slump, Malaysia and the Philippines suffered a reversal in export diversification, and the trend has continued to worsen.

The HHI ranges from 0.1 to 0.18, indicating moderate market concentration. In contrast, if the HHI is less than 0.01 and more than 0.18, it means a highly competitive market. According to Table 3, the diversification of exports in the member nations of SAARC has increased since 2008. From 2008 to 2014, the SAARC nations' HHI value was 0.464; from 2014 to 2016, it was 0.371; from 2019 to 2021, it was 0.267. The decrease in HHI demonstrates an improving tendency in the SAARC nations' export product diversification. The graph additionally demonstrates that Bangladesh witnessed the most diversification of any SAARC nation. Over the same period, Bangladesh's HHI declined to 0.338 from 0.375, whereas in the case of Pakistan, the HHI values decreased to 0.307 from 0.457, and for Sri Lanka, the experience was the same accounting for 0.321 from 0.353.

The member states of ASEAN together comprise an estimated population of approximately 600 million, representing 8.8% of the population pie of the world. As of 2022, the region's overall GDP hovered around $3.22 trillion. In Table 3, it is witnessed that ASEAN economies are more open economies by international standards. Between 1980 and 2013, GDP in ASEAN nations expanded at a 5.41% annual rate, while per capita GDP increased at a 6.93% annual rate. Furthermore, in accordance with the data, GDP expansion rates in Malaysia and Singapore have risen with an average yearly increase of 6.01% and 6.84%, respectively. These economies are growing at a quicker rate than the rest of ASEAN. Thailand with a growth rate of 4.34 and Singapore with 4.18% lead the ASEAN region in GDP growth. The majority of them had a significant increase

Table 3. HH Market Concentration Index of SAARC and ASEAN.

| Country Name | 2008 | 2010 | 2012 | 2014 | 2016 | 2018 | 2019 | 2021 |
|---|---|---|---|---|---|---|---|---|
| Afghanistan | 0.16 | 0.15 | 0.18 | 0.24 | 0.22 | 0.24 | 0.30 | 0.30 |
| Brunei | 0.24 | 0.26 | 0.25 | 0.24 | 0.22 | 0.18 | 0.16 | 0.17 |
| Cambodia | 0.27 | 0.19 | 0.15 | 0.11 | 0.10 | 0.06 | 0.07 | 0.08 |
| Indonesia | 0.07 | 0.07 | 0.07 | 0.07 | 0.07 | 0.06 | 0.07 | 0.07 |
| Malaysia | 0.07 | 0.08 | 0.08 | 0.08 | 0.08 | 0.08 | 0.08 | 0.09 |
| The Philippines | 0.11 | 0.10 | 0.10 | 0.11 | 0.10 | 0.10 | 0.10 | 0.10 |
| Singapore | 0.05 | 0.06 | 0.06 | 0.06 | 0.06 | 0.07 | 0.07 | 0.07 |
| Thailand | 0.05 | 0.06 | 0.06 | 0.06 | 0.06 | 0.06 | 0.06 | 0.06 |
| Vietnam | 0.08 | 0.07 | 0.07 | 0.06 | 0.06 | 0.08 | 0.09 | 0.09 |

*Source:* Authors compilation based on the data from WITS database.

in their trade portions of GDP, owing to the contribution of the policies aimed at export promotion, trade liberalisation and diversification.

## 4. Research Methodology

### 4.1 Measurement of Export Diversification

Export diversification can potentially be quantified through several approaches. The choice of a measure is often impacted by different definitions, dimensions, forms and degrees of diversity. Herfindahl, normalised Hirschmann and total difference measurements are the most common methods (Petersson, 2005; Pineres & Ferrantino, 1997). These indexes are used to assess the export diversity of various areas. The Herfindahl index is the first diversity index identifying changes in export revenue or regional concentration. According to Petersson (2005), it is computed as follows:

$$\text{SPEC} = \sum_i \left( E_{jit} \Big/ \sum_j E_{jit} \right) \tag{A1}$$

where $E_{jit}$ indicates the country $j$'s exports in sector $i$ at a given period $t$. The values range from 0 to 1, with 0 indicating comprehensive export diversity and 1 indicating export concentration or specialisation. The normalised HI index, based on Al-Marhubi (2000), is computed as follows:

$$H_{jt} = \left\{ \sqrt{\sum_{i=1}^{n} \left( \frac{X_{it}}{X_{jt}} \right)^2} - \left( \sqrt{\frac{1}{n}} \right) \right\} \Big/ \left\{ 1 - \left( \sqrt{\frac{1}{n}} \right) \right\}$$

where $X_{it}$ is the market value of sector $i$ in country $j$, $X_{jt}$ is the overall export volume of nation $j$ for a given time period $t$ and $n$ denotes the industry number. According to Al-Marhubi (2000) and Naqvi and Morimune (2005), one index indicates total export concentration, whereas values closer to zero indicate an extremely diversified export composition.

Based on Al-Marhubi's (2000) approach, the total variance of the country's share of total world exports is a third approach for measuring export diversification and is quantified as follows:

$$S_{jt} = \frac{\sum_i |h_{ijt}| - |h_{it}|}{2}$$

where '$it$' denotes the ratio of the sector $i$'s exports to total exports of nation $j$, and '$h_{it}$' denotes the proportion of the sector $i$'s exports to the rest of the world over a specific time period $t$. The estimated index score spans between 0 (complete concentration) and 1 (complete diversification). When there is evidence of export diversification due to changes in export content across industries, this measure is helpful. Furthermore, this measure could represent the two extremes (diversity and margins) as well.

## 4.2 Dataset and Econometric Framework

There are limited conceptual or empirical frameworks available to explain the variables of diversification of exports. Based on the insights from Parteka and Tamberi (2011) and Bebczuk and Berrettoni (2006), the low per capita levels of GDP correlate with a low level of comparative diversity within economic frameworks. As a result, the general form of the basic model is as follows:

$$HHI = f(GDPP) \tag{1}$$

Further to add, in export diversification, the country-specific impacts are relevant and substantial (Bebczuk & Berrettoni, 2006; Parteka & Tamberi, 2011). Additionally, there are other elements that have an impact on the export diversification process. As a result, model (1) may be modified as follows:

$$HHI = f(GDPP, FDI, GFCF, CPS, REER, MANU, H - CAPITAL, \\ EXP, R - DUMMY, FUEL) \tag{2}$$

The proportion of FDI to GDP is represented by FDI, the proportion of gross fixed capital formation to GDP is denoted by GFCF, the proportion of manufactured exports to overall exports is denoted by MANU, human capital is represented by H-Capital, the proportion of exports to GDP is denoted by EXP, the real effective exchange rate is denoted by REER, a regional dummy variable is denoted by R-Dummy, the credit to the private sector is reflected by CPS and proportion of fuel exports to total exports is denoted by FUEL. The overall specification encompassing these variables is set in a behavioural equation for estimation and is presented in Eq. (2) as follows:

$$HHI = \alpha_0 + \beta_0 FUEL_{it} + \beta_1 GDPP_{it} + \beta_2 CPS_{it} + \beta_1 MANU_{it} + \beta_5 GFCF_{it} \\ + \beta_6 REER_{it} + \beta_7 FDI_{it} + \beta_1 HCapital_{it} + \beta_9 EXP_{it} + \beta_{10} Dummy_{it} + \mu_{it} \tag{3}$$

where $\mu_{it}$ represents the disturbance term and $t$ and $i$ represent the time period and the countries, respectively. The prime focus is to evaluate the repercussions of various adjustments, such as banking and liberalisation of trade, as well as economic policies, in addition to the traditional elements that explain export diversification documented in the literature. The employed variables reflect and characterise macroeconomic efficiency and strength and improve enterprises' growth potential, which has consequences for export diversification (Alaya, 2012; Fonchamnyo & Akame, 2017; Ruane & Sutherland, 2005; Swathi & Sridharan, 2022; Vasilyeva et al., 2022).

## 4.3 Data Sources

The data have been collected mainly from the World Bank through the world development indicators. The research spans the years 2008–2021. A balanced panel is used in the dataset by employing a 4-digit Standard International Trading Classification (SITC) coding classification from the UNCOMTRADE database. Since the data availability is limited, the analysis is restricted to Afghanistan,

Bangladesh, India, Pakistan and Sri Lanka in the SAARC, whereas in the ASEAN, Indonesia, Malaysia, the Philippines, Singapore and Thailand have been selected for analysis.

# 5. Findings and Analysis

The primary need for determining an extended link between the diversification of exports and other regressor factors in the panel dataset is to investigate the order of integration of the variables. The results encompass a balanced panel sample of five ASEAN and five SAARC countries analysed over a 14-year period (2008–2021).

## 5.1 Empirical Findings Based on Unit Root

Although time periods are larger and of greater significance than cross sections, it is critical to investigate data unit root attributes. The test used to investigate unit root features of data is determined by the existence (or lack) of cross-sectional dependency among the nations studied. The Pesaran (2003) exam is used for this purpose. This test implies that measuring the factor loading is a simpler technique to reduce cross-sectional dependency. To quantify the cross-sectional variability caused by a single-factor method, the Augmented Dickey Fuller (ADF) test is utilised in conjunction with the latent cross-section mean and standard deviation. To address this, Table 5 displays the results of the Pesaran (2003) test. The ADF test corresponds to two hypotheses with the null hypothesis stating no cross-sectional dependency and the reverse of this in the alternate hypothesis.

Given that the null hypothesis is accepted, we look at the data's unit root properties. Specific widely unit root test options are offered when cross sections are independent. Im et al. (2003) are employed for the unit root test, as it restricts the impact of the Levin et al. (2002) test because it does not account for panel heterogeneity in unit root attributes.

Given that the null hypothesis is accepted, we investigate the unit root characteristics of the data. Specific widely unit root test alternatives are provided when cross sections are independent. Im, Pesaran and Shin (IPS) (2003) are presented in Table 4. This addresses the constraints of the Levin, Lin and Chu (LLC) test, such as the reality that LLC is limited since it cannot account for panel heterogeneity in terms of unit root properties.

In contrast to the alternative, using IPS as a unit root test states that every single period has a unitary root. Table 5 displays the IPS test results. Further to connect, Engle and Granger's (1987) tests developed by Kao and Pedroni are the

Table 4. Cross-Sectional Dependence Assessment.

|  | **Test Statistics** | **Probability** |
|---|---|---|
| IPS test | 1.231 | 0.2043 |

*Source:* Authors' compilation of the data output from the EViews 8.0.

Table 5. Results of the IPS Test.

| Variable | Level | | First Difference | | Order of Integration |
|---|---|---|---|---|---|
| | Intercept and Trend | P Values | Intercept and Trend | P Values | |
| CPS | −2.5101 | 0.5423 | −10.531 | 0.000*** | I(1) |
| REER | −0.0592 | 0.4753 | −4.432 | 0.012*** | I(1) |
| Manu | −3.5213 | 0.5213 | −9.7621 | 0.000*** | I(1) |
| FDI | −1.2379 | 0.1087 | −4.4123 | 0.021*** | I(1) |
| GDPP | −3.8515 | 0.9998 | −7.3161 | 0.005*** | I(1) |
| EXP | −3.6431 | 0.2143 | −9.6101 | 0.000*** | I(1) |
| GFCF | −1.2021 | 0.3032 | −2.5182 | 0.010*** | I(1) |
| FUEL | −2.0219 | 0.4021 | −7.3067 | 0.000*** | I(1) |
| H-Capital | −1.5312 | 0.4371 | −3.5121 | 0.001*** | I(1) |
| HI | −3.1129 | 0.0014 | −5.3034 | 0.001*** | I(1) |

*Source:* Authors' compilation of the data output from the EViews 8.0.
*Note:* The symbol *** denotes statistical significance at 1%.
$H_0$ indicates the presence of a unit root.
$H_1$: The lack of a unit root.

most sophisticated tests for co-integration. Pedroni tests assess if there is co-integration but do not offer a long-run estimate. Instead, the study has employed the Kao test, similar to the Pedroni test, to estimate a long-term connection within variables.

At the 1% significant level, the Kao ADF-*t* test reveals a long-run association between the variables (Table 6). As a result, the concern of erroneous regression is eliminated. The results have established the existence of a linear combination using the Kao (1999) co-integration test. Given this, ordinary least squares (OLS) estimators in a co-integrated panel will be biased and inconsistent; hence, an

Table 6. Results of the Co-integration Test.

| Variable | t-statistic | P Value |
|---|---|---|
| ADF Value | −2.0112 | 0.029*** |

Augmented Dickey-Fuller Test Equation (Dep. Variable: D (RESID))

| Variable | Coefficient | Standard Error | t-statistic | P Value |
|---|---|---|---|---|
| RESID(−1) | −0.231 | 0.07145 | −3.687 | 0.001*** |

*Source:* Authors' compilation of the data output from the EViews 8.0.
*Note:* The symbol *** denotes statistical significance at 1%.

alternative technique must be adopted. Consequently, we execute the panel using Pedroni's (2000) fully modified OLS (FMOLS). FMOLS, which applies a corrective technique, produces the estimated model's coefficients in the long run and is devoid of heterogeneity and correlation in series. As a result, we use FMOLS estimations to calculate the long-run effect of variables that do not have a serial correlation. These estimations provide consistent parameter estimates using a limited sample size and assist in adjusting for serial correlations while additionally considering the substantial diversity across the nations in both areas.

## 5.2 Fully Modified Least Squares Empirical Results

The adjusted OLS model results demonstrate that in the economies of the SAARC and ASEAN areas, the intensity of explanatory variables included in the model has a significant and favourable impact on export diversification. Under the plausible premise of a later effect on diversification, the values of the variables that are independent are one-year lag values. The results of the FMOLS are presented in Table 7.

The export GDP ratio's negative value implies a favourable association between export diversification and the economy's competitiveness in the global market for both areas. The findings confirm the notion that strengthening SAARC and ASEAN nations' competitiveness globally allows them to broaden their exports. The results of Sarin et al. (2022), Tovar Mora and Martínez Armas (2011) and Mayangsari and Handoyo (2017) all find a substantial and positive relationship between performance and diversification of exports.

The negative link between personal credit and GDP reinforces the hypothesis that growth in finance reduces export product concentration in both regions. In simple terms, economic advances help economies in the region broaden the products they export. These findings corroborate Acemoglu and Zilibotti's (1997) research findings. Furthermore, in both regions, FDI and export diversification are favourably linked (Table 7). The link demonstrates that FDI improves macroeconomic efficiency and diversifies product offerings. As a result, the country's exports are diversifying. Moran (2010) proposed in this respect that since FDI offers new ideas, expertise and practices for starting innovative businesses, the influx of FDI is expected to culminate in the diversification of exports. Furthermore, FDI may help enterprises in their home nations swiftly create networks and promote forward and backward connections. Moreover, supplying technical spillovers might assist the host nations in diversifying their exports, thereby strengthening their production line and foundation. These findings are supported by the findings of Debbarma et al. (2022), Egyir et al. (2020), Filipescu et al. (2013), Kowalski et al. (2015), Ngoc et al. (2022) and Yu et al. (2022).

Diversification of exports has become crucial to ensure effective engagement with the global trade system, as well as for growth and development (Egyir et al., 2020; Matthee & Naudé, 2007; Yu et al., 2022).

Globally, the trade pattern has evolved away from primary exports and towards manufactured exports, boosting the diversification of exports.

Table 7. FMOLS Results.

| Variable | Coefficient | Standard Error | t-Statistics | p Values |
| --- | --- | --- | --- | --- |
| CPS | −0.00044 | 0.00219 | −1.876 | 0.0045* |
| REER | −0.00086 | 0.00316 | −2.8661 | 0.0001* |
| FUEL | 0.000231 | 0.00127 | 2.0186 | 0.0005** |
| FDI | −0.00387 | 0.05310 | −2.1020 | 0.0007* |
| GDPP | −0.00218 | 0.01923 | −4.8458 | 0.0000* |
| GFCF | −0.00165 | 0.00121 | −3.7231 | 0.0005* |
| R-DUMMY | −0.08712 | 0.01821 | −4.7631 | 0.0001* |
| H-CAPITAL | −0.00421 | 0.05321 | −5.9084 | 0.0005* |
| MANU | −0.00156 | 0.02190 | −4.0967 | 0.0001* |
| EXP | −0.00110 | 0.01093 | −3.8741 | 0.0005* |
| C | 0.029871 | 0.03213 | 7.6076 | 0.0000* |

| | | | |
| --- | --- | --- | --- |
| $R$-squared | 0.835107 | Mean dependent variable | −0.169692 |
| Adjusted $R$-squared | 0.815077 | SD dependent variable | 0.052147 |
| SE of regression | 0.05052 | Sum squared residual | 0.007585 |
| Durbin-Watson stat | 1.87574 | Long-run variance | 0.000979 |

*Source:* Authors' compilation of the data output from the EViews 8.0.

*Note:* The symbols * and ** denote relevance at the 1% and 5% levels, correspondingly.
It is worth noting that as we move from 1 to 0, 'export diversity' grows; consequently, a negative connotation of coefficients denotes a gain in export diversity due to more offers to the private market.

ASEAN countries diversified their production divisions by making fundamental changes to improve their financial standing. These development approaches prioritise export diversification, and ASEAN countries have achieved greater maturity than SAARC economies (Shepherd, 2009). These results are also compatible with the findings of this study. The calculated model in Table 7 includes a regional dummy representing a simulation ASEAN area benchmark. A beneficial and significant effect reveals that the ASEAN region has a more significant and substantially better export diversification mechanism than the area encompassed by SAARC.

Growth in domestic investment has a statistically significant and favourable connection with the diversification of exports. Khan and Kumar (1997) agree with our conclusions. Both areas have a favourable and substantial association between human capital and export diversification. Our findings are supported by

Agosin et al. (2012). GDP per capita measures a country's institutional strength. Furthermore, our research results indicate that per capita GDP is positively and significantly connected to the diversification of exports, correlating with the findings of Hodey et al. (2015), Fonchamnyo and Akame (2017) and Siddiqui (2018). The data also show that the manufacturing-related exporting-to-total export percentage is positively and highly associated with export diversification, supporting the findings of Agosin (2007), Carrere et al. (2007) and Lim (2012).

The exchange rate coefficient's positive linkage suggests that SAARC and ASEAN are motivated to diversify their export product portfolios due to the actual depreciation of local currencies. Specialisation is reduced because depreciation boosts exports and drives even non-exporting enterprises to export. This study's results corroborate Rodrik's (1998) and Krugman's (1987) results. The FUEL coefficient has a positive sign. Natural resource exports have a considerable correlation with the diversification of exports. This further reveals the detrimental influence and supports the axioms of the resource curse conundrum, further leading nations to become sluggish or erratic. As a consequence, the attempts to diversify exports are minimised. These findings are in line with the results of Lederman and Maloney (2003), Qaiser and Mahmood (2016) and Sediqi et al. (2018).

# 6. Conclusion

This chapter investigated the determinants of export diversification in SAARC and ASEAN economies. The impact of variables such as institution resilience (strength), efficiency and competitiveness, national investment advancement, financial sector advancement, natural resources and macroeconomic performance on export diversification was explored. The empirical results reveal that all variables have a strong relationship with export diversification in both regions, except for the fuel-intensity variable. In the simplest terms, reliance on natural resource exports lessens the requirement for export diversification.

Consequently, we observed a natural resource curse in the ASEAN and SAARC countries. The result suggests that institutional capacity allows countries to promptly broaden their exports. In other words, if a country has an effectively developed physical infrastructure along with solid governance, it has a greater opportunity to diversify its exports. Additionally, FDI also promotes export diversification by fostering stable macroeconomic conditions and increasing efficiency in the economy via the transfer of technology and expertise. Similarly, increased domestic investment helps economies diversify their exports by providing the necessary domestic resources to diversify their production base. Simultaneously, increasing the financial industry, which offers required finance to privately owned companies, represents an advantage for the diversification of exports. Effective rates of exchange have also been crucial in diversifying exports, as real currency depreciation is lucrative, enhancing the competitiveness needed for export diversification.

*6.1 Policy Implications*

In light of the evidence presented above, we may deduce the following policy implications for the SAARC and ASEAN regions:

- Reform and strengthen institutions to aid in export diversification. It should improve institutional policymaking capacity and establish a business-friendly environment.
- Stimulate FDI by implementing suitable policies and incentives for tax simplification, flexible labour markets and improved infrastructure.
- Policymakers must diligently oversee resources to maximise their ultimate utilisation to reorganise markets and exports rather than waste them; they must safeguard macroeconomic equilibrium and strengthen every area of the economy to expand exports.
- Stabilise and maintain the realms of local currencies and price increases with the goal of boosting competitiveness in global marketplaces and achieving export diversification.

# Bibliography

Acemoglu, D., & Zilibotti, F. (1997). Was Prometheus unbound by chance? Risk diversification and growth. *Journal of Political Economy, 115*(4), 709–751.

Aghion, P., & Howitt, P. (1992). A model of growth through creative destruction. *Econometrica, 60*(2), 323–351.

Agosin, M. (2007). Export diversification and growth in emerging economies. https:// hdl.handle.net/11362/11322

Agosin, M. R., Alvarez, R., & Bravo-Ortega, C. (2012). Determinants of export diversification around the world: 1962–2000. *The World Economy, 35*(3), 295–315.

Ahmed, Z. S., & Zahoor, M. (2015). Afghanistan in SAARC: A critical assessment of organisational expansion. *South Asian Survey, 22*(2), 171–188.

Akbari, S. (2021). *The WTO transit regime for landlocked countries and its impacts on members' regional transit agreements: The case of Afghanistan's transit trade with Pakistan* (Vol. 17). Springer Nature.

Al-Marhubi, F. (2000). Export diversification and growth: An empirical investigation. *Applied Economics Letters, 7*(9), 559–562.

Alaya, M. (2012). The determinants of MENA export diversification: An empirical analysis. In *Corruption and Economic Development ERF 18th Annual Conference*. Cairo, Egypt.

Alemu, A. M. (2008). Determinants of vertical and horizontal export diversification: Evidence from sub-Saharan Africa and East Asia. *Ethiopian Journal of Economics, 17*(2).

Arawomo, D. F., Oyelade, A. O., & Tella, A. T. (2014). Determinants of export diversification in Nigeria: Any special role for foreign direct investment (FDI)? *Journal of Economics and Business Research, 20*(2), 21–33.

Arip, M. A., Yee, L. S., & Karim, B. A. (2010). *Export diversification and economic growth in Malaysia*. MPRA Paper No. 20588.

Baltagi, B. H. (2008). Forecasting with panel data. *Journal of Forecasting, 27*(2), 153–173.

Bebczuk, R. N., & Berrettoni, D. (2006). *Explaining export diversification: An empirical analysis.* Documentos de Trabajo.

Bolivian, S. (2009). *Export diversification and inclusive growth.* Policy Research Working Paper No. 127. The World Bank, Washington, DC.

Bonaglia, F., & Fukasaku, K. (2003). *Export diversification in low-income countries: An international challenge after Doha.* Working Paper No. 209. OECD Development Centre, Doha.

Carrere, C., Strauss-Kahn, V., & Cadot, O. (2007). *Export diversification: What is behind the hump?* Discussion Paper No. 6590. Centre for Economic Policy Research (CEPR), London.

De Benedictis, L., Gallegati, M., & Tamberi, M. (2009). Overall specialisation and development: Countries diversify. *Review of World Economics, 145*(1), 37–55.

De Ferranti, D., Perry, G. D., & Maloney, W. (2002). From natural resources to the knowledge of world economy. *The American Economic Review, 89*(5), 1234–1258.

Debbarma, J., Choi, Y., Yang, F., & Lee, H. (2022). Exports as a new paradigm to connect business and information technology for sustainable development. *Journal of Innovation & Knowledge, 7*(4), 100233.

Duru, I., & Ehidiamhen, P. (2018). Empirical investigation of the impact of export diversification on economic growth: Evidence from Nigeria, 1980–2016. *Journal of Economics, Management and Trade, 21*(7), 1–24.

Egyir, J., Sakyi, D., & Baidoo, S. T. (2020). How does capital flows affect the impact of trade on economic growth in Africa? *Journal of International Trade & Economic Development, 29*(3), 353–372.

Ekholm, K., Forslid, R., & Markusen, J. (2007). Export-platform foreign direct investment. *Journal of the European Economic Association, 5*(4), 776–795.

Elhiraika, A. B., & Mbate, M. M. (2014). Assessing the determinants of export diversification in Africa. *Applied Econometrics and International Development, 14*(1), 147–160.

Engle, R. F., & Granger, C. W. (1987). Co-Integration and error correction: Representation, estimation, and testing. *Econometica, 73*(5), 251–276.

Felipe, J., McCombie, J. S., & Naqvi, K. (2010). Is Pakistan's growth rate balance-of-payments constrained? Policies and implications for development and growth. *Oxford Development Studies, 38*(4), 477–496.

Ferdous, F. B. (2011). Export diversification in East Asian economies: Some factors affecting the scenario. *International Journal of Social Science and Humanities, 1*(1), 13–18.

Filipescu, D. A., Prashantham, S., Rialp, A., & Rialp, J. (2013). Technological innovation and exports: Unpacking their reciprocal causality. *Journal of International Marketing, 21*(1), 23–38.

Fonchamnyo, D. C., & Akame, A. R. (2017). Determinants of export diversification in Sub-Sahara African region: A fractionalized logit estimation model. *Journal of Economics and Finance, 41*, 330–342.

Gourdon, J. (2010). *FDI flows and export diversification: Looking at extensive and intensive margins in trade competitiveness of the Middle East and North Africa: Policies for export diversification.* The World Bank.

Grimwade, N. (2003). *International trade: New patterns of trade, production and investment*. Routledge.

Hausmann, R., Hwang, J., & Rodrik, D. (2007). What you export matters. *Journal of Development Economics, 12*(1), 1–25.

Heckscher, G., Heckscher, E. F., & Ohlin, B. (1991). *Heckscher-Ohlin trade theory*. MIT Press.

Herzer, D., & Nowak-Lehnmann, D. F. (2006). What does export diversification do for growth? An econometric analysis. *Applied Economics, 38*(15), 1825–1838.

Hesse, H. (2008). *Export diversification and economic growth*. Working Paper 21, Commission of Growth and Development. The World Bank, Washington, DC.

Hlatshwayo, S., & Saxegaard, M. M. (2016). *The consequences of policy uncertainty: Disconnects and dilutions in the South African real effective exchange rate-export relationship*. International Monetary Fund.

Hodey, L. S., Oduro, A. D., & Senadza, B. (2015). Export diversification and economic growth in Sub-Saharan Africa. *Journal of African Development, 17*(2), 67–81.

Hong, P. M. (2021). *The importance of export diversification for developing ASEAN economies*. ISEAS Publishing.

Im, K. S., Pesaran, M. H., & Shin, Y. (2003). Testing for unit roots in heterogeneous panels. *Journal of Econometrics, 115*(1), 53–74.

Iqbal, N., Abbasi, K. R., Shinwari, R., Guangcai, W., Ahmad, M., & Tang, K. (2021). Does export diversification and environmental innovation achieve the carbon neutrality target of OECD economies? *Journal of Environmental Management, 291*, 112648.

Jetly, R. (2003). Conflict management strategies in ASEAN: Perspectives for SAARC. *The Pacific Review, 16*(1), 53–76.

Kao, C., & Chiang, M. H. (1997). On the estimation and inference of a cointegrated regression in panel data. *American Journal of Mathematical and Management Sciences, 19*(12), 75–114.

Khan, M. S., & Kumar, M. S. (1997). Public and private investment and the growth process in developing countries. *Oxford Bulletin of Economics & Statistics, 59*(1), 69–88.

Klinger, B., & Lederman, D. (2004). *Discovery and development: An empirical exploration of new products*. The World Bank Policy Research Working Paper No. 3450. The World Bank, Washington, DC.

Koren, M., & Tenreyro, S. (2007). Volatility and development. *Quarterly Journal of Economics, 122*(1), 243–287.

Kowalski, P., Gonzalez, J. L., Ragoussis, A., & Ugarte, C. (2015). *Participation of developing countries in global value chains: Implications for trade and trade-related policies*. https://doi.org/10.1787/5js33lfw0xxn-en

Krugman, P. (1987). The narrow moving band, the Dutch disease, and the competitive consequences of Mrs Thatcher: Notes in the presence of dynamic scale economies. *Journal of Development Economics, 27*(2), 41–55.

Kumari, I. D., & Ocha, W. (2016). Effect of ASEAN on SAARC: The perspective of trade. *RSU International Journal of College of Government, 3*(1).

Kumeka, T. T., Uzoma-Nwosu, D. C., & David-Wayas, M. O. (2022). The effects of COVID-19 on the interrelationship among oil prices, stock prices and exchange rates in selected oil exporting economies. *Resources Policy, 77*, 102744.

Leamer, E. E., & Levinsohn, J. (1995). International trade theory: The evidence. *Handbook of International Economics*, *3*, 1339–1394.

Lederman, D., & Maloney, W. (2003). *Trade structure and growth*. Policy Research Working Paper No. 3025. The World Bank, Washington, DC.

Levin, A., Lin, C. F., & Chu, C. (2002). Unit root test in panel data: Asymptotic and finite sample properties. *Journal of Econometrics*, *108*(19), 1–25.

Lewis, S. B. (2004). Determinants of sustainability of trade liberalization: Export diversification. *Wharton Research Scholars Journal*, *4*(1), 1–58.

Lim, J. (2012). *Export diversification in a transitioning economy: The case of Syria*. Policy Research Working Paper, No. 5811. The World Bank, Washington, DC.

Machado, P. S., & Trigg, A. B. (2021). On absolute and comparative advantage in international trade: A Pasinetti pure labour approach. *Structural Change and Economic Dynamics*, *59*, 375–383.

Matthee, M., & Naudé, W. (2007). Export diversity and regional growth: Empirical evidence from South Africa (No. 2007/11). WIDER Research Paper.

Mayangsari, E. P., & Handoyo, R. D. (2017). Impact export diversification on exchange rate regime choice. *JDE (Journal of Developing Economies)*, *2*(2), 25–33.

Moran, R. (2010). The state and effective control of foreign capital: The case of South Korea. *World Politics*, *43*(1), 111–138.

Naqvi, H., & Morimune, K. (2005). *An empirical analysis of the sustainability of trade deficits*. Discussion Paper No. 072. Interfaces for Advanced Economic Analysis. Kyoto University, Kyoto.

Ndambendia, H. (2014). *Exports diversification and knowledge sharing from south-south and south-north economic cooperation: Evidence from the Central and West Africa*. https://mpra.ub.uni-muenchen.de/id/eprint/71571

Ngassam, S. B., Ngameni, J. P., Tiwang, G. N., & Kemmanang, L. F. (2022). Export diversification in economic communities of Central African countries: The role of infrastructure. *Asian Journal of Economic Modelling*, *10*(3), 160–177.

Ngoc, P. T. B., Vu, H. Q., & Dinh Long, P. (2022). Domestic total factor productivity with trade and heterogenous foreign direct investment in developing countries: A case of Vietnamese manufacturing. *International Journal of Emerging Markets*. https://doi.org/10.1108/IJOEM-08-2021-1333

Nguse, T., Oshora, B., Fekete-Farkas, M., Tangl, A., & Desalegn, G. (2021). Does the exchange rate and its volatility matter for international trade in Ethiopia? *Journal of Risk and Financial Management*, *14*(12), 591.

Noureen, S., & Mahmood, Z. (2016). Explaining trends and factors affecting export diversification in ASEAN and SAARC regions: An empirical analysis. *NUST Journal of Social Sciences and Humanities*, *2*(1), 1–28.

Parteka, A. (2010). Employment and export specialisation along the development path: Some robust evidence. *Review of World Economics*, *145*, 615–640.

Parteka, A., & Tamberi, M. (2011). *Export diversification and development-empirical assessment*. Universita'Politecnica delle Marche Dipartimento di Scienze Economiche e Sociali Working Paper, (359).

Pedroni, P. (1999). Critical values for co-integration tests in heterogeneous panels with multiple regressors. *Oxford Bulletin of Economics & Statistics*, *61*(1), 653–670.

Pedroni, P. (2000). Fully modified OLS for heterogeneous cointegrated panels. *The Review of Economics and Statistics*, *83*(4), 727–731.

Pesaran, M. H. (2003). A simple panel unit root test in the presence of cross-section dependence. *Journal of Applied Econometrics, 22*(2), 265–312.

Petersson, L. (2005). Export diversification and intra-industry trade in South Africa. *South African Journal of Economics, 73*(4), 785–802.

Pineres, G., & Ferrantino, M. (1997). Export diversification and structural dynamics in the growth process: The case of Chile. *Journal of Development Economics, 52*(2), 375–391.

Prebisch, R. (1950). *The economic development of Latin America and its principal problems.* United Nations Document No.E/CN. 12/89/Rev.1, New York.

Qaiser, R., & Mahmood, Z. (2016). *Natural resource dependence and human capital accumulation – An analysis for the selected SAARC, ASEAN and OPEC countries.* Working Paper Series Number 07:2016.

Rath, B. N., & Akram, V. (2017). Export diversification and total factor productivity growth in the case of the South Asian region. *Journal of Social and Economic Development, 19,* 196–210.

Ricardo, D. (1817/2001). *Principles of political economy and taxation.* Batoche Books.

Rodrik, D. (1998). *Trade policy and economic performance in Sub-Saharan Africa.* NBER Working Paper 6562. National Bureau of Economic Research, Cambridge, MA.

Ruane, F., & Sutherland, J. (2005). Export performance and destination characteristics of Irish manufacturing industry. *Review of World Economics, 141,* 442–459.

Sabhasri, C., Cheewatrakoolpong, K., & Bunditwattanawong, N. (2013). *Impact of the ASEAN economic community on ASEAN production networks.* ADBI Working Paper 409. Asian Development Bank Institute, Tokyo.

Saleem, R., Nasreen, S., & Azam, S. (2022). Role of financial inclusion and export diversification in determining green growth: Evidence from SAARC economies. *Environmental Science and Pollution Research, 29*(40), 60327–60340.

Sarin, V., Mahapatra, S. K., & Sood, N. (2022). Export diversification and economic growth: A review and future research agenda. *Journal of Public Affairs, 22*(3), e2524.

Sediqi, M. M., Ibrahimi, A. M., Danish, M. S. S., Senjyu, T., Chakraborty, S., & Mandal, P. (2018). Optimisation analysis of cross-border electricity trading between Afghanistan and its neighbouring countries. *IFAC-PapersOnLine, 51*(28), 25–30.

Sekkat, K. (2016). Exchange rate misalignment and export diversification in developing countries. *The Quarterly Review of Economics and Finance, 59,* 1–14.

Shepherd, B. (2009). *Enhancing export diversification through trade facilitation.* United Nations Economic and Social Commission for Asia and the Pacific (ESCAP), Bangkok.

Siddiqui, A. H. (2018). Export diversification and growth in Pakistan: An empirical investigation from 1972 to 2015. *Business and Economic Review, 10*(1), 107–131.

Singer, H. (1950). The distribution of gains between investing and borrowing countries. *The American Economic Review, 40*(2), 473–485.

Singla, N. (2016). Regional trade barriers in South Asia: SAARC lagging behind ASEAN. *SAMVAD12,* 54–61.

Smith, A. (1776/1977). *An inquiry into the nature and causes of the wealth of nations.* University of Chicago Press.

Swathi, M., & Sridharan, P. (2022). Determinants of export diversification: Evidence from fractional logit estimation model. *Foreign Trade Review, 57*(2), 160–177.

Tovar Mora, J. A., & Martínez Armas, L. R. (2011). *Diversification, networks and the survival of exporting firms.* http://hdl.handle.net/1992/8242

Vasilyeva, R. I., Voitenkov, V. A., & Urazbaeva, A. R. (2022). Modelling of the influence of regional determinants on export diversification in Russia. *Journal of Applied Economic Research, 21*(1).

Voon, J. P. (1998). Export competitiveness of China and ASEAN in the US market. *ASEAN Economic Bulletin, 19*(3), 273–291.

Wani, N. U. H. (2019). Nexus between openness to trade and economic growth: An empirical investigation of Afghanistan. *South Asia Economic Journal, 20*(2).

Wani, N. U. H., & Rasa, M. M. (2023). Dynamics of trade specialization and performance of SAFTA: A case study of Afghanistan. *South Asia Economic Journal, 24*(2).

Wondemu, K. A., & Potts, D. J. (2016). *The Impact of the real exchange rate changes on export performance in Tanzania and Ethiopia.* http://hdl.handle.net/10454/10336

Wu, F. (1991). The ASEAN economies in the 1990s and Singapore's regional role. *California Management Review.* https://doi.org/10.2307/41166686

Yama, M., & Wani, N. U. H. (2021). Nexus between export diversification and economic growth: A case study of Afghanistan. *Kardan Journal of Economics and Management Sciences, 3*(3), 45–67.

Yasmin, B., Tufail, S., & Naz, F. (2020). Impact of terms of trade and sectoral competitiveness on export diversification in Pakistan. *Pakistan Journal of Social Sciences, 40*(1), 415–431.

Yokota, K., & Tomohara, A. (2009). A decomposition of factors influencing horizontal and vertical FDI: A separate analysis. *Eastern Economic Journal, 35*, 462–478.

Yu, H., Zhang, J., Zhang, M., & Fan, F. (2022). Cross-national knowledge transfer, absorptive capacity, and total factor productivity: The intermediary effect test of international technology spillover. *Technology Analysis & Strategic Management, 34*(6), 625–640.

Chapter 5

# Trade Costs of Afghanistan With Its Major Trading Partners: Measurement and Its Determinants

## Abstract

The trading expenses encountered domestically and across borders have a detrimental influence on global trade. Higher trade costs hamper trade and limit the benefits of trade liberalisation. The current research applies Novy's micro-founded trade cost measure (2013) to estimate global trade costs connected with Afghanistan, along with the factors that influence trade costs. Based on the investigation, trade in agriculture costs is significantly higher compared to the non-agricultural. As a consequence, focusing on agricultural trade facilitation would be advantageous.

Furthermore, enhancing and expediting trade facilities in trading areas are top priorities for government intervention to reduce trade costs. Focusing on free trade agreements and better shipment communication with trade partners increases transportation routes efficiently, cutting time and other expenses. The study proposes that the World Trade Organization's trade facilitation agreement be effectively implemented, administrative burdens at entry points minimised, non-tariff barriers (NTBs) be simplified and harmonised and soft infrastructures be established utilising current technologies.

*Keywords*: Trade costs; Afghanistan; South Asia; determinants; measurement

*JEL Codes*: F14; F19

## 1. Introduction

In the economic literature, trade costs encompass all expenses involved in delivering the product to the end customer, except the marginal cost of production. These include policy obstacles (tariffs and non-tariff barriers [NTBs]), transit,

Policy Solutions for Economic Growth in a Developing Country, 105–127
Copyright © 2024 Nassir Ul Haq Wani
Published under exclusive licence by Emerald Publishing Limited
doi:10.1108/978-1-83753-430-220241006

costs associated with communication and other information, regulation and foreign exchange costs, administrative and regulating costs and regional costs for transportation (Anderson & Van Wincoop, 2004; Li & Whalley, 2014; Singh & Mathur, 2014). Pursuant to the sources, trade costs are classified into two distinct categories. The initial category comprises solely bilateral isolation components between the seller and buyer, determined by external factors such as geographic separation, shared frontier and language instead of typical policy actions. The endogenous trade costs of international connections (transport facilities by sea or air), trade impediments and other trade-facilitating variables (Sanitary and Phytosanitary (SPS) measures and Technical Barriers to Trade (TBT) transparency) are included in the second category.

The subject matter related to trade costs is deemed critical by international trade economists, as it helps in determining trade volume and direction. The research has widely appraised the consistent drop in trade costs as typical agents of international trade expansion. Data demonstrate that international trade volume has surged in recent years in comparison with earlier decades. International trade stood at almost $25 trillion in 2019 and escalated to $28 trillion in 2021. The value of international trade is predicted to reach over US$ 32 trillion by the end of 2022, up nearly 26% from pre-pandemic levels in 2019 (Aiyar et al., 2022).

With the emergence of regionalism, evidence shows that governments have drastically reduced tariffs, with an average of below 5% for developed countries and between 10% and 20% in case of developing countries (Beverelli & Ticku, 2022; Keen & Ligthart, 2002). With considerable tariff reductions, on the one hand, certain new trade barriers limit trade performance on the other. Aside from trade barriers, infrastructural quality issues also have a key role in affecting the intensity of trade, referred to as policy obstacles collectively. Failing institutional setup and weak infrastructures impede trade strategy, which emphasises traditional tariffs, quota systems, infrastructure and logistics, which are frequently referred to as 'behind-the-border issues'. As a result, apart from differences in the size of the economy and resource endowment, variations in the cost of trade, which function as an impediment to trade, are the main reasons for the difference in trading intensities across economies.

Trade costs are significant from a policy standpoint in an increasingly globalised and networked society given that they determine the framework of international investments and trade, as well as the distribution across the globe. However, costs to trade vary across countries and are likely to be greater in emerging economies compared to advanced economies owing to numerous barriers, inadequate infrastructure, as well as inefficient transportation and operations.

The prevalence of these concerns is observed in Afghanistan as well; however, the country's abundant natural resources are a matter of relief, thereby saturating its position in the trade. Its trading partners are diverse encompassing partners in Central Asia, South Asia, the European Union and Gulf nations. Afghanistan also has strong trading relations with Asian countries such as Pakistan, India, China, Turkey, Uzbekistan, Tajikistan, the United Arab Emirates, Saudi Arabia and the European Union. Afghanistan's current trade size must precisely represent its trade potential as the trajectory of Afghanistan's global trade defined by the cost of trade has been consistent since 2001. Given Afghanistan's strategic importance, it is vital to understand the variables driving trade costs. Afghanistan requires careful consideration of trade costs so as to enhance its position in international trade and manufacturing systems. Comprehensive research on the drivers and computation of trade costs can assist in identifying the areas that require particular attention to identifying policies and actions that substantially impact trade costs and prioritise them, therefore altering the trade trajectory and composition. In light of these objectives, the present research empirically examines the drivers of trade costs endured by Afghanistan in the trade of agricultural and non-agricultural commodities at the HS (4) commodity classification with primary trading partners namely India, Pakistan, Turkey, Iran, China, the United Arab Emirate, Saudi Arabia, Germany, the United States and the United Kingdom. In the case of Afghanistan, this area is essentially unexplored. As a result, a research study is required to illustrate Afghanistan's position in trade costs and determine its drivers. Such research may produce findings that, if properly focused on, might reduce trade costs and assist in the development of impact policies aimed at improving overall trade and increasing Afghanistan's position in the international trade system. This study further adds to the existing scholarship by classifying trade based on agricultural and non-agricultural commodities involving significant trading partners.

## 2. Literature Review

Researchers are increasingly interested in trade costs. Much economic literature on trade cost revolves around its theoretical underpinnings and practical analyses. In this sense, it is critical to understand which variables cause a particular economy's trade costs. Existing work highlights some of the most critical variables of trade costs. Samuelson (1954) is credited with making significant contributions to this problem by characterising trade transportation expenses as costs of icebergs, whereby only a fraction of the exporting country's goods arrive at their destination, the rest melts away along the route. Tinbergen (1962), in his renowned gravity model formulation, employed distance as an approximation substitute for costs associated with trade. Some studies have highlighted and illustrated the exchange of trade costs between the two nations using the ratio (cif/fob)−1 (Limao & Venables, 2001), whereas Obstfeld and Rogoff (2000) investigate iceberg costs for shipping in a basic two-country situation and create a precise estimate of the trade cost using a Constant elasticity of substitution (CES) utility function.

Other studies have included external bilateral barriers to trade within their gravity framework and proposed that border barriers and geographical distance influence bilateral trade costs (Anderson & van Wincoop, 2003). The usage of other extraneous variables as proxies to measure the penetration of trade costs included geographical separation, adjacency, preferential trade membership, shared language and various other variables.

Venables and Limao (1999) employed the Tobit model to identify the components that determine the cost of transportation and its linkage with geographic proximity and infrastructure development. The study suggests that landlocked nations have high transportation costs, which might be reduced with enhanced infrastructure. It is claimed that decreasing transportation expenses by 50% intensifies the trade volume by 5 times.

Following the same analysis, Arvis et al. (2013) calculated the cost of being landlocked. Since the landlocked countries face huge uncertainty associated with transit time and high freight expenses, thereby raising the trading costs. The study emphasised the need for comprehensive logistical services, which must be addressed by constructing a transit infrastructure. Along the same note, Novy (2006) investigated the patterns in trade costs between the United Kingdom and the United States, including 31 trading partners. The findings revealed that the trade costs that are tariff equivalents for the United States have fallen, resulting in enhanced trade. It is pertinent to mention that the United Kingdom's bilateral trade expenses have risen dramatically over time. Novy calculated trade costs by employing a micro-founded trade cost measure encompassing the geographic, historical and institutional characteristics as the primary drivers of trade costs.

In terms of the reduction in ocean freight and air transportation costs, Hummels (2007) investigated the impact on trade flows from 1952 to 2004. The findings reflect that there has been a significant fall in air transportation prices, which has worked as a crucial factor in boosting global trade in the later part of the 20th century. The trade cost models given, on the other hand, were difficult since a specific trade cost function was defined, which may only effectively represent certain significant trade barrier features. Novy (2013a) addresses these difficulties by developing a micro-founded measure based on openly accessible export statistics. Therefore, specifying a trade cost function is not needed.

Furthermore, previous research employed distance as a trade cost estimate that remains constant over time, excluding the use of data (time series or panel). Novy's method, on the other hand, could potentially be utilised for both datasets. Novy's technique was chosen for trade cost modelling due to considerable improvements over earlier models. A key point to bear in mind is that the model does not suggest seamless local trade. As a result, under this paradigm, the equivalent tariff measures of bilateral trade costs accrue to domestic trade costs. The notion of tariff equivalence accounts for factors that increase international business transaction costs above and beyond local trade and thus is compatible with the theories of Chaney (2008) and Melitz and Ottaviano (2008).

Other studies, like the one by Gaurav and Mathur (2015), employed Novy's (2013) trade cost measurement to investigate India's comparative bilateral costs of trade with EU nations. The benefit of such a model is that trade expenditures can only be calculated with observable trade data. According to the data, India's tariff compared to its key EU trade partners declined by 20% from 1995 to 2010. The majority of this trade expansion, according to Novy's model, can be attributed to a decrease in the bilateral cost of trade, which has been partially offset by a decrease in multifaceted terms, which has redirected trade with other trading partners. Other studies have employed other models to evaluate the impacts of trade costs on trade flows. Using the dynamic gravity framework, Noureen and Mahmood (2021) evaluated changes in bilateral trade costs, especially those associated with policy impediments, for exporters. The empirical data indicate that trade costs are typically dropping internationally; but, in the case of developing economies, the pace of decrease is quite slow.

In a nutshell, these studies have ardently worked on the basis of Novy's (2013) model or the gravity model approach for estimations of trade costs in different countries. However, there is not a single study in the Afghanistan context; thus, further research is needed to quantify Afghanistan's trade costs and investigate trade cost issues with its important trading partners. Consequently, the analysis is even more important in bridging the academic gap in the literature.

## 3. Overview of Trade Costs in Afghanistan

Afghanistan's path to economic resilience has been fraught with global and local problems since the Taliban's overthrow in 2001. Despite the dire conditions, the nation gained pace. From this perspective, the decade of the 2010s was Afghanistan's golden era, with impact trade policies concentrating on manufacturing and industrial growth and promoting exports. Numerous enticements, such as tax rebates, exemptions and export bonuses, contributed to a phenomenal increase in the volume of exports, with shipments increasing at a rate of 16.19% annually.

Afghanistan began the process of trade reforms in the late 2010s in response to increasing economic pressures and globalisation factors, and its intensity rose in the first part of the 2010s. In the agriculture sector, extensive reform efforts began in 2014. The government cut average tariffs to 12% in 2017 from a peak of 29% in 2015 (WTO, 2017). Afghanistan's trade volumes surged dramatically in the 2010s. The trade volume climbed from $540 million in 2008 to $870 million in 2021 (UNCTAD, 2021).

An assessment of Afghanistan's trade costs with its trading partners for agricultural and non-agricultural businesses finds that, on average, Afghanistan has high trade costs despite considerable international tariff decreases. The standards and state of institutions and infrastructure facilities vary for each country, resulting in differences in trade and associated costs. As a result, trade policy now extends beyond conventional tariff and quota systems to address a wide range of policies that might influence the quantity and structure of trade with and between developing nations. These occurrences often result in 'behind-the-border' concerns, emphasising the significance of infrastructure and regulation in sustaining an effective global economy. Many studies, for example, imply that liberalising international transport services, similar to tariff liberalisation, improves international trade (Baier & Bergstrand, 2007; De, 2006). The trade cost equivalent projections have decreased during the course of the study, resulting in higher global trade volumes in Afghanistan (Table 1). Due to regulatory limitations, such as substantial tariffs and non-tariff constraints, agriculture experienced higher tariffs than non-agriculture. Furthermore, agricultural commodities have higher processing and storage costs than industrial consumer goods.

As demonstrated in Table 1, Afghanistan experienced a decline in trade costs in both agricultural and non-agricultural commodities from 2008 to 2021, owing

Table 1. Trade Cost Trends of Afghanistan.

| Year | Trade Cost (Agriculture) | Trade Cost (Non-Agriculture) | LSCI | Afg Tariff | ΔER | TV(US$ Million) |
|------|--------------------------|------------------------------|-------|------------|----------|-----------------|
| 2008 | 203.07 | 160.44 | 18.21 | 15.91 | 0.008 | 23,485 |
| 2009 | 201.70 | 155.41 | 21.27 | 15.27 | 0.021 | 27,987 |
| 2010 | 196.27 | 156.50 | 22.38 | 15.71 | 0.012 | 34,998 |
| 2011 | 195.08 | 151.10 | 22.28 | 15.89 | 0.085 | 45,541 |
| 2012 | 197.47 | 152.53 | 25.81 | 15.91 | 0.143 | 47,815 |
| 2013 | 193.23 | 149.09 | 25.81 | 14.28 | 0.186 | 59,319 |
| 2014 | 194.09 | 152.75 | 27.47 | 14.48 | 0.049 | 52,641 |
| 2015 | 190.21 | 147.98 | 30.03 | 14.61 | 0.014 | 54,087 |
| 2016 | 191.37 | 146.13 | 31.34 | 14.25 | 0.082 | 65,296 |
| 2017 | 188.51 | 143.97 | 30.86 | 13.89 | 0.095 | 68,587 |
| 2018 | 194.67 | 150.09 | 26.58 | 14.78 | 0.049 | 52,586 |
| 2019 | 199.13 | 149.23 | 29.48 | 14.51 | 0.014 | 54,078 |
| 2020 | 190.39 | 147.83 | 30.54 | 14.25 | 0.082774 | 65,224 |
| 2021 | 187.7 | 144.94 | 31.97 | 13.98 | 0.09536 | 68,540 |

*Source:* Except for LSCI, the authors' estimates are based on World Bank (2018) average tariffs and UNCOMTRADE trade volume (different issues).

*Note:* Trade cost trends apply to both agricultural and non-agricultural trade. Further to add, the positive changes in the currency rate imply depreciation, whereas negative changes represent appreciation. LSCI refers to the liner shipping connectivity index, whereas PIP stands for port infrastructure and TV stands for trade volume.

to reductions in tariffs. Tariffs boost the prices of imported supplies and act as a covert tax on exporting goods, raising the price of imports and deterring exports. As a result, lowering the mean tariff from 15.91% in 2008 to 13.98% in 2021 boosted both imports and exports, which is correlated with lower costs of trade. An assessment of changes in the rate of exchange (ER) reveals a decline in the currency exchange rate during the research timeframe. The lowering in the ER has increased trade between nations relative to local trade, resulting in a reduction in the overall trade cost. As a consequence, the falling value of the ER is an element assisting in lowering the cost of trade.

### 3.1 Costs of Sectoral Trade

The dual trading experience between Afghanistan and Pakistan encounters low trade costs, with an average of 46.4% and 54% for agricultural and non-agricultural commodities, respectively, as presented in Tables 2 and 3. Several variables contribute to reduced trade costs including the frontier

Table 2. Trade Cost Estimate Equivalents (Agricultural Sector).

| Year | IND | PAK | BGD | UAE | CHN | IRN | TUR | GMY |
|------|--------|--------|--------|--------|--------|--------|--------|--------|
| 2008 | 241.26 | 151.18 | 167.51 | 148.28 | 222.76 | 217.26 | 200.31 | 224.92 |
| 2009 | 239.87 | 156.65 | 199.07 | 148.19 | 219.47 | 215.38 | 201.76 | 224.27 |
| 2010 | 217.54 | 150.09 | 199.33 | 142.31 | 207.87 | 210.65 | 199.33 | 220.86 |
| 2011 | 196.67 | 158.92 | 192.41 | 144.37 | 217.21 | 208.85 | 203.25 | 216.73 |
| 2012 | 222.88 | 151.07 | 222.76 | 148.86 | 196.07 | 208.87 | 199.07 | 218.59 |
| 2013 | 217.54 | 150.09 | 219.47 | 142.31 | 207.87 | 210.65 | 199.33 | 220.86 |
| 2014 | 218.38 | 151.24 | 207.87 | 147.27 | 207.21 | 197.99 | 192.41 | 214.41 |
| 2015 | 221.74 | 150.12 | 217.21 | 146.92 | 206.35 | 199.52 | 180.85 | 212.57 |
| 2016 | 219.91 | 149.04 | 196.07 | 142.73 | 203.41 | 196.37 | 185.8  | 208.57 |
| 2017 | 213.5  | 149.82 | 207.87 | 149.18 | 199.91 | 206.34 | 179.77 | 209.42 |
| 2018 | 212.88 | 149.01 | 207.21 | 147.2  | 191.78 | 202.98 | 179.84 | 208.68 |
| 2019 | 221.74 | 150.12 | 206.35 | 146.92 | 206.35 | 199.52 | 180.85 | 212.57 |
| 2020 | 219.91 | 149.04 | 222.76 | 142.73 | 203.41 | 196.37 | 185.8  | 208.57 |
| 2021 | 213.5  | 149.82 | 219.47 | 149.18 | 199.91 | 206.34 | 179.77 | 209.42 |
| Avg. | 218.66 | 151.71 | 165.6  | 146.53 | 206.62 | 204.42 | 192.24 | 209.76 |

*Source:* Calculations by the author.

*Note:* IND represents India, PAK represents Pakistan, BGD represents Bangladesh, UAE represents the United Arab Emirates, CHN represents China, IRN represents Iran, TUR represents Turkey and GMY represents Germany.

proximity closeness, close cultural and traditional ties, huge energy supply (such as coal) and the lowest corporation taxes.

Another interesting finding from the trade costs research is that the tariff analogues reflecting costs of trade between Afghanistan and India are among the lowest, at 30%, for both the agricultural and non-agricultural sectors (Tables 2 and 3). The discriminatory use of NTBs by India, such as regulatory and compliance norms, minimises Afghan export flows to India. Political ambiguity, stringent licencing permit procedures, and visa complications constitute trade barriers, increasing trade costs. As shown by high trade costs (TC), India has a restrictive trade policy, notably in the agricultural sector. India and Afghanistan signed a Preferential Trade Agreement (PTA) in March 2003, under which India gave massive tariff reductions ranging from 50% to 100% on certain types of Afghan dried fruit. Afghanistan responded by offering reciprocal incentives to Indian items such as tea, sugar, cement and medicines. At the SAARC Council in November 2011, India reduced key customs rates for all SAARC low-income nations, allowing major Afghan items (excluding tobacco and alcohol) duty-free entrance into the Indian market.

Table 3. Trade Costs Estimate Equivalents.

| Year | IND | PAK | BGD | UAE | CHN | IRN | TUR | GMY |
|---|---|---|---|---|---|---|---|---|
| 2008 | 164.32 | 103.23 | 124.56 | 153.62 | 137.68 | 157.7 | 165.9 | 151.17 |
| 2009 | 174.46 | 103.62 | 137.68 | 158.8 | 135.74 | 157.75 | 163.74 | 149.79 |
| 2010 | 171.49 | 103.06 | 135.74 | 152.93 | 130.7 | 147.88 | 163.32 | 145.96 |
| 2011 | 169.34 | 101.52 | 130.7 | 154.58 | 131.8 | 148.71 | 163.63 | 147.88 |
| 2012 | 172.11 | 100.48 | 131.8 | 154.64 | 127.84 | 139.88 | 158.63 | 142.73 |
| 2013 | 185.64 | 109.32 | 127.84 | 160.49 | 147.19 | 160.33 | 165.9 | 160.3 |
| 2014 | 174.46 | 103.62 | 147.19 | 158.8 | 135.74 | 157.75 | 163.74 | 149.79 |
| 2015 | 171.49 | 103.06 | 135.74 | 152.93 | 130.7 | 147.88 | 163.32 | 145.96 |
| 2016 | 169.34 | 101.52 | 130.7 | 154.58 | 131.8 | 148.71 | 163.63 | 147.88 |
| 2017 | 172.11 | 100.48 | 163.32 | 154.64 | 127.84 | 139.88 | 158.63 | 142.73 |
| 2018 | 174.46 | 103.62 | 163.63 | 158.8 | 135.74 | 157.75 | 163.74 | 149.79 |
| 2019 | 171.49 | 103.06 | 158.63 | 152.93 | 130.7 | 147.88 | 163.32 | 145.96 |
| 2020 | 182.6 | 106.39 | 171.49 | 153.83 | 148.71 | 158.85 | 164.03 | 160.52 |
| 2021 | 162.07 | 105.77 | 182.6 | 148.3 | 144.82 | 152.83 | 165.49 | 161.97 |
| Avg. | 176.12 | 103.72 | 162.07 | 154.66 | 139.33 | 154.2 | 164.01 | 154.04 |

*Source:* Authors' calculations.

*Note:* The trade cost estimates are related to the non-agricultural sector.

With USAID's assistance, an exhibition primarily targeting India–Afghanistan Trade and Investment Passage to Prosperity' (P2P) has been held continuously for 3 years. The first P2P was held in New Delhi in 2017, the second in Mumbai in 2018 and the third in New Delhi in 2019. The trade displays have allowed Afghan businesspeople to present their goods and sign memorandums of understanding (MoUs) and agreements with Indian partners, thereby increasing economic connections between India and Afghanistan and promoting the country's status as a World Trade Organization (WTO) member nation. Afghanistan's WTO entrance in 2015 opened new opportunities for collaboration between Afghanistan and Pakistan. Due to political issues, Afghanistan has yet to reap the benefits of being a WTO member. Articles 125 (1) and 125 (2) of the UNCLOS explicitly stipulate that both parties (in this example, Afghanistan and Pakistan) must achieve an agreement in order to constitute the 'legal right' of access to and from the sea, assuring freedom of passage (Akbari, 2021). Based on these, Pakistan is only obliged to provide Afghanistan access to the sea as a landlocked country after the bilateral arrangements between the two countries. The UNCLOS and the GATT articles aim to enhance global trade by encouraging the principles of lowering tariff and NTBs (Shaw, 2013). The Afghanistan Transit Trade Agreement (ATTA) codified and regulated transit arrangements mentioned in the articles of the GATT between Afghanistan and Pakistan for the first time in

1965. Consequently, Afghanistan could use Torkham and Chaman as exit points and Port Qasim and Karachi as an entrance. However, the internal crossing roads in both countries remained unspecified and Afghan trucks could not enter Pakistan soil and vice versa. All domestic transportation was carried by domestic mechanisms/firms between the two states.

While ATTA was an essential agreement of its time and was signed before 1982 UNCLOS, it could not efficiently respond to the development of the 21st century. With the fall of the Soviet Union in 1991 and the establishment of new Central Asian republics (CARs), along with the development of technology, transportation facilities and legal procedures, the connectivity context of the region changed. These new circumstances required a more comprehensive new transit agreement between the two neighbours. Thus, the negotiations for the new agreement, Afghanistan–Pakistan Transit and Trade Agreement (APTTA), started in 2008 and was signed in 2010, becoming effective in 2011. The APTTA contains provisions and discussions on rights/limits of transit trade, transport corridors, facilitation of transiting trade, requirements, conditions for road vehicles, customs and other controls, including taxes, duties and payment arrangements. This transit agreement also lays the foundation for establishing APPTCA, the joint coordination authority to implement the agreement terms and resolve disputes.

There are five security levels under APTTA to ensure unauthorised transit is prevented. These include insurance guarantees, tracking services, vehicle bank guarantees, bonded carrier licences and container security deposits. While inhibiting cross-border smuggling, all limiting the smooth trade flow between the two countries. The volume of Afghan transit trade declined through Pakistan between 2011 and 2014, the post-APTTA period (Rauf & Ahmad, 2019). However, the difference in transit trade reported by the two countries also fell from $2.9 bn to $1 bn in 2014 post-APTTA. The guarantee schemes curb illegal trade and negatively affect Afghan transit trade.

The critics on both sides of the border are not satisfied and consider the impediments that come with APTTA too high, especially for Afghan traders. APTTA allows Afghanistan to access the sea, China and India (although limited) via Pakistan, allowing Pakistan to access five Central Asian Countries and Iran via Afghanistan. More specifically, Afghan merchants can use the following three ports in Pakistan for import and export: Qasim, Karachi and Gwadar. The routes are pre-specified in the agreement, too, via Peshawar/Azakhel to Torkham and via Chaman to Spin Boldak. The consistent push by Afghan merchants to have full access to Wagah (Pakistan–India) border crossing - has been a contentious issue (Masood et al., 2023).

Through Afghanistan, Pakistani merchants can access Ai Khanom and Sher Khan Bandar (to Tajikistan), Hairatan (with Uzbekistan), Aqina and Torghundi (to Turkmenistan), Islam Qala and Zaranj (to Iran). The specific entry points and cities that trucks will have to go through to reach these exit points are also pre-determined (Rauf & Ahmad, 2019). If fully operationalised and utilised, APTTA is crucial in connecting the region. On the other hand, a trade agreement is different from a trade transit agreement. Until 2004, Afghanistan and Pakistan were part of no trade agreements, only after signing the regional SAFTA, which became effective in 2006.

Afghanistan and China share a common border and enjoy voracious trading relations. However, bilateral trade costs (TC) remain high between the two nations. China's government encourages domestic spending via structural tax cuts, and domestic demand is strong in China. Despite significant bilateral commerce flows between the two nations, China's customs processes still need harmonisation. Furthermore, its tariff regimes have not changed much, which may explain the escalated costs of trade. Furthermore, based on security concerns and ethical standards, China imposes limits, licencing and bans on certain products from Afghanistan and as such these factors influence the magnitude of trade costs. The trade costs can further be reduced if the Karakoram National Highway, which travels via Pakistan and is the easiest land route connecting the two nations, is improved. Furthermore, the creation of a commercial corridor is envisioned as a tremendous opportunity to save time and distance. Lengthy transportation and shipping routes connecting the two countries increase costs associated with trade, which could potentially be decreased by constructing an immediate corridor from *Kashgar* to *Gwadar*. Linking it to Afghanistan is anticipated to reduce existing trade costs by one-third compared to the current level of trade costs.

Afghanistan and the European Union have significant and rapidly developing trade links. For our trade cost investigation, two EU countries are chosen: the United Kingdom and Germany. Despite the absence of a shared culture or physical closeness between Afghanistan and selected member nations of the European Union, average trade costs are modest. Afghanistan is expected to benefit from the European Union's 'Everything but Arms' (EBA) policy for least developed countries, which will result in further price reductions. The World Bank classifies Afghanistan as a low-income economy, with a per-capita income of $368.8 in 2021. Afghanistan's preferential imports to the European market are expected to be valued at $10.6 million in 2021.

As seen in Table 3, Afghanistan and Bangladesh still need to reduce their bilateral trade costs significantly. Afghanistan's exports to Bangladesh have climbed at an annualised rate of 1.85% during the previous 22 years, from $209k in 2008 to $313k in 2019. In comparison, Bangladesh's exports to Afghanistan have climbed at a 2.69% annualised pace, from $3.99M in 2008 to $7.15M in 2019. To further minimise trade expenses, trade facilitation solutions must be developed. The two nations have no direct flight connectivity, particularly between Kabul and Dhaka. The movement of products between Afghanistan and Bangladesh needs to be improved by fostering shipping agreements between the two nations.

Afghanistan also enjoys amicable trade ties with Turkey, and there is enormous potential for trade latency between the two nations. In the case of Afghanistan–Turkey trade relations, costs to trade are quite high. The import laws, relevant standards and quarantine procedures make exporting Afghan goods, particularly food items, even more complex. Afghan exports are also more distant from the market than rivals such as Iran, India and CARs, which raises transportation costs and delays product delivery. Turkish importers, on the other hand, seek limited quantities with quick shipment deadlines. Both countries have to tackle these barriers to trade. Turkish importers, on the other hand, seek limited quantities with quick shipment deadlines. Both countries have to tackle these barriers to trade.

In contemporary times, developed nations are considering trade costs as an indicator of national trade growth and economic efficiency. The concerned governments are critically assessing and exploring efficient trade cost-cutting initiatives. On the other hand, emerging nations have been largely clueless, and few governmental measures have been undertaken to address this problem. Afghanistan is comparable to other poor countries. Based on international trade forecasts, Afghanistan still faces elevated international costs for trade in contrast to its important counterparts, reflecting the government's absence of regulatory emphasis on promoting and facilitating trade. Afghanistan continues to export a significant amount of agricultural goods. The associated costs for agriculture trade for Afghanistan, on the other hand, are much higher than non-agricultural trade costs, reflecting sectoral imbalance and regulatory prejudice. Thus, identifying the principal causes of trade costs and determining how the authorities ought to accomplish to tackle these is critical for trade to continue at a high rate of economic growth over an extended period of time.

## 4. Research Methodology

### 4.1 Theoretical Framework

Trade costs have a deep impact on global trade flows. In gauging the impact, the gravity model is an appropriate tool based on the trends and patterns of costs of trade. Since the framework offers a crucial link between the movement of goods and obstacles to trade, international trade is best suited for determining factors that impact trade costs (Baier & Bergstrand, 2007; Evenett & Hutchinson, 2002). The gravity model has become essential to applied international economics. It is inspired by Newton's gravitational law, which states that distance and mass dictate the gravitational force between two bodies. Tinbergen's pioneering work (1962) in international economics popularised this paradigm. It correlates trade between nations with GDP, geographical separation and various other variables such as culture, language, currency rates and trade restrictions. This model has been widely utilised by Abbas et al. (2023), Ahmad and Wani (2018), Dhami et al. (2020), Jin et al. (2023), Limao and Venables (2001), Martínez-Martínez et al. (2023), Masood et al. (2023), and Wani and Yasmin (2023) to determine trade movement implications of entities like exchange rate, ethnic and cultural adjustments, cultural and language identities and frontiers or boundaries.

This study in light of the objectives hinges on Novy's (2006) approach. This framework has been frequently employed to estimate trade between countries. It serves as a global trade workhorse, integrating economic transactions between countries based on their macroeconomic strengths and trading costs. This measurement method satisfies the mathematical gravity theory for trade cost elements that describe global trade restrictions quantitatively. Novy (2006) presented a detailed analytical approach for the international trade barrier parameters following addressing the trade costs equation. Novy's trade cost metric has the benefit of allowing the long-term tracking of bilateral trade barriers. Using publicly accessible production and trade data in tradable goods categories, we can assess and clarify the causes of reciprocal border consequences. This strategy is based on the assumption that modifications in barriers to trade impact domestic as well as international trade. In fact, when a country lowers or lowers trade tariffs, some items produced for home use are shipped to other nations, signalling trade restrictions. Since they neglect to account for the non-tradable (domestic trade) sector, traditional grounded in-theory forms of the gravity equation underestimate boundary barrier costs. Trade barriers influence domestic as well as international trade. This argument's premise is self-evident. Trade obstacle adjustments create a resource movement across marketable and non-marketable sectors (import-competing), causing adjustments in global trade flows. This is particularly true for the multilateral response of nations that trade, which is based on domestic trade.

As a result, it emphasises the relevance of the home prejudice by adding local trade to the gravity framework. Novy's approach (2013a, 2013b) addressed the limitations of the gravity model proposed by Anderson and Van Wincoop (2003). By including multilateral trade barrier components, the theory-driven gravity expression enhanced the classic gravity formulation. The benefit in Novy's framework is the reality that it allows for long-term tracking of trade barriers. Using publicly accessible production and trade statistics for tradable goods categories, we can assess and explain the causes of bidirectional boundary consequences.

Using a multi-country generalised equilibrium method, Anderson and Van Wincoop (2003) developed the following trade cost measurement model based on micro-founded assumptions:

$$X_{ij} = \frac{y_i y_j}{y_w} \left( \frac{t_{ij}}{\Pi_i P_j} \right)^{1-\sigma} \tag{1}$$

where $X_{ij}$ represents the trade flow from country $i$ to country $j$; $y_i y_j$ denotes the incomes of country $i$ to country $j$, $t_{ij}$ represents the global income, $\Pi_i$ is the outward multilateral resistance (OMR is a weighted-average aggregate of all bilateral trade costs for goods producers in each country) of country $i$ and $P_j$ is a bilateral trade cost measurement and is the product elasticity of substitution. The inclusion of price indices ($P$) in the approach reflects that trade is impacted both by the bilateral cost of trade and the trade resistance that countries face with their trading partners. Equation (1) captures the country $i$'s intra-national trade as:

$$X_{ii} = \frac{y_i y_j}{y_w} \left( \frac{t_{ij}}{\Pi_i P_j} \right)^{1-\sigma} \tag{2}$$

Additionally, rephrase it as:

$$\Pi_i P_i = \left( \frac{X_{ii}/Y_i}{Y_i/Y_\omega} \right)^{\frac{1}{\sigma-1}} t_{ii} \tag{3}$$

which overcomes the nation $i$'s OMR. When we multiply Eq. (1) by $X_{ji}$, we get:

$$X_{ij} X_{ji} = \left( \frac{y_i y_j}{y^w} \right)^2 \left( \frac{t_{ij} t_{ji}}{\Pi_i P_i \Pi_j P_j} \right)^{1-\sigma} \tag{4}$$

Substituting Eq. (3) in Eq. (2) helps in determining the costs of trade bilaterally in comparison to national costs of trade expressed as tariffs equivalent by differencing 1 as shown in Eq. (5) as follows:

$$X_{ij} = \left( \frac{t_{ij} t_{ji}}{t_{ii} t_{jj}} \right)^{\frac{1}{2}} - 1 = \left( \frac{X_{ii} X_{jj}}{X_{ij} X_{ji}} \right)^{\frac{1}{2(\sigma-1)}} - 1 \tag{5}$$

where $\tau_{ij}$ represents the tariff analogous costs of trade (comparison of domestic and bilateral trade); $t_{ij}$ denotes the cost associated with global trade between $i$ and $j$, $t_{ii}$ and $t_{jj}$ represent the intra-national trading costs of country $i$ and $j$, respectively. It should be noted that $t_{ij}$ is a dual trade cost measurement. It intuitively assesses the cost of trade between nations. Intuitively, costs related to trade advance as nations deal in intra-trade than inter-trade. The gravity equation is a remarkable accomplishment in terms of dealing with the empirical side of economics. It defines the value of international trade, which is determined by the economic size (GDP of the country) along with the geographical proximity (distance) between the countries (Lili, 2011). As trade gets more complex and incurs transaction costs, the significant distance between trading partners will likely diminish trade flows. The basic gravity model is as follows:

$$T_{ij} = G \left( \frac{Y_i Y_j}{D_{ij}} \right) \tag{6}$$

where $T_{ij}$ represents the total trade between countries (exports and imports), $Y_i$ and $Y_j$ is the GDP of country $i$ and $j$, respectively, and $D_{ij}$ is the geographical proximity between the two countries. $G$ denotes a constant that has a connection to a standard gravity equation in the form illustrated below. Eq. (6) may be linearised in parameters since it is multiplicative in nature:

$$\ln T_{ij} = \ln G + \alpha_1 \ln GDP_i + \alpha_2 \ln GDP_j - \alpha_1 \ln D_{ij} + \varepsilon_{ij} \tag{7}$$

Given the scarcity of data on all of the elements involved, establishing the nexus between costs to trade and their enticements is time-consuming. To study the sources of trade expenses, we used several parameters, including distance, infrastructure intensity, exchange rate, tariffs, geographical area, trading partner closeness and Free Trade Agreement (FTA).

### 4.2 Empirical Model

The aggregated measurements of non-bilateral factors for countries $i$ and $j$ are exemplified by adopting Novy's (2006) methodology. This measurement is adopted by multiplying the single-country variables, resulting in symmetrical and perpetually interacting consequences.

$$\tau_{ij} = f(\text{Dist}, \text{Tariff}, \text{Exch}, \text{LSCI}, \text{Area}, \text{Cont}, \text{FTA}) \tag{8}$$

The elements in Eq. (8) include the $\tau_{ij}$ variable representing the tariff equivalent of trade costs, DIST is the distance that exists between Afghanistan and the other partner nation, TARIFF is an amalgamation of tariffs employed by Afghanistan and other trading nations and EXCH is the official ER regarding Afghanistan (derived in current US dollars). The liner shipping connectivity index (LSCI) is Afghanistan's and the partner nation's liner shipping connectivity index, and AREA is the product of trade partners' land areas.

Since the gravity model utilises distance as an analogue for alienation or the cost of transportation, the distance factor is projected to impact trade costs favourably. The LSCI is employed to examine the infrastructural development of trade nations. A dummy variable is also incorporated in our model symbolising a shared boundary with the trade partner. Contiguity is a unitary value of a dummy variable that represents countries that share a boundary. The shared border is a reference for transport and information expenses, which are cheaper for close counterparts as they are fully cognizant of their consumer needs and possibilities for trade, reducing the overall expenses for shared trade. It is anticipated that the coefficient of proximity is negative. On the other hand, a huge land area signifies a large economy and population with strong domestic needs. Foreign items are also acceptable to meet that high demand; developed nations have higher cultural diversity and citizens are more accepting of a range of cultures, necessitating varied imports (Masood et al., 2023). As a result, trade flow flourishes and expands when the costs of trade decrease. The coefficient of the trade partners' area is projected to be negative. Furthermore, a dummy variable for FTA is included to analyse its impact on the cost of trade and is anticipated to increase trade costs.

Tariffs and the exchange rate of the currency are the additional two factors with regard to policy. Trade flow limitations are evaluated utilising tariffs placed by partners in trade. Tariff increases imposed by trading nations are anticipated to raise bilateral trade costs. Tariffs on raw materials influence imports but harm exports. Duty drawback concerns increase the total amount of trade expenditures even more. Consequently, global trade is declining while intra-trade increases, raising the costs of trade. Furthermore, the utilisation of the exchange rate to gauge competitiveness in international trade flows is also taken care of. The study employs the official exchange rate to calculate trade expenditures and its impact on trade costs is assumed positive. Due to the inverse relationship between trade flows and costs, a rise in trade flows combined with a nominal depreciation conduces to reduced costs related to trade. As a result, the expected exchange rate coefficient is negative.

### 4.3 Mathematical Connotation

The basic framework in Eq. (8) is converted into the empirical connotation that follows, which relates tariff equivalents of trade costs to their drivers:

$$\tau_{ij} = \beta_0 + \beta_1 \text{Exch}_{ijt} + \beta_2 \text{TR}_{it} * \text{TR}_{jt} + \beta_3 \text{Dist}_{ij} + \beta_4 \text{LSCI}_{jt} + \beta_5 \text{Cont}_{ij} \\ + \beta_6 \text{Area}_i * \text{Area}_j + \beta_7 \text{FTA}_{ijt} + \varepsilon_{it} \tag{9}$$

The model in Eq. (8) assists us in determining the influence of these factors on Afghanistan's trade costs. The conclusions of this model have substantial policy ramifications since it can assist policymakers in determining which sectors result in considerable reductions in trade costs and prioritise programmes appropriately.

## 5. Discussion and Results

### 5.1 Summary Figures

Summary figures provide a numerical account of the main components of the study data. In Table 4, an account of Afghanistan's trade costs for the factors studied is summarised. Afghanistan has the most significant average value of overall trade expenditure at 138.50%, having a highest value of 191.8% and a lowest of 98.4%.

The initial procedure is to investigate the time-series characteristics of the parameters to see whether there is a long-term connection between costs to trade and other associated independent variables. The panel unit root test is based on the concept that co-integration tests are done when the panel data components are non-stationary (Levin et al., 2002).

Table 4. Descriptive Statistics Summary.

| Variable | Mean | Median | Std. Dev | Minimum | Maximum |
|---|---|---|---|---|---|
| TC | 123.6 | 129.47 | 21.207 | 97.9 | 189.7 |
| TARIFF | 0.831 | 0.7213 | 0.626 | 0.208 | 3.39 |
| DIST | 4512.17 | 3764.79 | 2265.11 | 589.287 | 10851 |
| AREA | 1085211 | 567100.7 | 866723.6 | 3421991' | 286310 |
| LSCI | 35.0421 | 37.697 | 12.875 | 8.914 | 67.121 |
| *Dummy Variables* | | | | | |
| CONT | 0.214 | 0 | 0.41 | 0 | 1 |
| FTA | 0.285 | 0 | 0.451 | 0 | 1 |

*Source:* Authors' compilation of the data output from the EViews 8.0.

## 5.2 Unit Root Test Results

We utilised Eviews-8 to execute an aggregated unit root examination. Table 5 displays the stationarity test findings, which reveal that the variables are stationary at the initial difference, i.e. I(1). Since countries and geographical areas are time-independent, the distance between them has no effect.

## 5.3 Results of Co-Integration Test

Developed by Kao in 1999, it helps in assessing the nature and order of integration and whether a long-run relationship exists or not. Table 6 satiates the existence of a long-run association, thereby eliminating the risk of inaccurate findings. The co-integration tests reveal that the dependent and explanatory variables have a long-term connection. As a result, the OLS approach yields biased and inconsistent outcomes. Due to the endogeneity issue, the fixed effects model cannot be used for models including time-dependent factors like distance. As an outcome, a new technique for estimating the co-integrated panel is incorporated as suggested by Pedroni (2000). The method is the Panel fully modified ordinary least squares (FMOLS) approach, which employs an adjustment process to account for extraneous variables and yields coefficients over the long run for the estimated model's parameters while taking into account heterogeneity and correlation between variables. FMOLS outperforms previous approaches in that it can estimate similar co-integration parameters simultaneously considering

Table 5. LLC Test for Stationarity.

| Variable | Level | | Difference at First Level | | Order of Integration |
|---|---|---|---|---|---|
| | Stat. | Prob. | Stat. | Prob. | |
| TC | −2.308 | 0.0916 | −8.877 | 0.000 | I(1) |
| TARIFF | 0.1546 | 0.57443 | −4.744 | 0.000 | I(1) |
| EXCH | −26.043 | 0.0010 | −4.872 | 0.000 | I(1) |
| LSCI | 0.365 | 0.6653 | −5.271 | 0.000 | I(1) |

*Source:* Authors' compilation of the data output from the EViews 8.0.

Table 6. Co-Integration Test Estimation.

| KCT | Dependant variable: D (RESID) | | |
|---|---|---|---|
| Variable | Coefficient | *t*-statistic | *P* Value |
| RESID(−1) | −0.221 | −2.954 | 0.0004 |

*Source:* Authors' compilation of the data output from the EViews 8.0.

*Note:* H$_0$: No co-integration.

spatial and longitudinal heterogeneity (Pedroni, 2000). As a consequence, the obtained estimations are more reliable and devoid of serial correlations and inconsistency.

## 5.4 Empirical Findings Based on FMOLS

The FMOLS model results reveal that the explanatory factors contained within the framework exhibit significant impacts on Afghanistan's selected trading partners' trade cost equivalents. Table 8 shows the anticipated results of trade cost variables for total goods trade with Afghanistan's key trading partners. The logarithm trade costs equivalent to total goods trade is the explained variable.

According to the data, the foreign currency exchange rate (EXCH) is statistically important at 1% and has a negative trend. Trade expenditures and nominal exchange rate depreciation are negatively connected. To put it another way, as the exchange rate falls, so does the overall trade. As trade expands, so does intra-national trade, resulting in lower trade costs. According to the exchange rate coefficient (Table 8), a 1% decrease in the ER decreases the costs of trade by 0.023%, thus aligning with the findings of Beckmann et al. (2020) and Neumann and Tabrizy (2021). As a consequence of currency depreciation, an increase in global trade greater than an increase in intra-national trade implies that countries deal globally rather than locally, demonstrating a reduction in the cost of trade. As the ER drops, total trade connections with selected countries expanded by 32.3% from 2008 to 2021, outpacing the 17.8% growth in intra-national trade.

Tariffs are always a hindrance to international trade, raising trade costs. As a consequence, an increase in tariffs reduces overall trade flow. In this scenario, the scope of market accessibility in the two countries is demonstrated by tariffs on products levied by Afghanistan and its economic partner, resulting in higher trade costs. This variable's estimated coefficient value is positive while statistically unimportant. The data reveal that a 1% tariff increase enhances trade expenditures by 0.02% (Table 7) and these findings align with the findings of Novy (2013) and Beverelli et al. (2023). Geographic factors of the cost of trade include geographical separation, locale or land area and shared boundary. The physical transportation cost is influenced by the distance between trade partners. To increase bilateral trade flows, the geographical distance between trading nations must be minimised. According to the projected findings, Afghanistan's geographic distance from its trading partners is positively associated with the costs of trade. It illustrates that a 1% rise in geographical distance intensifies the cost of transactions by 0.27%, thus colliding with Our findings are consistent with the research findings of Duan and Grant (2012), Yao et al. (2022) and Oglend et al. (2022).

The land area variable is negative and statistically significant at a 1% confidence level, and thus, a 1% increase results in a decrease in trade costs by 0.13% as shown in Table 7. The core concept is that nations with wide geographical areas have massive economies and populations, which results in substantial consumer demand. As a consequence, the indigenous populace embraces foreign products, triggering transactions. In addition, large economies are distinguished by immense variation in culture. Residents are increasingly open to diverse cultures, particularly foreign cultural products, which results in an increase in cultural product imports (Salim & Mahmood, 2014). As a result, global trade volumes rise while costs for trade shrink. The empirical results of the present study are congruent with the findings from Lili (2011).

Dummy parameters FTA possesses an adverse and considerable impact on costs associated with trade. According to the econometric outcomes (Table 7), including Afghanistan within a liberal trade agreement decreases trade costs by 0.16%. A free trade zone decreases exchange barriers and boosts international trade through specialisation, division of labour and comparative advantage. Due to the free trade agreement lowering trade costs, international trade escalates, and thus our results are congruent with Novy's (2006).

Table 7. Results of FMOLS.

| Var | Coeff | S. Error | $t$-Stat | $p$ Values |
|---|---|---|---|---|
| TARIFF (TRi*TRD) | 0.0196 | 0.051249 | 0.3836 | 0.702 |
| EXCH | −0.028 | 0.009666 | −2.9270 | 0.0042* |
| LSCI $(LSCI_i*LSCI_j)$ | −0.166 | 0.045527 | −3.939 | 0.0002* |
| DIST | 0.2781 | 0.071994 | 3.8622 | 0.0002* |
| AREA$(Area_i*Area_j)$ | −0.047 | 0.015814 | −3.1590 | 0.0031* |
| CONT | −0.1314 | 0.099674 | −1.3231 | 0.1888 |
| FTA | −0.1667 | 0.071971 | −2.317 | 0.0224** |
| C | 2.6444 | 0.553275 | 4.7796 | 0.0000* |
| $R$-squared | 0.6785 | Mean dependent var | 4.9165 | |
| Adjusted $R$-squared | 0.6563 | SD dependent var | 0.1816 | |
| SE of regression | 0.115 | Sum squared resid | 1.236 | |
| Durbin–Watson stat | 0.597 | Long-run variance | 0.028 | |

*Source:* Authors' compilation of the data output from the EViews 8.0.

*Note:* * Significant at 1%, ** significant at 5%.

R-square evaluates the efficacy of the regression for identifying the outcomes of the variables that are dependent. Our model is efficient in general, with independent factors accounting for more than half of the variance in the dependent variable. The updated R-square is 0.66, suggesting that the drivers are responsible for 67% of trade cost variations. The dependent variable's deviation from the mean is lower, making the results appear more plausible. The framework is additionally updated to account for serial relationships and potential endogeneity issues caused by FMOLS. Tables 8–10 show the estimated findings for

Table 8. FMOLS-Based Empirical Results (Agricultural Sector).

| Variable | Coeff | Std. Error | *t*-Stat | *p* Value |
|---|---|---|---|---|
| TARIFF | 0.072242 | 0.052622 | 1.372851 | 0.1732 |
| EXCH | −0.052983 | 0.01158 | −4.575206 | 0.0000* |
| LSCI | −0.171619 | 0.054041 | −3.175734 | 0.0020* |
| DIST | 0.14925 | 0.071237 | 2.095166 | 0.0389** |
| AREA | −0.059225 | 0.012518 | −4.731075 | 0.0000* |
| CONT | −0.040529 | 0.030851 | −1.313729 | 0.1922 |
| FTA | −0.144177 | 0.067401 | −2.139099 | 0.0351** |
| C | 4.578977 | 0.260851 | 17.55403 | 0.0000* |
| *R*-squared | 0.586571 | Mean dependent var | | 5.257956 |
| Adjusted *R*-squared | 0.554769 | SD dependent var | | 0.146936 |
| SE of regression | 0.098044 | Sum squared resid | | 0.874743 |
| Durbin–Watson stat | 0.728349 | Long-run variance | | 0.021633 |

*Source:* Authors' compilation of the data output from the EViews 8.0.
*Note:* * Significant at 1%, ** significant at 5%.

Table 9. FMOLS-Based Empirical Results (Non-Agricultural Sector).

| Variable | Coefficient | Std. Error | *t*-Statistics | *p* Values |
|---|---|---|---|---|
| Tariff | 0.004116 | 0.03763 | 0.131385 | 0.8965 |
| Exchange rate | −0.027271 | 0.018943 | −2.021432 | 0.0462** |
| LSCI | −0.186991 | 0.070096 | −2.657421 | 0.0094* |
| Distance | 0.2824316 | 0.069651 | 4.0708732 | 0.0001* |
| Geographical area | −0.048191 | 0.012487 | −3.9707310 | 0.0001* |
| Contiguity | −0.007494 | 0.079229 | −0.1237512 | 0.902 |
| Free trade agreement | −0.295929 | 0.077192 | −3.7844317 | 0.0003* |
| C | 6.168743 | 1.114465 | 5.55098 | 0.0000* |
| *R*-squared | 0.528904 | Mean dependent var | | 5.660031 |
| Adjusted *R*-squared | 0.488021 | SD dependent var | | 0.149255 |
| SE of regression | 0.106890 | Sum squared resid | | 1.037896 |
| Durbin–Watson stat | 0.520971 | Long-run variance | | 0.029268 |

*Source:* Authors' compilation of the data output from the EViews 8.0.
*Note:* * Significant at 1%, ** significant at 5%.

Table 10. Cross Model Coefficients Based on Z-Scores.

| Variable | Z-Score |
| --- | --- |
| Tariff | 1.132 |
| Exchange rate | −1.320 |
| LSCI | 0.185 |
| Distance | 5.631 |
| Geographical area | 0.641 |
| Contiguity | 0.420 |
| Free trade agreement | 0.763 |

Source: Authors' compilation of the data output from the EViews 8.0.

agricultural and non-agricultural trade cost equivalents, as well as the cross-model coefficients comparisons of $z$-test results. Statistically speaking, the selected explanatory variables have a similar connection with the explained variable of trade.

# 6. Conclusion and Policy Suggestions

This study used panel data estimate methods to examine trade cost projections for Afghanistan's overall trade with its key counterparts in Asia, Europe and North America from 2008 to 2021. Regardless of the reality that the global economy has become increasingly interconnected, the investigation of tariff alternatives for trade costs reveals substantial untapped gains could be realised by narrowing the gap between the price for producing suitable and accessible goods and the final price paid by the consumer, i.e. by lowering trade costs. Based on trade cost estimates, Afghanistan's expenses are disproportionate to those of its trading partners. While the predictions show significant reductions in trade-related expenses, they also show significant potential for further reductions. This necessitates efficient cost-cutting measures between Afghanistan and its commercial partners. To boost the country's actual and comparative position in global trade, policymakers must deal with the changing conditions of growing trade expenditures. It is recommended that agricultural trade expenditures be preferred above non-agriculture trade costs at the sectoral level. Given that agricultural trade costs outnumber non-agriculture trade costs in many developing countries, concentrating on agricultural facilitation measures would be especially beneficial to Afghanistan. This is also in compliance with the rules of the WTO's trade promotion agreement, which promotes easing the delivery of perishable goods as promptly as appropriate.

Based on other variables like geographical proximity, transit and trade facilitation all have an impact on trade costs. It is proposed that government engagement in trade structures and envisioning trade areas (free) with other nations could possibly significantly reduce the costs of trade. The Liner shipping link is a stronger determinant of trade costs than tariff barriers. Improved cargo communication with trading partners optimises transportation routes, saving time and money. Similarly, open trade through FTAs greatly lowers the costs of trade.

### 6.1 Policy Recommendations

The overall trend of investment and trade between nations is shaped by the costs of trade, thus impacting a nation's capacity to engage in global trade. In light of trade cost's cosmic importance in understanding the intensity and trade trajectory, the subject matter is appealing as of now. Higher trade costs limit competitiveness, lowering the potential benefits of trade. On the other hand, trade liberalisation resulted in reduced trade barriers (tariff and non-tariff), but inadequate institutional and infrastructure performance has impeded trade performance. Despite global economic integration, enormous latent advantages may be achieved by minimising trade costs. Although considerable reductions in trade costs guarantee increased trade flow and thus demand effective cost-cutting methods. Afghanistan is a developing nation, and trade could assist the country in achieving sustainability and economic well-being if the high trade costs are acknowledged. If appropriate policy changes are adopted, the analysis indicates a sufficient possibility for reduced trade costs. The results of the research have several policy enunciations which are underlined as follows:

- Afghanistan needs to engage in WTO's trade advocacy and collaboration agreements while also eliminating administrative hurdles at border crossings.
- Perishable agricultural products should be shipped as promptly as possible, and discharging these items promptly may assist in cutting trade costs.
- Intensify the level of infrastructure by expediting the port connection, handling of cargo and transportation modes including roadways, railroads and air routes and corridors.
- In order to lower trade costs, NTBs must be removed and harmonised in addition to tariff reduction.
- Long-distance transportation's effect may be reduced by constructing physical and soft infrastructures utilising contemporary technical means such as the internet, public relations campaigns and electronic media.

## References

Abbas, S., Shtun, V., Sapogova, V., & Gleb, V. (2023). Russian global export flow and potential: Evidence from augmented gravity model. *International Journal of Emerging Markets.* https://doi.org/10.1108/IJOEM-02-2022-0285

Ahmad, S. S., & Wani, N. U. H. (2018). Trade potential of Afghanistan against SAARC: An application of gravity model approach. *Kardan Journal of Economics and Management Sciences, 1*(4), 1–19.

Aiyar, M. S., Malacrino, M. D., Mohommad, M. A., & Presbitero, M. A. F. (2022). *International trade spillovers from domestic COVID-19 lockdowns* (No. 17395). International Monetary Fund.

Akbari, S. (2021). Implications of WTO rules on freedom of transit and security exceptions for Afghanistan–Pakistan transit trade. In *The WTO transit regime for landlocked countries and its impacts on members' regional transit agreements: The case of Afghanistan's transit trade with Pakistan* (pp. 203–215). Springer International Publishing.

Anderson, J. E., & Van Wincoop, E. (2004). Trade costs. *Journal of Economic Literature, 42*(3), 691–751.

Anderson, J. E., & Wincoop, E. V. (2003). Trade costs. *Journal of Economic Literature, 42*(3), 691–751.

Arvis, J. F., Duval, Y., Shepherd, B., & Utoktham, C. (2013). *Trade costs in the developing world: 1995–2010*. World Bank Policy Research.

Baier, S. L., & Bergstrand, J. H. (2007). Do free trade agreements actually, increase members' international trade? *Journal of International Economics, 71*(1), 72–95.

Beckmann, J., Czudaj, R. L., & Arora, V. (2020). The relationship between oil prices and exchange rates: Revisiting theory and evidence. *Energy Economics, 88*, 104772.

Beverelli, C., Gourevich, I., Heiland, I., Keck, A., Larch, M., & Yotov, Y. (2023). *Trade and welfare effects of the WTO trade facilitation agreement* (No. ERSD-2023-04). WTO Staff Working Paper.

Beverelli, C., & Ticku, R. (2022). Reducing tariff evasion: The role of trade facilitation. *Journal of Comparative Economics, 50*(2), 534–554.

Chaney, T. (2008). Distorted gravity: The intensive and extensive margins of international trade. *The American Economic Review, 98*(4), 1707–1721.

De, P. (2006). Why trade costs matter? In *Asia-Pacific research and training network on trade*. Working Paper Series 26.

Dhami, J. K., Wani, N. U. H., & Sidana, N. (2020). Trade potential of India against BRCS economies: An empirical analysis based on gravity model. *Kardan Journal of Economics and Management Sciences, 3*(2), 13–26.

Duan, S., & Grant, J. H. (2012). *Agricultural trade costs: 1965–2010*.

Evenett, S. J., & Hutchinson, W. K. (2002). *The gravity equation in international economics: Theory and evidence*. Available at SSRN 343194.

Gaurav, A., & Mathur, S. K. (2015). Trade costs between India and the European Union. *The Journal of Industrial Statistics, 4*(2), 178–193.

Hummels, D. (2007). Transportation costs and international trade in the second era of globalisation. *The Journal of Economic Perspectives*, 131–154.

Jin, F., Lee, L. F., & Yu, J. (2023). Estimating flow data models of international trade: Dual gravity and spatial interactions. *Econometric Reviews, 42*(2), 157–194.

Kao, C. (1999). Spurious regression and residual-based tests for cointegration in panel data. *Journal of Econometrics, 90*(1), 1–44.

Keen, M., & Ligthart, J. E. (2002). Coordinating tariff reduction and domestic tax reform. *Journal of International Economics, 56*(2), 489–507.

Levin, A., Lin, F., & Chu, C. J. (2002). Unit root tests in panel data: Asymptotic and finite sample properties. *Journal of Econometrics, 108*, 1–24.

Li, C., & Whalley, J. (2014). China and the trans-pacific partnership: A numerical simulation assessment of the effects involved. *The World Economy, 37*(2), 169–192.

Limao, N., & Venables, A. J. (2001). Infrastructure, geographical disadvantage, transport costs, and trade. *The World Bank Economic Review, 15*(3), 451–479.

Martínez-Martínez, A., Esteve-Pérez, S., Gil-Pareja, S., & Llorca-Vivero, R. (2023). The impact of climate change on international trade: A gravity model estimation. *The World Economy*, *46*(9), 2624–2653.

Masood, S., Khurshid, N., Haider, M., Khurshid, J., & Khokhar, A. M. (2023). Trade potential of Pakistan with the South Asian countries: A gravity model approach. *Asia Pacific Management Review*, *28*(1), 45–51.

Melitz, M. J., & Ottaviano, G. I. (2008). Market size, trade, and productivity. *The Review of Economic Studies*, *75*(1), 295–316.

Neumann, R., & Tabrizy, S. S. (2021). Exchange rates and trade balances: Effects of intra-industry trade and vertical specialization. *Open Economies Review*, 1–35.

Noureen, S., & Mahmood, Z. (2021). The effects of trade cost components and uncertainty of time delay on bilateral export growth. *Heliyon*, *8*(1), e08779.

Novy, D. (2006). Is the iceberg melting less quickly? International trade costs after World War II. In *International trade costs after World War Ii (October 2006). Warwick economic research paper* (p. 764).

Novy, D. (2013a). Gravity redux: Measuring international trade costs with panel data. *Economic Inquiry*, *51*(1), 101–121.

Novy, D. (2013b). International trade without CES: Estimating translog gravity. *Journal of International Economics*, *89*(2), 271–282.

Obstfeld, M., & Rogoff, K. (2000). The six major puzzles in international macroeconomics: Is there a common cause? *NBER Macroeconomics Annual*, *15*, 339–390.

Oglend, A., Asche, F., & Straume, H. M. (2022). Estimating pricing rigidities in bilateral transactions markets. *American Journal of Agricultural Economics*, *104*(1), 209–227.

Pedroni, P. (2000). Fully modified OLS for heterogeneous cointegrated panels. *The Review of Economics and Statistics*, *83*(4), 727–731.

Rauf, S., & Ahmad, S. (2019). Pak Afghan border management: Developments and controversies. *Journal of Contemporary Studies*, *8*(1), 35–51.

Samuelson, P. A. (1954). The transfer problem and transport costs, II: Analysis of effects of trade impediments. *The Economic Journal*, *64*(254), 264–289.

Shaw, T. M. (2013). *Asymmetric trade negotiations*. Ashgate Publishing, Ltd.

Singh, S., & Mathur, S. K. (2014). *Trade costs of India within Asia: Measurement and its determinants*. Working Paper No: p. 746.

Tinbergen, J. (1962). *Shaping the world economy; suggestions for an international economic policy*. Oxford University Press.

Venables, A., & Limao, N. (1999). Infrastructure, geographical disadvantage, and transport costs. *World Bank Economic Review*, *15*, 451–479.

Wani, S. H., & Yasmin, E. (2023). India's trade with South and Central Asia: An application of institution-based augmented gravity model. *Future Business Journal*, *9*(1), 77.

World Bank. (2018). *World development report 2019: The changing nature of work*. The World Bank.

WTO. (2017). *World trade report: Trade in a globalizing world*. World Trade Organization.

Yao, B. H., Shanoyan, A., Schwab, B., & Amanor-Boadu, V. (2022). Mobile money, transaction costs, and market participation: Evidence from Côte d'Ivoire and Tanzania. *Food Policy*, *112*, 102370.

Part IV

# Policy Concerns: Some Insights

Chapter 6

# Incidence of Reverse Capital Flight to Afghanistan: An Empirical Examination

## Abstract

Afghanistan has experienced capital flight, which has long perplexed poli-cymakers and planners. There have been widespread concerns about capi-tal's 'paradoxical' character, which jeopardises national welfare. In this regard, this study envisages examining the nature and prevalence of reverse capital flight in Afghanistan by employing two methods viz direct approach (Cuddington's Model) and indirect approach (World Bank approach and Morgan approach). The findings highlight four main reasons for reverse capital. These include facilitating the whitening of black money (money laundering) which has been previously illegally flown out of the country; second, it allows import tax evasion and the realisation of unnecessary export rebates and refunds; third, it facilitates the avoidance and incidence of Non-Tariff Measures (NTMs) on imported goods; and finally, it allows for the concealment of investment in the underground economy. The study recommends maintaining a thorough record of illegal cash flows in Afghanistan since the nature of trade in Afghanistan is difficult owing to the simultaneous flow of illicit capital. Furthermore, the unrecorded private investments must be adjusted for illegal capital flows resulting from trade mis-invoicing, thus crucial for policy enunciation.

*Keywords*: Capital flight; Afghanistan; illicit capital movement; trade mis-invoicing; export under-invoicing

*JEL Codes*: F11; F13; F17

## 1. Introduction

Capital flight over the years has attracted attention from policymakers and researchers alike (World Bank, 1985, 1993). Several explanations exist for capital flight, which encompass all outflows or are limited, trying to exclude certain

Policy Solutions for Economic Growth in a Developing Country, 131–154

Copyright © 2024 Nassir Ul Haq Wani

Published under exclusive licence by Emerald Publishing Limited

doi:10.1108/978-1-83753-430-220241007

'normal' flows of foreign transactions. Authors have brought attention to the extent of this problem by using estimates of capital flight from poor nations (Almounsor, 2017; Badwan & Atta, 2019; Bashir et al., 2022; Geda & Yimer, 2017; Mahmood, 2013; Mpenya et al., 2015). Studies have suggested the occurrence of capital flight due to external pull factors as the driving forces. These forces range from portfolio considerations, elevated tax burdens, substantial exchange rate alterations and macroeconomic complexities to political instability. The elements assisting the illicit outflow of money are remittances channelled via the Hawala system, under-invoicing and over-invoicing of export and import bills and capital transfers via undocumented valuable metals, and antiques (Aziani, 2018; Forstater, 2018; Ogunwole et al., 2023; Shahzad, 2017). The incidence of these substantial private capital outflows has posed a fundamental macroeconomic concern for many emerging nations during the last two decades. The reversal of capital flight in various South Asian nations in the early 1990s brought a new dimension to this problem. However, capital flight remains a poorly known element of these nations' economies, and determining the scale of capital flight is difficult. Consequently, a better understanding of historical capital flights and a credible forecast of likely reverse capital flight in recent decades could prove important in the accurate evaluation of current opportunities for greater development and investment in underdeveloped nations like Afghanistan.

Afghanistan remained poor after the hundreds of billions of foreign non-refundable inflows (Akbari, 2021; Wani & Rasa, 2023). From late 2001 to August 2021, Afghanistan received 145.8 billion US dollars only from American agencies, government and humanitarian organisations (SIGAR, 2021). Such funds were aimed at filling the Afghan government budget gap, besides partial contributions to other internal revenue mobilisation for Afghanistan. These large inflows resulted in lousy governance, a broken and disparate distribution system, low aid efficacy and corrupt practices, resulting in black money generation. However, the more significant impact of the yearly GDP equivalent aids (or a more significant portion of domestic output) on the infrastructure of Afghanistan should not be ignored, which resulted in the abrupt progress of the economy from 2005 and later. However, the injection of foreign aid later moved away from Afghanistan through importation, overseas transfer of earnings of non-domestic contracting parties and outgoing remittances through Hawala (Hogg et al., 2013). In addition to these reasons, studies have also suggested that trade mis-invoicing (over-invoicing and under-invoicing of import and export bills) and precious minerals and artefacts smuggling are the other factors of capital outflow from a country (Mahmood, 2013). For transferring these funds outside the domestic market, the foreign currency is exchanged for domestic currency, resulting in lower economic well-being. Finally, it attracts the attention of external funding agencies to limit the reverse inflow of previously remitted assets abroad (Mahmood, 2013).

The study illustrates that private individuals' motives for avoiding trade taxes and regulations tend to exceed the reasons for developing foreign assets in Afghanistan. Consequently, rather than a net capital flight exiting the nation, an opposite flow of capital is occurring. Afghanistan witnessed a variety of currency rate regimes between 2008 and 2021, ranging from a fixed exchange rate to adjustable exchange rates. During this time, Afghanistan executed numerous trade policy reform programmes, including substantial tariff rate reductions, NTMs and export promotion incentives, and assessing their inter-relationship is thus worth investigating. Afghanistan permitted full current account convertibility and partial capital account convertibility; thus leaving leverage for illicit capital flows. This regulation on foreign exchange positions is under the authority granted to Da Afghanistan Bank (DAB) by Article 35.2.5 and Article 72 of the Decree Law of Banking in Afghanistan (Banking Law and DA Law).

The tendency and the nature of the private citizens' reasons to dodge trade levies and avoid trade regulations exceed the incentives to amass overseas assets in Afghanistan. As a consequence, rather than a net capital flight from the nation, there is a net reverse capital flight. The primary reason for reverse capital is that most reverse money ends up in the informal (underground) sector, where owners of illicit assets may easily escape domestic taxes. As a result of these activities, capital owners under-invoice imports to reclaim unlawful money. They utilise illicit capital stashed outside the nation or foreign cash obtained via *Hawala* firms. To avoid detection by domestic tax officials, they invest illegal funds in the informal sector, disguised as imported plants and equipment. Surprisingly, this happens even though owners of unlawful money may swiftly repatriate funds via legitimate banking systems. They dodge import taxes and keep unlawful capital concealed from tax and other authorities by transferring back illegal capital via under-invoiced imports. They seek to make deposits in the underground economy, avoid paying domestic taxes and charge indefinitely. Of course, this is done with the assistance of tax and other authorities. The widely held belief is that providing foreign help to countries like Afghanistan may be harmful if it results in the flight of capital. In contrast to this assumption, Afghanistan is experiencing a net reverse flight of capital. Although the flow is indirect, these illegal inflows greatly augment the country's resources through foreign loans, investment and currency revenues. This influx of illegal wealth is invested in the underground economy as taxation is not applicable. Industries in Afghanistan indulge in understating their installed capacity by under-invoicing their machinery and other assets, resulting in an inaccurate reporting of the true size (D'Souza, 2011). Eventually, this practice aids industries in evading sales taxes and helps in the procurement of domestic inputs, and generating revenues becomes easier. It is observed that there is a synchronisation between reverse capital flight and trade liberalisation, offering room for private individuals to plunder trade and foreign exchange restrictions. Surprisingly, unrecorded (illegal) currency transit is bidirectional. Private individuals' wealth held abroad is imported at the appropriate time and even recently policymakers have recognised the necessity to combat the capital flight caused by remittances (Ndikumana et al., 2020).

Misrepresenting commercial flows in Afghanistan enables the illegal inflow and outflow of private capital. In 2014, the Afghan Parliament (*Wolsey Jirga*) signed and approved the anti-money laundering (AML) legislation to combat the flight of capital (Ghanizada, 2014). The prevalence is so familiar and easy that in 2012, Afghan passengers leaving Kabul for Dubai transferred approximately 4.6 billion

U.S. dollars through Hamid Karzai Airport (Najafizada, 2012). UAE has been a haven for capital flight from Afghanistan, and not only does the UAE welcome wealthy Afghans, but India is also inclined to attract them (Schmeidl, 2014). The laws governing the operations for the investment procedures are even bleak as there are no import taxes on the production apparatus. Similarly, unprocessed materials imported into Afghanistan by offshore businesses are tariff-free. The foreign businesses are permitted to operate independently and invest up to 3 million US dollars without obtaining official permission from the Higher Commission of Investment (HCI); investments exceeding 3 million require a review by the HCI, with a land leasing opportunity for the 50 years (Barcelona NA, 2022). The literature shows no evidence of the reverse capital flight in Afghanistan; however, this study covers the analysis from 2008 to 2021, the entire tenure of the Republican government established following the US invasion of Afghanistan. Throughout this period, Afghanistan received large amounts of humanitarian financial assistance and war funds, which aided the country's membership in the World Trade Organization (WTO) and other regional transit trade cooperation bodies, trade expansion and infrastructure development, and the development of legal frameworks by international standards, particularly the establishment of trade and monetary policies, the unification of domestic currency, and the selection of the mana. Due to the prevalence of trade-related mis-invoicing in Afghanistan, unlawful money flows both ways (Nyasulu et al., 2023).

In Afghanistan, the announcement by the American Congress regarding the withdrawal of US forces from Afghanistan in 2014 resulted in a more significant capital flight from Afghanistan (Qais et al., 2022). Fortunately, the outflow of black money is reversed when the domestic market is advantageous for the illicit capital owner and through money transfers of national labourers from abroad. Furthermore, the two main situations that allow return capital flight are underfunding imported goods and overpaying for exported goods. The fundamental reasons for return capital flight are; laundering of black market income; a logical way to avoid paying tax on imported goods and repayment of overfunded amounts on goods sold abroad; and it allows the capital owner to limit Non-tariff-measures or NTMs when bringing goods into the domestic market (Mahmood, 2013). The scenario in Afghanistan presents the same picture. Misrepresenting commercial flows allows for the illegal inflow and outflow of private capital.

Additionally, the underground economy is Afghanistan's primary capital flight market, allowing for tax evasion. Black market traders underpay import bills and pay higher customs taxes to return black assets abroad (,). The bills for those goods are paid with capital already illegally flown abroad or remittances abroad via Hawala companies. The money obtained through unpaid import bills is then invested in the black market, leaving the tax administration in the dark(). Despite the availability of formal banking transfers, the inflow of capital flight back to the home country facilitates tax evasion. Simultaneously, reinvesting capital in the black market is a method of hiding it from tax authorities.

## 2. Literature Review

The literature provides three possible explanations for the predominance of capital flight. It helps to whiten previously transferred illicit money, allows import tax cheating, realises superfluous export rebates and refunds and supports the avoidance of taxes in the form of NTMs on imports. Research studies have pointed out two strands about the connection between capital flight and economic growth. Some studies have focused on the linkage, while others used quantitative approaches to assess the detrimental impact of capital flight on economic growth.

Studies have analysed the connections across countries, investigated capital flight determinants and evaluated the magnitude of capital flight's influence. Capital flight granger drives economic development in Indonesia, Nigeria, Jordan and Palestine (Badwan & Atta, 2019; Erhijakpor, 2019; Refai et al., 2015; Wahyudi & Maski, 2012). A growing body of research has highlighted the detrimental effects of capital flight on economic growth in several countries (Baharumshah & Thanoon, 2006; Bailliu, 2000; Beja, 2007; Bredino et al., 2018; Sodji, 2022; Wujung & Mbella, 2016). Other studies, however, have shown a negative link between capital flight and economic development in the short run but a favourable relationship in the long run (Agyeman et al., 2022; Faza & Badwan, 2023; Olawale & Ifedayo, 2015).

## 3. Afghanistan Trade Arrangements and Regimes Thereof

Assessing the flow of illegal financials can be elaborated efficiently after looking at the changes in Afghanistan's trade and exchange rate regimes. For the sake of paucity, the patterns in illegal money flows are delineated for simplicity, ensuring that the development of Afghanistan's trade and exchange control regimes may be portrayed analytically and meaningfully. In this perspective, we define four distinct stages from 2001 to 2021 as follows:

*Phase 1: The Interim Government Era (Late 2001–mid-2004)*
In this phase, the new government by the leadership of Hamid Karzai replaced the government of the Taliban on 22 December 2001, after the Afghan parties signed the Bonn Agreement on 05 December 2001 (The Bonn Agreement, 2001). Afghanistan needed a proper banking system and a lack of central bank governance on currency controls, no or less trade with other nations and poor infrastructure and investment due to consecutive decades of war. A lack of public certainty about the stability of the national currency led to the use of foreign currencies. Trade transfers were taking place through the national *Hawala* system. A negligible amount of agricultural and essential manufacturing products were exported to Pakistan and Iran (their imports include products from other nations like Korea and Japan). Later, in 2002, the United States captured the maximum share of the export pie. Besides the official currency (the currency left to the Taliban by the previous government), non-original copies with the already in-use notes' serial numbers and two other currency notes (these notes were exchangeable at a 50% discount in the Kabul exchange market) printed by commanders in

northern Afghanistan; altogether totalled to 16 trillion different notes of Afghanis (IMF, 2003).

The new government started efforts to improve the economic situation, public certainty on national currency through central bank governance on issuing money, and the desire of external financing parties to get certainty for efficiently spending their money and not affected by increasing price levels (inflation) in the country. This was only possible by issuing a new currency or replacing a foreign currency, either the currency of adjacent countries or United States dollars. The government decided to print a new currency as the use of the dollar cannot be reversed easily after new notes are printed. However, the International Monetary Fund (IMF) suggested using dollars only for government expenditures and letting the people use their preferred currency until the new currency is designed, printed and delivered and asked for designing a sound monetary policy and legal support for keeping the newly issued notes valuable in the market. As a result, the design works finalised by the Taliban government got approved for printing 27.9 billion new notes, and the first stock of the new currency was delivered on 04 September 2002. The exchange of old and new money commenced on 07 October 2002, for 2 months in 47 locations in Afghanistan. However, after a devaluation in November resulted from the people's stress for not being able to exchange their old money for new money, this process continued for 1 month. It ended on 02 January 2003, exchanging 15.6 billion new Afghanis for 19 trillion old Afghanis (1,000 old Afghanis = 1 new Afghani). The exchange rate was pretty fixed throughout these 3 months in the market (IMF, 2003).

The government planned to have a fixed exchange rate to increase the certainty of Afghan residents. During the old and new money exchange periods, the value of new Afghani notes was not volatile. However, on careful evaluation, the government followed a managed floating exchange rate regime (a fixed range, and within the range, volatility is allowed; simply a mix of changing and constant regimes) (IMF, 2003). Furthermore, the value of Afghani appreciated from 52.82 to 50.01 between 2003 and 2004 (Da Afghanistan Bank, 2004).

Furthermore, the more significant inflows of external funds to build essential infrastructure in Afghanistan, especially building smooth roads for inter-connecting Afghanistan simplified trade, cheaper and efficient goods delivery, and rebuilt the old transit pathways that can absorb transit traders to transfer goods through Afghanistan and welcome foreign direct investments (IMF, 2003; Wani, 2019). As a result, the Afghan government signed trade and transit agreements with regional nations, such as Afghanistan–Pakistan Transit Trade Agreement (APTTA), Economic Cooperation Organisation Trade Agreement (ECOTA) and transit agreements with the Central Asian region. The trade administration system was revisited largely in response to IMF recommendations, and the tariffs on basic and capital-intensive products were lowered as well. All export subsidies were eliminated except for tax breaks and export funding. Instead, export tariffs on numerous intermediate inputs were imposed to stimulate businesses, however later repealed. Aside from these adjustments to policy, the import licencing mechanism was simplified, with all permissible imports attached to one of two lists: the 'Free List' or the 'Tied List'. Both the accounts (current and capital) were tightly monitored during this period. The aforementioned economic reform attempts had a limited impact, primarily due to rising prices within the nation. The Afghani currency (AFN) proved overvalued once again, especially after the strengthening of the US dollar. Instead of depreciating the AFN, the government attempted to balance the trade via subsidies for exports and quantitative import limitations. The licencing processes were tightened once again. Commercial and industrial users were subject to different import duty rates. All of these policies exacerbated the government's anti-export stance.

*Phase 2: The Hamid Karzai Era (2004–2014)*
In this era, the transitional government commenced efforts to choose a democratic president by collecting votes for 18 candidates in the first election campaign on 09 October 2004 (The White House, 2009). Finally, the elections board consisting of United Nations and Afghan bodies under the supervisory of Zakim Shah announced that the 'US-backed president Hamid Karzai' became the president of Afghanistan for the next 5 years (Jay & Agencies, 2003). Moreover, the exchange rate policy did not change from a managed floating exchange rate regime (Da Afghanistan Bank, 2004).

During this era, the government continued developing legal frameworks for trade, facilitating entrepreneurial activities and trade and transit to absorb international investments and collect revenues from import taxes and transit tolls. In addition, the government also planned to develop frameworks for limiting illegal trade and bribery popularised for these unlawful trade activities. Furthermore, the government planned to become part of the WTO, revise currently signed trade and transit contracts and facilitate new agreements with other nations, improve customs and ports systems through computerised systems, scanning machines and other modern facilities by controlling bribery and officers' dishonest dealings. In addition, investment in infrastructure, e.g. energy, health, transit routes, public safety and security and private business support, was enhanced (IMF, 2006).

In the year 2012, the roles and responsibilities of security transferred to Afghan authorities from foreign troops (World Bank, October 2012b), based on the conferences of Kabul and Lisbon agreements of authority transmission between NATO forces and the Afghan National government in 2010 (World Bank, May 2012a). The economic growth rose to about 10% this year due to rains and agricultural productivity. Therefore, food was enough for the domestic market; thus, the inflation rate did not grow more than 4.6%. Moreover, opportunities existed to welcome international investments, and the mining sector also grew this year (World Bank, October 2012b).

*Phase 3: The Muhammad Ashraf Ghani Era (2014–Aug 2021)*
The first-ever noted peaceful transition of power in the last century's history in Afghanistan was from Hamid Karzai to the newly elected president, Muhammad Ashraf Ghani, which took place in 2014 (Murtazashvili, 2015). This era opened some new doors for facilitating international trade and brought changes in the governmental structure of Afghanistan. Furthermore, foreign financing parties

extended their financial support for Afghanistan due to the London Conference in December 2014 (IMF, 2015). The government followed the managed exchange rate regime (Da Afghanistan Bank, 2015). With weak money transfer channels, deposit money remains the strategic instrument for monetary policy to keep inflation low; however, inflation is anticipated to speed up as demand rises before reforms lead to a supply-side reaction. Hence a changing rate of exchange can help exchange-rate policy to manage the recurring shocks. For a powerful monetary transmission mechanism, exchange rate policy can be aided with higher use of domestic currency and limiting the use of foreign currencies, e.g. the dollar (IMF, 2016). Moreover, curbing inflation and keeping the exchange rate pliable to maintain foreign currency reserves and limit more significant exchange rate variations were the main goals of the monetary policy of Afghanistan. Accordingly, the fiscal policy aimed to improve government revenue and adjust cash in the public treasury (IMF, 2015).

Afghan economy continually grew each year with the growing Afghanistan population, hence no growth effectiveness. Trade relationships strengthened; the Chabahar Agreement was signed with Iran and India. Finally, Afghanistan became a WTO member in 2016 (World Bank, 2016). Afghanistan opened air corridors with Kazakhstan, Turkey and UAE in 2017. The air corridors expanded its projects with Europe, China, Russia and India, which solved 80% of the export concerns of Afghanistan. About USD 1 billion worth of Afghan goods were exported in 2017 (ACCI, n.d.).

Moreover, it is worth mentioning that for international trade and investment support in the country, the first National Trade Policy of Afghanistan was also developed for 2019–2023 by the Ministry of Industries and Commerce (Ministry of Industries and Commerce, 2019). The lower humidity in 2017 and 2018 resulted in lower crop production in 2019. Moreover, increasing unpredictability has decreased investment inclination resulting from higher deaths and other problems provoked due to the 2018 elections, uncertainty about the period and degree of foreign security support and peace debates with the Taliban. In addition, population growth surpassed economic growth and affected the per capita national income in Afghanistan (World Bank, June 2019).

*Phase 4: Taliban 2.0 (Aug 2021–present)*
After the Taliban's re-emergence to power in late 2021, the nation experienced political turmoil in the early months of 2021, as well as economic sanctions imposed by Western countries. According to Article 69 of the Da Afghanistan Bank statute, one of the key tasks of Da Afghanistan Bank is to formulate, adopt and implement an exchange rate policy. Da Afghanistan Bank has introduced the Managed Floating Exchange Rate system. The currency rate is governed by market demand and supply considerations under this system, and its extreme swings are managed as much as feasible by DAB.

The economy's economic position determines this exchange rate regime, the balance of payments, and the degree of openness (currency inflow and outflow). It is pertinent to mention that DAB does not target the currency rate under this system.

### 3.1 Trade Mis-Invoicing

The disparity of the recorded international trade figures between emerging economies and advanced economy nations is defined as trade mis-invoicing (Tandon & Rao, 2017). It happens when international businessmen report wrong information through customs invoices, internationally transfer funds illicitly, escape taxes and tariffs, money laundering, avoid currency regulations and conceal earnings deposited in foreign banks (Global Financial Integrity, 2021). Accordingly, higher tariffs and premiums in the underground economy are the main reasons for making mis-invoicing happen worldwide (Buehn & Eichler, 2011). On the contrary, Patnaik et al. (2012) see poor economic situations and increasing rates of tariffs as less credible factors for fast-growing developing economies. Instead, the liberalisation of capital accounts, interest rate variations, stabilisation of the political situation, lawbreaking, arrearage and the regime of the exchange rate in the country are the primary reasons for mis-invoicing between nations. Mis-invoicing accounts for 1.6 trillion US dollars among illegal monetary transfers between 134 rich (36) and developing nations (98) from 2009 to 2018 (Global Financial Integrity, 2021).

Moreover, mis-invoicing contributes to more than 1/5 of the commerce between emerging and advanced economy countries (Umer, 2023). Afghanistan is ranked first for suffering a higher risk of money laundering and terrorist financing by the Basel Anti-Money Laundering Index in 2021 (Basel Institute on Governance, 2021), which shows that Afghanistan still has higher rates of mis-invoicing trade with the world.

Under-invoicing is one type of mis-invoicing. It is defined that the imports are reported undervalued, but the supplier abroad receives the actual amount of money, which is greater than the reported amount (Bhagwati, 1974). The remaining unreported amount is transferred through *Hawalla* systems or cryptocurrency (Morshed & Rahman, 2021). Under-invoicing happens when rents and tariffs for the numerically limited goods cost higher than the higher premia received by the importing trader to buy foreign currency in the free or underground market to transfer to the foreign supplier. Accordingly, importers see an opportunity for undervaluation when the currency market is non-regulated, but international business is limited by the state (Mahmood, 1997).

Furthermore, traders under-invoice import controlled goods with having higher premia than the black market premia, especially when under-reporting is probably more accessible and more convenient (Bhagwati, 1974). Even though the trader is rewarded for the under-reporting activity after returning the capital to the home country, counting this and the cost of unpaid import taxes will further broaden the concern. At the same time, it leads to depleting national foreign currency deposits (Mahmood, 2013). Secondly, over-reporting is the inclination of the trader to withdraw illicit capital from the country that takes place similar to under-reporting. More significant tariffs are paid to reach the capital withdrawal purpose of money laundering in some future time after transferring the illegal money to a secure foreign nation. Paying more tariffs to the exporter reveals this fraudulent motivation that the domestic and international trade policy is highly protective of (Mahmood, 2013).

Importers are usually involved in under-invoicing their imports if the tariffs and rents on imports surpass the surcharge on the free (or black) market currency rate. Whenever there are no currency limitations but barriers to trade, there is a temptation to under-invoice imports (Mahmood, 1997). Under-invoicing items and engaging in unlawful foreign currency transactions, on the other hand, pose hazards. Thus, under-invoicing will occur only if the gap between the tariffs on imports equivalent and the free-floating premium on foreign currency is larger than the anticipated risk of discovery by law enforcement authorities (Cassara, 2015). This usually occurs when money is bought into the country and then profited from the transaction (reverse capital flight). The difference increases when this apparent gain is combined with the savings in import tariffs due to import under-invoicing. Import under-invoicing brings money into the nation while bypassing foreign currency reserves of the country.

Over-invoicing of imported goods, which involves paying increased customs duties to move wealth, or 'black money', outside the country, can be a misleading signal that the trade regulatory regime is more protectionist or limiting. Under-invoicing of exports is used to transfer illegal funds out of the nation, allowing exporters to forgo export subsidies or avoid paying export taxes. This practice results in the government losing foreign currency profits. Some exporters also overcharge for their goods, seeking to illegally profit from subsidies for export and use a reverse flight of capital to convert black money and transfer it out of the country and exporters obtain it via foreign-based correspondence system (*Hawala*) exchange firms. If the difference is greater than the perceived risk of being detected, the exporter indulges in over-invoicing, which leads to government agencies obtaining more foreign currency and requiring additional spending owing to higher subsidies given for over-invoiced exports.

## 4. Research Methodology

Scholarly works have highlighted two methods (direct and indirect) for measuring the intensity of illegal capital outflows. The direct method (Cuddington approach) involves the utilisation of data from the Balance of Payments (BOP) accounts, describes capital flight as immediate financial outflows and is a private individual's reaction to risks associated with investing in the nation. It refers to individual individuals' immediate (speculative) reaction to unpredictable economic circumstances or similar policy-induced risks associated with investments. These assets often react quickly to political or financial crises, as well as expectations of increased capital account restrictions or currency depreciation in their home country. As a result, rather than focusing on the private sector acquiring all external claims, the Cuddington model concentrates only on private non-bank investors purchasing net acquisition of non-bank private short-term capital (NAC) and errors and omissions (Net errors and Omissions). Capital flight (KFCUD) is defined as follows:

$$KF_{CUD} = -NEO - NAC \qquad (1)$$

In contrast, other scholars have an aversion to directly quantifying capital flight. The critics believe in the inclusion of long-term foreign financial assets along with short-term capital flows as these are near replacements due to exceptionally active secondary markets in long-term financial assets, for short-term assets. Unrecorded flows and statistics abnormalities are examples of mistakes and inaccuracies usually called errors and omissions. In light of this criticism, further anti-capital-flight measures are being recommended. Approaches proposed by the World Bank (1985) and Morgan (1986) are the widely accepted indirect frameworks for quantifying the plight of capital flight. As per these approaches, the drivers of capital flight range from advances or changes in international/external debt (CED), net foreign direct investment (NFDI), changes in foreign currency reserve (COR), and the current account deficit balance (CAB). The first two factors (external debt and NFDI) should be sufficient to cover the latter two outflows (FCR and Current Account Deficit (CAD)) and the discrepancy between these two flows implies capital flight. The World Bank, on the other hand, defines capital inflows to a country as elevated outside debt and NFDI. This difference is used by private persons to validate their claim on foreign assets. In simple terms, if the inflows of capital do not sustain the CAD or official reserve accumulation (i.e. the recorded use of foreign money), it departs the country in the shape of capital flight. As a result, the World Bank defines capital flight (KFWB) as follows:

$$KF_{WB} = CED + NFDI + CAB + COR \qquad (2)$$

The Morgan definition, like the World Bank definition, measures foreign capital outflows based on factors like current account balance (CAB), changes in external debt (CED), establishing foreign official currency reserves (COR), net foreign direct investment (NFDI) and boosting the net acquisition foreign assets (NAFA). As a result, the Morgan description (KFMOR) is as follows:

$$KF_{MOR} = CED + NFDI + CAB + COR + NAFA \qquad (3)$$

## 4.1 Adjustment of Capital Flight With Trade Mis-Invoicing

Trade mis-invoicing is incentivised when there are restrictions on trade and foreign currency coupled with lax regulatory enforcement leading to a two-way flow of capital. Surprisingly, the disparity in trade statistics between the trading partners (the partner and the reporter country) typically aids in identifying this issue. For gauging the capital flight estimates, data statistics of partner countries are employed as explained in the equations below:

$$KF_{WB} = KF_{WB} + MI$$

$$KF_{MOR} = KF_{MOR} + MI$$

$$KF_{CUD} = KF_{CUD} + MI$$

where
  $MI = MI_X + MI_m$ represents the total trade mis-invoicing.
  MI represents the export mis-invoicing. If $MI_X = 0$, then the country indulges I over-invoicing of exports, and if it exceeds 0, then it is the case of under-invoicing.
  On the other hand, the import mis-invoicing is denoted by $MI_m = M_{pic} - X_{icp} * Ad$ and if $MI_m$ is greater than 0, then it is the case of Import over-invoicing and if equalling 0, then it is the case of under-invoicing. Furthermore, $M_{icp}$ denotes the industrial country imports from Afghanistan (cif) and $X_{pic}$ are Afghanistan's exports to industrial nations (fob); $M_{pic}$ reflects the Afghanistan imports from industrial nations (cif); $X_{icp}$ denotes the industrial nations' exports to Afghanistan (fob); and Ad is the adjustment factor, often known as the ratio of *cif* and *fob*. Furthermore, the study employs data sets from the BOP accounts, IMF and World Bank ranging from 2001 to 2021.

## 5. Discussions and Results

### 5.1 Capital Flight Estimates

How large are the illegal money flows in Afghanistan? Between 2001 and 2021, Afghanistan received more than $30 billion in (net) illegal money inflows (or reverse capital flight). Capital flight (reverse) in 2009 accounted for 74% of unsettled foreign debt and constituted 18% of GDP. Such enormous capital flight (reverse) runs counter to generally held and exaggerated beliefs concerning the nation's net financial loss. Individuals with various behaviours and interests participate in illegal cash flow operations. Their motivation is to exploit economic policy to maximise their gain. The intensity and direction of illegal capital flow alter when economic policies change to fulfil the economy's developmental goals. The following study demonstrates that illegal financial movement is an issue that successive Afghan administrations have yet to address.

  Table 1 reflects the under-invoiced exports during the first phase (2001–2004), amounting to an average of $29.58 million per year. It demonstrates a definite incentive to withdraw money from the nation. It was the time when capital account limits were at their most severe. Export tariffs were used to limit inter-mediate input exports. Exporters may therefore avoid capital controls and export limitations with the help of customs officials. During the same time period, the

Table 1. Trade Mis-Invoicing.

| Period/Phase | Exports | Imports | Total Trade |
| --- | --- | --- | --- |
| Late 2001–Mid-2004 | 427.2 | 16,821 | 16393.8 |
| 2004–2014 | 617 | 7660.2 | 7043.2 |
| 2014–Aug 2021 | 534 | 6337.5 | 5805.5 |

*Source:* Data from WITS, OEC and IMF.

*Note:* The figures are expressed based on the annual average in million US$.

level of under-invoiced imports stood at $248.64 million. In this instance, the goal was to transfer illegal wealth back into the nation and avoid heavy import tariffs. During the first phase, as a result of trade mis-invoicing, a net reverse capital flight of $219.06 million occurred each year. Furthermore, Table 1 also reveals the patterns of over-invoicing (exports) and under-invoicing (imports) in the other stages. As a consequence of the floating and flexible exchange rates, Afghanistan witnessed an infusion of illegal cash via trading accounts. The third phase (2014–August 2021) witnessed the highest export over-invoicing (average annual figures). This era was marked by a decline in foreign exchange reserves, economic repercussions enacted by Western countries, the suspension of foreign currency finances, the implementation of different rates of exchange and ultimately, the establishment of the filthy exchange rate system as well as the implementation of subsidies for export. Exporters blocked government entities from getting further incentives for over-invoiced shipments while the administration required finances. However, the administration was pleased since the over-invoiced export revenues increased foreign currency reserves simultaneously.

The second period (2001–2004) witnessed the largest rate of capital under-invoicing because tariffs and NTBs were especially high, motivating importers to evade trade-related restraints and engage in import under-invoicing activities, pushing illicit money home as shown in Table 1. The average yearly import under-invoicing percentages were also exceptionally high in the third phase (2014–Aug 2021). Tariff rates were modest during this period yet high enough to keep importers active in such operations. Although NTBs decreased during this time, NTMs surged due to corruption and poor governance. The total illegal capital influx was the largest net during the fourth phase. This illustrates that, even with less trade restrictions and the expansion of accounts (current and capital) in the fourth phase, illegal capital movement could not be restricted. It means that implicit trade and capital account constraints persisted, motivating individuals to disobey them to reap advantages. The essential issue is how this significant infusion of illegal wealth was funded. The explanation is Hawala, a financing conduit for trade mis-invoicing. Furthermore, illegal funds that had previously fled the country became an important driver of the reversal of capital flight subsequently.

Table 2 displays unadjusted estimations of the flight of capital generated by the three previously addressed methods. The assessments determined by these

Table 2. Representation of Capital Flight Based on Unadjusted Estimates.

| Period/Phase | World Bank | Morgan | Cuddington |
|---|---|---|---|
| Late 2001–Mid-2004 | 27.2 | −15.73 | −36.23 |
| 2004–2014 | 51.9 | −680.21 | −304.32 |
| 2014–Aug 2021 | −73.4 | −1337.5 | −780.55 |

*Source:* Authors' calculations based on the data from WITS, OEC and IMF.

*Note:* The figures are expressed based on the annual average in million US$.

approaches need to be more accurate, rendering consensus challenging. The estimates based on Morgan and Cuddington's approaches agree in each of the initial three phases but disagree in the final one (fourth phase). The estimates based on the $KF_{WB}$ approach vary from the estimates based on Morgan and Cuddington's approaches.

The World Bank approach estimates a net outflow of funds from Afghanistan in the initial two stages; however, Morgan and Cuddington's methodologies reveal a net influx of illegal cash (Table 2). The World Bank and Cuddington techniques predict a reversal of capital flight in the third phase, but the Morgan method predicts an additional capital flight from the country. The growth is mostly owing to commercial banks' massive purchases of overseas holdings, which aligns with the World Bank's method. Although commercial banks' purchase of foreign assets may not be termed capital flight, therefore, Morgan's estimates deserve to be treated with caution.

For gauging the adjusted estimates of capital flight, the forecasts remain comparable across all methods and stages, except Morgan's framework in stage three as shown in Table 3. The level of reverse capital flight has increased as the currency regimes and liberalisation of trade evolved, in accordance with the World Bank's methodology. Cuddington's technique yields equivalent results. This tendency has emerged as a consequence of the lower price of illegal funding operations. This is primarily a result of trade and financial accounts liberalisation, especially when enforcement agencies were ineffective in executing regulations. The third phase on the other hand witnessed the huge capital flight reversal.

Since we have discussed the trends and patterns of illegal cross-border transfer of funds, therefore, estimating the impact of illegal capital flows on GDP, exchange rate gains, deficits in current accounts and foreign debt will provide additional details of the intensity. The proportion of Reverse Capital Flow (RCF) to GDP, for example, represents investments in the shadow economy; the proportion to foreign currency profits illustrates the importance of illicit vs authorised capital inflows; the proportion to CAD indicates CAD growth; the ratio to external debt measures the intensity of RCF in relation to the amount of the nation's foreign debt.

The average yearly RCF to Afghanistan in the third phase (2018–2021) is highlighted by the numbers from Table 4. However, using the World Bank's technique, the projections of RCF to GDP in the second phase (2004–2014) show the greatest discharge, subsequently followed by the first and third phases.

Table 3. Adjusted Capital flight (Average per Annum, US$, Millions).

| Period/Phase | World Bank | Morgan | Cuddington's |
| --- | --- | --- | --- |
| Late 2001–Mid-2004 | −212.2 | −235.73 | −326.93 |
| 2004–2014 | −851.9 | −380.21 | −1324.12 |
| 2014–Aug 2021 | −1731.4 | −1034.5 | −1080.51 |

*Source:* Authors' calculations based on the data from WITS, OEC and IMF.

Table 4. Illegal Flows of Capital to Afghanistan.

| Period | GDP | | | Foreign Exchange Earnings | | | Current Account Deficit | | | External Debt | | |
|---|---|---|---|---|---|---|---|---|---|---|---|---|
| | WB | MGN | CGN | WB | MGN | CGN | WB | MGN | CGN | WB | MGN | CGN |
| Late 2001–Mid-2004 | −1.943 | −1.443 | −1.732 | −12.54 | −1.8 | −1.448 | −1.562 | −13.143 | −16.943 | −21.343 | −30.132 | −22.143 |
| 2004–2014 | −1.231 | −2.763 | −1.531 | −9.097 | −11 | −21.713 | −1.331 | −9.087 | −13.231 | −22.703 | −31.091 | −19.087 |
| 2014–Aug 2021 | −1.431 | −1.326 | −1.701 | −4.321 | −19 | −11.126 | −1.841 | −5.121 | −17.431 | −28.306 | −31.905 | −14.101 |

*Source:* Data output from the equations.

*Note:* W.B. stands for World Bank; MGN stands for Morgan and CGN stands for Cuddington's; and the figures are expressed in percents.

What do these forecasts imply? These figures account for around 2% of GDP. Based on the insights from the second phase, it is worth noting that Afghanistan initiated policy reforms aimed at economic expansion, liberalisation and denationalisation along with structural adjustment programmes with donor assistance. Furthermore, Afghanistan's shift to a managed float exchange rate offered a chance to convert illegal capital (domestic as well as the capital held abroad) along with the provision of currency accounts (foreign) to its citizens. These policy shifts resulted in the movement of capital, making it cheaper for individuals to retrieve the funds held abroad. To avoid possible governmental enforcement actions, the majority of this capital has entered the nation illegally rather than lawfully.

Looking at the data figures from Table 4, the first phase had the highest proportion of reversed flight of capital to foreign exchange gains. It was a period when the country focused largely on import substitution, controlled floating exchange and nationalisation policies with strict capital account constraints. Remittances were small in size but growing. With such strict regulations in place, it was perfect for individuals to participate in illegal activities, returning around 17% of offshore earnings to the country in reverse capital flight. This percentage fell as foreign currency earnings climbed. The percentage of reversed flight of capital compared to the CAD is significant in the second phase, followed by the second and first phases.

What does this ratio imply? The CAD represents the gap in the economic resources but not the total economic resource imbalance (formal plus underground economy). It should be emphasised that official numbers do not cover the underground economy. Considering that reversed flight of capital contributes to over 50% of the subsequent current account deficit, it is plausible to suppose that this phenomenon is having a considerable impact on the actual economy. It is evident in the country's growing number of automobiles as well as thriving retail and commercial real estate sectors. Otherwise, the formal sector of the economy continues in dire circumstances. The reversal of the flight of capital to international debt accumulation proportion was highest in the third phase when reversing capital flight contributed to roughly 42.8%. It denotes that the movements in illegal money movements brought back an amount equivalent to or more than the foreign debt accumulated throughout the period.

## 6. Conclusion and Policy Suggestions

The study focused on the prevalence of capital flight in Afghanistan, ranging from 2001 to 2021. As of 2021, the country's overall long-term financial obligation stands at US$ 3.5 billion, whereas real capital outflow totalled US$ 1.5 billion, or 42.8% of the debt. The study findings challenge the generally held assumption that providing foreign funds to countries such as Afghanistan may be counterproductive if it results in the flight of capital. In contrast to this statement, reverse capital occurred on a continual net basis in Afghanistan. These unauthorised flows improve the country's resources, which include foreign loans, foreign investment and foreign currency earnings. Due to tax relaxations, these earnings are diverted for investments in the underground economy, notably the real estate market. Furthermore, because of the selective tax benefits offered to businesses, there is a prevalence of underreporting of the capacity installed, and thus report misleading representation of the establishment's true capacity. Eventually, this practice aids industries in evading taxes.

The flight of capital complicates national economic issues, leading to an unfavourable investment climate. In such situations, the country needs a robust economy with an amicable economic environment. The inflows of reverse capital flight portray the growth of the economy as markets and infrastructure are booming and growing, making the atmosphere more conducive.

Furthermore, official data provide a confused image; for example, total investment has fallen in recent years. Despite issues like law and order and conflict, economic growth is steady. Reverse capital flight needs to be documented in official statistics; its consequences for the country's socioeconomic progress cannot be deduced directly. During trade and exchange liberalisation, reverse capital also increased. This provided an impetus for private individuals to exploit the norms in the absence of strong regulatory bodies.

### 6.1 Policy Suggestions

Based on the findings, the paper suggests the following policy approaches to restrict capital flight:

- Enact policies and create strategies to combat illegal flight of capital, such as improving tax administration and trade law enforcement, instituting governance reforms, improving customs administration, simplifying tariff structure and appointing pre-shipment inspection firms. Furthermore, Hawala (correspondent) related individuals or businesses should be followed via the use of banking reform legislation or guidelines.
- Trade mis-invoicing has been used to illegally transfer money overseas. As a result, the government should implement port personnel training programmes to detect trade mis-invoicing.
- To boost domestic investor confidence and limit capital flight, the government must collaborate with international organisations to expose opacity in offshore financial jurisdictions, strengthen regularity capabilities and implement a rigorous transparency and accountability system to manage the government's finances.
- To facilitate business, the Afghan government should design investment-friendly regulations and implement a VAT system.
- Improving tax administration and effectively applying trade norms may assist in the management of unlawful money flows. Money obtained via corruption is a key source of illegal payments carried across borders. As a result, urgent governance improvements are required to combat the country's widespread corruption, which undermines sanctioned activities.

- The main source of illegal capital flows is regulatory agencies' poor application of capital and trade prohibitions. Private individuals who violate trade and foreign currency restrictions and take advantage of trade advantages face severe penalties. As a result, effective trade and exchange laws are likely to discourage capital flight. In this context, it would be positive if the handling of customs was improved, and the tariff system could be streamlined by rendering it more uniform.
- The 'government's Remittances Initiative Scheme' may be a policy tool that encourages rather than discourages capital undervaluation in the country. Under-invoicing of imported plant and equipment would become less popular. The study opines a policy of accelerated depreciation allowance as a compensation factor for under-invoicing.
- Enact agreements with other countries to exchange information on private individuals' financial accounts and trade-related activities.
- The capital account, unlike the current account, is not convertible. This duality must be eradicated by establishing suitable and efficient processes to guarantee identical results.

## Bibliography

ACCI. (n.d.). *Afghanistan opens air cargo corridors with Europe, Russia, China, and UAE*. https://acci.org.af/en/538-afghanistan-opens-air-cargo-corridors-with-europe-russia-china-and-uae.html#:~:text=Sector%20Proposed%20Suggestion-,Afghanistan%20opens%20air%20cargo%20corridors%20with%20Europe%2C%20Russia%2C%20China%2C,and%20other%20cities%20o

Adedoyin, I. L., Promise, K. K., Adeoti, J. O., Godswill, O. O., Sunday, A., & Bamidele, I. (2017). Capital flight and the economic growth: Evidence from Nigeria. *Binus Business Review*, *8*(2), 125–132.

Adeleye, N., Osabuohien, E., Bowale, E., Matthew, O., & Oduntan, E. (2018). Financial reforms and credit growth in Nigeria: Empirical insights from ARDL and ECM techniques. *International Review of Applied Economics*, *32*(6), 807–820.

Agyeman, G., Sakyi, D., & Oteng-Abayie, E. F. (2022). External debt and economic growth in selected sub-Saharan African countries: The role of capital flight. *Research in Globalization*, *5*, 100091.

Ajayi, S. I. (2014). Capital flight and economic development in Africa. In *Capital flight from Africa: Causes, effects, and policy issues* (pp. 55–80). https://doi.org/10.1093/acprof:oso/9780198718550.003.0003

Akanbi, O. B. (2015). An econometric approach to the short and long-run analysis of the Nigerian economy – Capital flight in Nigeria. *International Journal of Research in Humanities and Social Studies*, *2*(12), 83–89.

Akbari, S. (2021). *The WTO transit regime for landlocked countries and its impacts on members' regional transit agreements: The case of Afghanistan's transit trade with Pakistan* (Vol. 17). Springer Nature.

Almounsor, A. (2005). A development comparative approach to capital flight: The case of the Middle East and North Africa, 1970–2002. In *Capital flight and capital controls in developing countries* (pp. 234–261). Edward Elgar Publishing.

Almounsor, A. H. (2017). A new analysis of capital flight from Saudi Arabia: The relation with long-term economic performance. *Applied Economics and Finance*, *4*(6), 17–26.

Ani, C., Inuwa Dauda, M., & Andekujwo Baajon, M. (2018). Capital flight and economic growth in Nigeria: An empirical analysis. *International Journal of Humanities, Art and Social Studies*, *3*(3), 1–11.

Aziani, A. (2018). *Illicit financial flows: An innovative approach to estimation.* Springer.

Badwan, N., & Atta, M. (2019). Empirical investigation of capital flight and illicit financial flows, economic growth in Palestine. *Journal of Economics, Management and Trade*, *25*(5), 1–15.

Baharumshah, A. Z., & Thanoon, M. A. M. (2006). Foreign capital flows and economic growth in East Asian countries. *China Economic Review*, *17*(1), 70–83.

Bailliu, J. (2000). *Private capital flows, financial development, and economic growth in developing countries* (No. 2000-15). Bank of Canada.

Bakare, A. S. (2011). The determinants and roles of capital flight in the growth process of the Nigerian economy: Vector autoregressive model approach. *British Journal of Management & Economics*, *1*(2), 100–113.

Barcelona, N.A. (2022, November). *Foreign direct investment (FDI) in Afghanistan.* Lloyds Bank. https://www.lloydsbanktrade.com/en/market-potential/afghanistan/investment

Basel Institute on Governance. (2021). *Basel AML Index 2021: 10th Public Edition: Ranking money laundering and terrorist financing risks worldwide.* Basel AML Index.

Bashir, M. F., Khan, T., Bin Tariq, Y., & Akram, M. (2022). Does capital flight undermine growth: A case study of Pakistan. *Journal of Money Laundering Control*, *26*(6), 1131–1149.

Beja, E. J. (2007). *Capital flight and economic performance: Growth projections for the Philippines.* Munich Personal RePEc Archive.

Benhabib, J., & Spiegel, M. M. (1994). The role of human capital in economic development evidence from aggregate cross-country data. *Journal of Monetary Economics*, *34*(2), 143–173.

Bhagwati, J. N. (1974). On the under-invoicing of imports. In *Illegal transactions in international trade* (pp. 138–147). Elsevier.

Bhagwati, J. N. (1964). On the under-invoicing of imports. *Bulletin of the Oxford University Institute of Statistics*, *27*(4), 389–397.

Bobye, A. L. (2012). Capital flight and Nigeria economic growth. *Asian Journal of Finance & Accounting*, *4*(2), 277–289.

Boyce, J. K., & Ndikumana, L. (2001). Is Africa a net creditor? New estimates of capital flight from severely indebted sub-Saharan African countries, 1970–96. *Journal of Development Studies*, *38*(2), 27–56.

Boyce, J. K., & Ndikumana, L. (2012). *Capital flight from sub-Saharan African countries: Updated estimates, 1970–2010.* PERI Research Report. https://doi.org/10.2139/ssrn.2202215

Bredino, S., Fiderikumo, P., & Adesuji, A. (2018). Impact of capital flight on economic growth in Nigeria: An econometric approach. *Journal of Business and Economic Development*, *3*(1), 22–29.

Buehn, A., & Eichler, S. (2011, August 24). Trade mis-invoicing: The dark side of world trade. *The World Economy*, *34*(08), 1263–1287.

Cassara, J. A. (2015). *Trade-based money laundering: The next frontier in international money laundering enforcement*. John Wiley & Sons.

Cuddington, J. T. (1986). *Capital flight: Estimates, issues, and explanations* (Vol. 58). International Finance Section, Department of Economics, Princeton University.

D'Souza, J. (2011). *Terrorist financing, money laundering, and tax evasion: Examining the performance of financial intelligence units*. CRC Press.

Da Afghanistan Bank. (2004). *1382 annual financial statements Da Afghanistan Bank* (pp. 1–20). Da Afghanistan Bank. http://dab.gov.af/sites/default/files/2019-01/1382ANNUALFINANCIALSTATEMENTS28122013150536668553325325.pdf

Da Afghanistan Bank. (2015). *Exchange rate policy*. Da Afghanistan Bank. https://dab.gov.af/Exchange-Rate-Policy

Eggerstedt, H., Hall, R. B., & Van Wijnbergen, S. (1995). Measuring capital flight: A case study of Mexico. *World Development, 23*(2), 211–232.

Engle, R. F., & Granger, C. W. (1987). Cointegration and error correction: Representation, estimation, and testing. *Econometrica: Journal of the Econometric Society*, 251–276.

Erhijakpor, A. E. O. (2019). Effect of capital flight on economic growth: Evidence from Nigeria. *West African Journal of Business and Management Sciences, 8*(2), 249–264.

Eryar, D. (2005). Capital flight from Brazil, 1981–2000. In *Capital flight and capital controls in developing countries* (pp. 210–233). Edward Elgar Publishing.

Faza, M., & Badwan, N. (2023). The risk of capital flight on economic growth and national solvency: An empirical evidence from Palestine. *Asian Journal of Economics, Business and Accounting, 23*(7), 28–48.

Forstater, M. (2018). Illicit financial flows, trade misinvoicing, and multinational tax avoidance: The same or different. *CGD Policy Paper, 123*(29).

Gautier, T. T., & Luc, N. N. (2020). Capital flight and economic growth: The case of ECCAS, ECOWAS and SADC countries. *Economic Research Guardian, 10*(1), 1–11.

Geda, A., & Yimer, A. (2017). Effects of capital flight on growth and poverty reduction in Ethiopia: Evidence from a simulation-based analysis. In *Economic transformation for poverty reduction in Africa* (pp. 167–184). Routledge.

Ghanizada, A. S. (2014, June 24). *Afghan senate house approve anti-money laundering law*. Khama Press New Agency. https://www.khaama.com/afghan-senate-house-approve-anti-money-laundering-law-6251/

Glaeser, E. L., La Porta, R., Lopez-de-Silanes, F., & Shleifer, A. (2004). Do institutions cause growth? *Journal of Economic Growth, 9*(3), 271–303.

Global Financial Integrity. (2021, December 16). *Report finds trade misinvoicing continues to be a massive and persistent problem*. GFI. https://gfintegrity.org/press-release/report-finds-trade-misinvoicing-continues-to-be-a-massive-and-persistent-problem/

Gusarova, V. (2009). *The impact of Capital flight on economic growth*. Unpublished Master's Thesis of the KYIV School of Economics.

Henry, A. W. (2013). Analysis of the effects of capital flight on economic growth: Evidence from Nigerian economy (1980–2011). *European Journal of Business and Management, 5*(17), 21–32.

Hogg, R., Nassif, C., Osorio, C. G., Byrd, W., & Beath, A. (2013). *Afghanistan in transition: Looking beyond 2014*. World Bank Publications.

IMF. (2003, September 21). *Monetary and exchange rate policy in a post-conflict environment: Simple rules and flexibility*. International Monetary Fund. https://www.elibrary.imf.org/view/journals/002/2003/299/article-A005-en.xml?rskey=PbAS1j&result=5&ArticleTabs=fulltext

IMF. (2006, June 01). *Islamic republic of Afghanistan interim poverty reduction strategy paper: Summary report*. International Monetary Fund. https://doi.org/10.5089/9781451800272.002.A001

IMF. (2015, June 02). IMF managing director approves a staff-monitored program for the Islamic republic of Afghanistan. *Afghanistan Staff Monitored Program, 2015*(140). https://www.elibrary.imf.org/view/journals/002/2015/140/article-A003-en.xml?rskey=4lH5RB&result=6

IMF. (2016, July 27). *Arrangement under the extended credit facility*. Arrangement Under the Extended Credit Facility-Press Release; Staff Report; and Statement by the Executive Director for The Islamic Republic of Afghanistan, 2016(252). https://doi.org/10.5089/9781498389990.002

Jay, A., & Agencies (2003, November 03). Karzai confirmed as Afghan president. *The Guardian*. https://www.theguardian.com/world/2004/nov/03/afghanistan.afghanistantimeline

Johansen, S. (1988). Statistical analysis of cointegration vectors. *Journal of Economic Dynamics and Control*, *12*(2/3), 231–254.

Khan, M. K., Teng, J.-Z., & Khan, M. I. (2019). Effect of energy consumption and economic growth on carbon dioxide emissions in Pakistan with dynamic ARDL simulations approach. *Environmental Science and Pollution Research*, *26*(23), 23480–23490.

Kim, D.-H., Lin, S.-C., & Suen, Y.-B. (2012). The simultaneous evolution of economic growth, financial development, and trade openness. *Journal of International Trade & Economic Development*, *21*(4), 513–537.

Kolapo, F. T., & Oke, M. O. (2000). Nigerian economic growth and capital flight determinants. *Asian Journal of Business and Management Sciences*, *1*(11), 76–84.

Lan, S. K. (2009). *Effects of capital flight on economic growth in selected ASEAN economies*. Unpublished PhD thesis. University Putra Malaysia.

Le, Q. V., & Rishi, M. (2007). Corruption and capital flight: An empirical assessment. *International Economic Journal*, *20*(4), 523–540.

Lessard, D. R., & Williamson, J. (1987). *Capital flight and the third world debt*. Institute for International Economics.

Loayza, N. V., & Rancière, R. (2006). Financial dependence and growth. *Journal of Money, Credit, and Banking*, *38*(4), 1051–1076.

Mahmood, Z. (1997). Determinants of under invoicing of imports in Pakistan. *Journal of International Development*, *9*(1), 85–96.

Mahmood, Z. (2013, Spring). Reverse capital flight to Pakistan: Analysis of evidence. *Pakistan Development Review*, *52*(1), 1–15.

Majafizada, E. (2012). Afghans start to take the money and run. *Bloomberg Businessweek*, *12*.

Makova, T., Kadira, G., Muhoyi, E., Mukura, T., & Ndedzu, D. (2014). The impact of capital flight on economic growth in Zimbabwe. *University of Zimbabwe Business Review*, *2*(1), 16–19.

Ministry of Industries and Commerce. (2019). *Afghanistan national trade policy 2019–2023*. Ministry of Industries and Commerce. https://moci.gov.af/sites/default/files/2020-02/Afghanistan%20NTP%2010_web.pdf

Morgan, G. T. C. (1986). LDC capital flight. *World Financial Markets*, 2(1), 13–16.

Morshed, M. M., & Rahman, T. (2021). *"The phenomenon of trade-based money laundering in Bangladesh"–A critical review* (pp. 1–15). Dhaka University.

Mpenya, H., Clarisse, M., & Epo, B. N. (2015). *The effects of capital flight from oil and wood sectors on economic growth in cameroon.* https://doi.org/10.2139/ssrn.3176473

Murtazashvili, J. B. (2015). Afghanistan in 2014: Year of transition. *Asian Survey*, 55(1), 21–32.

Najafizada, E. (2012). Afghans start to take the money and run. *Bloomberg Businessweek, 12.*

Narayan, P. (2004). *Reformulating critical values for the bounds, F-statistics approach to cointegration: An application to the tourism demand model for Fiji* (Vol. 2, No. 04). Monash University.

Narayan, P. K., & Smyth, R. (2006). What determines migration flows from low-income to high-income countries? An empirical investigation of Fiji–Us migration 1972–2001. *Contemporary Economic Policy*, 24(2), 332–342.

Ndiaye, A. S. (2014, June). Is capital flight decisive in explaining economic growth performance in the African franc zone? In *GDN 15th Annual Global Development Conference on Structural Transformation in Africa and Beyond* (pp. 18–20).

Ndikumana, L. (2014). Capital flight and tax havens: Impact on investment and growth in Africa. *Revue d'Économie du Développement*, 22(HS02 (2014)), 99–124.

Ndikumana, L., & Boyce, J. K. (2003). Public debts and private assets: Explaining capital flight from sub-Saharan African countries. *World Development*, 31(1), 107–130.

Ndikumana, L., Naidoo, K., & Aboobaker, A. (2020). *Capital flight from South Africa: A case study.* https://doi.org/10.7275/28043202

Nyasulu, A., Maga, A., Marshall, A., & Bekenov, C. (2023). *Estimating illicit financial flows from trade mis-invoicing: Introducing the 'Grey Re-exports' method (The case of Kyrgyzstan).* https://hdl.handle.net/20.500.12870/5688

Nyong, M. O. (2003). Capital flight and economic growth in four African countries. In *Nigeria, Cote d'Ivoire, Morroco and Ghana, DMO Monthly Seminar Series* (No. 2). https://www.sciencepublishinggroup.com/article/10.11648.j.eco.20160505.11

Obidike, P., Uma, K., Odionye, J., & Ogwuru, H. (2015). The impact of capital flight on economic development: Nigeria in focus. *British Journal of Economics, Management and Trade*, 10(3), 1–13.

Ogunwole, A. E., Adebayo, A. M., & Jimoh, S. A. (2023). Illicit financial flows, trade misinvoicing and multinational tax avoidance: Exploratory approach. *KIU Journal of Social Sciences*, 8(4), 7–16.

Okonkwo, O. N., Ojima, D. O., & Manasseh, C. O. (2020). Capital flight and economic growth in Nigeria (1981–2017). *International Journal of Advanced Science and Technology*, 29(11), 467–479.

Olawale, O., & Ifedayo, O. M. (2015). Impacts of capital flight on economic growth in Nigeria. *International Journal for Innovation Education and Research*, 3(8), 10–46.

Olczyk, M., & Kordalska, A. (2017). International competitiveness of Czech manufacturing – A sectoral approach with error correction model. *Prague Economic Papers*, 26(2), 213–226.

Olugbenga, A. A., & Alamu, O. A. (2013). Does capital flight have a force to bear on Nigerian economic growth? *International Journal of Developing Societies, 2*(2), 80–86.

Onodugo, V. A., Kalu, I. E., Anowor, O. F., & Ukweni, N. O. (2014). Is capital flight healthy for Nigerian economic growth? An econometric investigation. *Journal of Empirical Economics, 3*(1), 10–24.

Orimolade, E. M., & Olusola, A. B. (2018). Capital flight and the growth of Nigerian economy: An autoregressive distributed lag (ARDL) modelling. *International Journal of Economics and Business Management, 4*(2), 1–15.

Orji, A., Ogbuabor, J. E., Kama, K., & Anthony-Orji, O. I. (2020). Capital flight and economic growth in Nigeria: A new evidence from ARDL approach. *Asian Development Policy Review, 8*(3), 171–184.

Owusu, F. A. (2016). *The impact of capital flight on economic development: Ghana and Nigeria compared.* Doctoral Dissertation. http://hdl.handle.net/20.500.11988/177

Patnaik, I., Sen Gupta, A., & Shah, A. (2012). Determinants of trade misinvoicing. *Open Economies Review, 23*, 891–910. https://doi.org/10.1007/s11079-011-9214-4

Peev, E., & Mueller, D. C. (2012). Democracy, economic freedom and growth in transition economies. *Kyklos, 65*(3), 371–407.

Pesaran, M. H., Pesaran, M. H., Shin, Y., & Smith, R. P. (1999). Pooled mean group estimation of dynamic heterogeneous panels. *Journal of the American Statistical Association, 94*(446), 621–634.

Pesaran, M. H., Shin, Y., & Smith, R. J. (2001). Bounds testing approaches to analysing level relationships. *Journal of Applied Econometrics, 16*(3), 289–326.

Qais, T., Wang, C., Noorullah, R., Khwaja Bahman, Q., Mohammad Shabir, S., & Muhammad Shekaib, H. (2022). The impact of tax evasion on Afghanistan's economy. *Journal of Asian Finance, Economics and Business, 9*(9), 317–325. https://doi.org/10.13106/jafeb.2022.vol9.no9.0317

Refai, M. F., Al Abdelhadi, S., & Aqel, S. (2015). Empirical investigation of capital flight and economic growth in Jordan. *International Journal of Statistics and Systems, 10*(2), 321–333.

Rigobon, R., & Rodrik, D. (2005). The rule of law, democracy, openness, and income: Estimating the interrelationships. *The Economics of Transition, 13*(3), 533–564.

Saheed, Z. S., & Ayodeji, S. (2012). Impact of capital flight on the exchange rate and economic growth in Nigeria. *International Journal of Humanities and Social Science, 2*(13), 247–255.

Salandy, M., & Henry, L. (2013). The impact of capital flight on investment and growth in Trinidad and Tobago, 1971–2008. *Guide to Modern Econometrics, 4*, 65–91.

Samson, O., & Edeme, R. (2012). Capital flight and Nigeria's economy. *Jorind, 10*(2), 304–320.

Schmeidl, S. (2014). *Going, going... once again gone? The human capital outflow from Afghanistan post 2014 election.* Paper, Barcelona Centre for International Affairs.

Schmidt, S. (2014). *Going, going... once again gone? The human capital outflow from Afghanistan post-2014 election.* Paper, Barcelona Centre for International Affairs.

Shahzad, A. (2017). *Capital account liberalization and development in Pakistan.* Unpublished Master's Dissertation. Lahore School of Economics.

Shekaib, H. (2022). The impact of tax evasion on Afghanistan's economy. *Journal of Asian Finance, Economics, and Business, 9*(9), 317–325.

SIGAR. (2021). *Reconstruction update*. Special Inspector General for Afghanistan Reconstruction. https://www.sigar.mil/pdf/quarterlyreports/2021-10-30qr-section3.pdf

Sodji, K. (2022). Capital flight and its impact on economic growth: The case of WAEMU countries. *African Journal of Economic Review, 10*(3), 48–62.

Solow, R. M. (1956). A contribution to the theory of economic growth. *Quarterly Journal of Economics, 70*(1), 65–94.

Tahir, M., Jan, A. A., Shah, S. Q. A., Alam, M. B., Afridi, M. A., & Tariq, Y. B. (2020). Foreign inflows and economic growth in Pakistan: Some new insights. *Journal of Chinese Economics and Foreign Trade Studies, 13*(3), 97–113.

Tahir, M., & Khan, I. (2014). Trade openness and economic growth in the Asian region. *Journal of Chinese Economics and Foreign Trade Studies, 7*(3), 136–152.

Tandon, S., & Rao, R. (2017, July 04). Trade misinvoicing what can we measure? *National Institute of Public Finance and Policy*, (200), 1–23. https://nipfp.org.in/media/medialibrary/2017/07/WP_2017_200.pdf

The Bonn Agreement. (2001). *Agreement on provisional arrangements in Afghanistan pending the re-establishment of permanent government institutions*. United Nations Security General (pp. 1–12). United Nations Peacemaker. https://peacemaker.un.org/afghanistan-bonnagreement2001

The White House. (2009, October 08). *Fact sheet elections in Afghanistan*. https://georgewbush-whitehouse.archives.gov/news/releases/2004/10/20041008-6.html

Umer, B. (2023). Effects of trade mis-invoicing on money laundering in developing economies. *Journal of Money Laundering Control, 26*(1), 60–68.

Wahyudi, S. T., & Maski, G. (2012). A causality between capital flight and economic growth: A case study Indonesia. In *The Eight Annual Conference Asia Pacific Economic Association APEA*, Singapore.

Wani, N. U. H. (2019). Nexus between openness to trade and economic growth: An empirical investigation of Afghanistan. *South Asia Economic Journal, 20*(Issue 2).

Wani, N. U. H., & Rasa, M. M. (2023). Dynamics of trade specialization and performance of SAFTA: A case study of Afghanistan. *South Asia Economic Journal, 24*(2).

World Bank. (1985). *World Bank Report*. World Bank.

World Bank. (1993). *Global development finance. Vol. 1: Analysis and summary tables*. World Bank.

World Bank. (2012a, May). *Afghanistan in transition*. World Bank. https://doi.org/10.1596/27334

World Bank. (2012b, October). *Afghanistan economic update, October 2012*. World bank. https://doi.org/10.1596/27070

World Bank. (2016, October). *Afghanistan development update*. World Bank Group. https://doi.org/10.1596/25350

World Bank. (2019, June). *Afghanistan development update, June 2019*. World Bank. https://elibrary.worldbank.org/doi/abs/10.1596/32144

Wujung, V. A., & Mbella, E. (2016). Capital flight and economic development: The experience of Cameroon. *Economics, 5*(5), 64–72.

Zobeiri, H., Akbarpour Roshan, N., & Shahrazi, M. (2015). Capital flight and economic growth in Iran. *International Economic Studies, 45*(2), 9–20.

Chapter 7

# Afghanistan's Regional and Bilateral Free Trade Agreements: An Evaluation of Trade Effects, Diversion and Creation

## Abstract

The increased participation of economies in regional and bilateral free trade agreements (FTAs) has resulted in welfare effects. This chapter attempts to determine the welfare implications of preferential reductions in tariffs and free-trade zones on Afghan imports by adopting the Magee (2016) framework. This approach separates the consequences of tariff hikes triggered by FTAs from the general equilibrium effects (GEEs) caused by unknown variables impacting the country's imports (historical links, shared language and culture, landlockedness, etc.). This method evaluates whether preferential tariff reductions favouring partner countries would benefit or harm member countries. The results indicate that the magnitude of the effects of trade creation (TC) is significantly higher than those of trade diversion. TC resulting from GEEs unexpectedly surpasses TC resulting from tariff preferences extended to member nations. Afghanistan's FTAs are not harmful but enhance living conditions. This chapter recognises South Asian Free Trade Area's (SAFTA's) potential for trade expansion by focusing on commitment to regional integration and increasing liberalisation by implementing a more easily upgraded tariff framework and trade facilitation system. The findings are relevant since World Trade Organisation (WTO) members are often sceptical about regional trade agreements (RTAs) or Bilateral Free Trade Agreements (BFTAs) as agents harming well-being.

*Keywords*: Preferential and bilateral trade agreements; Afghanistan; South Asian Association for Regional Cooperation; trade creation; trade diversion

*JEL Codes*: F11; F13; F16

Policy Solutions for Economic Growth in a Developing Country, 155–179
Copyright © 2024 Nassir Ul Haq Wani
Published under exclusive licence by Emerald Publishing Limited
doi:10.1108/978-1-83753-430-220241008

# 1. Introduction

The 1990s witnessed a decline in the multilateral trading structure due to the delay in Doha Round discussions; prompting nations to pursue trade arrangements like free Trade Agreements (FTAs), more generally referred to as Preferential Trade Agreements (PTAs) or Regional Trade Agreements (RTAs). This paper carries a definition of RTAs which are preferential trade agreements in which more than two PTA participants participate reciprocally. Although referred to as RTAs by the WTO, we refer to them as PTAs. A new phase of the integration of regional economies has ensued as a consequence (Akbari, 2021; Akhter & Ghani, 2010; Ali & Talukder, 2009; Anderson & Wincoop, 2001; Bergstrand et al., 2016; Rodrik, 2018; Yang & Martinez-Zarzoso, 2014). The trend of globalisation is transitioning towards regional economic integration due to the deteriorating performance of the multilateral trade system established by the World Trade Organisation (WTO). Over the previous two decades, PTAs have grown (Bao & Wang, 2019; Deme & Ndrianasy, 2017; Park, 2020). To promote economic integration, economies in Asia (particularly South Asia and South East Asia) established several key initiatives like ASEAN Free Trade Area (AFTA) in 1992, Bay of Bengal Initiative for Multi-Sectoral Technical and Economic Cooperation (BIMSTEC) in 2004 and South Asian Free Trade Area (SAFTA) in 2006, to improve inter-trade latency.

Globally speaking, as per the estimates from the WTO, there were around 82 distinctive PTAs in operation. In contrast, the PTAs have tripled in the preceding 20 years. Despite the distinction between total PTA registrations and total PTAs in effect, the expanding tendency illustrates the progress of regional economic integration. In recent years, Bilateral Free Trade Agreements (BFTAs) and RTAs have expanded at an unprecedented rate. This expansion raises the intriguing issue regarding whether preferential tariff reductions for the benefit of RTA and BFTA countries would improve or hurt the welfare of the trading nations. The insights from Afghanistan's trade reveal a growing trend, although the trade rather than global is limited to regional partners. Between 2010 and 2021, the global experience of other South Asian and East Asian countries reveals that South Asian Free Trade Agreement (SAFTA) and ASEAN member countries' exports increased by 6.4% and 8.9%, respectively. These changes have been a result of the signing of FTAs. With the proliferation of trade ties through FTAs, consumers have access to cheaper and higher quality goods and simultaneously exporters also intensify growth with partner countries. However, the import industry is partially harmed by duty-free imports following FTA implementation. The present analysis attempts to estimate the effect of the SAFTA and BFTAs on Afghan imports by employing industry-level trade flows. Following this mechanism, the study will exemplify how the FTAs impact Afghanistan's imports by utilising the most favoured country (MFN) tariff and tariff considerations. This will further illuminate the disparities between FTA member and non-member countries with regard to MFN tariff rates and tariff advantages. Previous studies employing the fixed effects method to study the impact of RTAs failed to distinguish between trade diversion (TD) and trade creation (TC). In order to surmount this obstacle, Cheong et al. (2015) and Magee (2016) accounted for exporters-industry, exporters-year and exporters-year as fixed-effect variables when determining the creation and diversion of trade.

Building the arguments from the Magee (2016) model, we differentiate the consequences of adjustments to tariffs resulting from FTAs along with the general equilibrium impacts of FTAs on the trade environment. Viner (1950) stated that the intrinsic welfare consequences of RTA are dependent on the creation and diversification of trade, and the TDs induced by a RTA reduce global effectiveness (the welfare effect). Considering the diversion of trade, Bhagwati et al. (1998) proposed a mechanism as to how a country could improve welfare. Consumers are of the opinion that transferring imports to the RTA members accruing higher trade costs facilitates the purchase at a more affordable proportional price, comparable to its 'absolute' global pricing.

Consequently, the gains in secondary purchasing resulting from the diversion of trade could surpass the losses incurred over the course of trade. A thorough statistical evaluation is necessary to understand trade formation and diversion phenomena. Following Magee (2016), this study constructs the empirical model based on the gravity model, although there have been critics around as well of the gravity model of international trade. The previous studies employing gravity frameworks have attributed the increase and decrease of intra and inter-trade with RTAs. Still, there is no immediate relationship with a policy change triggered by bilateral or regional agreements. This study employs the gravity framework to demonstrate the immediate connection between changes in policy (tariff preferences) generated by regional and bilateral agreements and the ensuing shift in imports with respect to TC and diversion. Furthermore, the study also evaluates the overall balancing effects of RTA and BFTA in the Afghanistan context.

Prior research has neglected to consider the implications of RTA for general equilibrium, thereby omitting a crucial element that contributes to TC consequences. The present study analyses import data at the sector level, which encompasses a limited amount of trade with regional and bilateral trading partners compared to the collective base. The benchmark criteria for inclusion at the aggregate level should be satisfied; however, some minor sector trade numbers are eliminated (due to the zero small trade round-off). Data enable the industrial level to absorb lost trade values, eventually contributing to TC. The present study is vital for policy dialogue, given that unnoticed variables impacting a nation's import levels, such as historical ties, common language and landlockedness, thus leaving the immediate effects of Bilateral Trade Agreements (BTAs) and RTAs roughly scattered. For gauging these effects, the study is conceivable if we delineate the impacts of MFN tariffs and preferences for tariffs in BTAs and RTAs.

## 2. Afghanistan's Economy: Regional and Bilateral Trade Agreements

The overall trade balance of Afghanistan remained in deficit from 2001–2020. However, post-collapse in 2021, Afghanistan experienced a trade surplus as the level of exports (FoB) was 2,501 million, whereas the total value of imports (CIF) was 2,475 million. The trade deficit decreased from $8209.1 million in 2013 to U$4457.7 billion in 2020. However, the previous two decades have experienced exports growing and imports increasing more than exports. As of 2021, exports from Afghanistan have been stagnant and concentrated around low value-added agricultural products (raw materials, 13.05%, vegetables, 19.38% and consumer goods, 28.89%), accounting for 61.32% of total exports. Following the enactment of bilateral FTAs and RTAs, there has been a noticeable shift in Afghanistan's trade flows. Almost 83% of Afghanistan's imports came from regional, neighbouring and South Asian countries. After signing the FTA with South Asian Association for Regional Cooperation (SAARC), the PTA with India and the Transit Trade Agreement (APTTA) with Pakistan, these countries emerged as top export destinations for Afghanistan as shown in Table 1. Table 1 presents the trade volume of Afghanistan with other member countries as part of their BTAs and RTAs.

### 2.1 Trade With SAFTA Countries

SAFTA came into effect at the 12th SAARC conference and is regarded as a key success of the SAARC mission. On 22 March 2006, the SAARC secretariat issued a statement officially declaring the entrance into the SAFTA agreement, which was finalised by 1 January 2016; however, Afghanistan joined SAFTA in 2011.

The trade liberalisation programme is the tariff reduction method under Article 7 of the agreement. SAFTA permits member nations to keep their

Table 1. Major Export Markets of Afghanistan 2021 (000 USD).

| Trading Partner | Exports | Imports |
|---|---|---|
| Turkmenistan | 1174.52 | 690214.12 |
| United Kingdom | 1690.92 | 18912.31 |
| Russian Federation | 2021.83 | 260518.34 |
| Uzbekistan | 2077.58 | 433352.86 |
| United States | 3006.28 | 783751.66 |
| Tajikistan | 5084.96 | 119466.54 |
| Germany | 11704.68 | 89702.14 |
| Iran, Islamic Rep. | 15053.04 | 1247167.95 |
| United Arab Emirates | 24944.87 | 154010.06 |
| Turkey | 25152.2 | 291170.12 |
| China | 31001.9 | 1192426.52 |
| Pakistan | 298635.06 | 1102989.06 |
| India | 410135.57 | 453695.6 |

*Source:* Trade data from WITS.

sensitive list without making any sacrifices. Contracting members may give tariff savings ranging from 0% to 5% for products not on the sensitive list. The trade between Afghanistan and SAARC increased by 41.3% from 416.05 million USD in 2015 to 709 million USD in 2021. Afghanistan's imports, on the other hand, climbed by 10.5% from 1481.09 million USD in 2015 to 1565 million USD in 2021.

### 2.2 Afghanistan–India FTA (AIFTA)

The AIFTA was signed on 6 March 2003, in New Delhi, and envisioned to foster the positive growth of economic connections between India and Afghanistan through trade growth, establish equal opportunity for trade between India and Afghanistan, pay attention to the principle of reciprocity and aid in the compatible growth and broadening of world trade by removing trade barriers.

### 2.3 Afghanistan–Pakistan Transit Trade Agreement (APTTA)

APTTA superseded the 1965 Agreement ATTA, which was signed in October 2010 and came into effect on 12 June 2011. This agreement aims to promote transit trade for Afghanistan and provide a gateway to Central Asia for Pakistan. Through connectivity to seaports and land crossing sites, Afghanistan obtains access to Indian and Chinese markets.

## 3. Methodology

The study hinges on Magee's (2016) technique, primarily employing the gravity model as an econometric framework.

### 3.1 Theoretical Structure

The gravity framework of international trade is a workhorse for analysing bilateral trade flows and was introduced by Tinbergen in 1962, inspired by Newton's gravitational law.

$$F_{ij} = G \frac{m_i * m_j}{d_{ij}^2} \qquad (1)$$

Newton's law states that the gravitational force is equivalent to the combined effect of the two bodies' masses and is inversely related to the square root of the distance. Building on the same connotations, in practice, this means the following in the case of international trade flows.

$$\text{IMP}_{ij} = A \frac{Y_i * Y_j}{d_{ij}^2} \qquad (2)$$

Where $IMP_{ij}$ is the trade flow across the two nations, $y_i y_j$ is the economic size (GDP) of the two countries, and $d_{ij}^2$ is their separation in geography. Tinbergen (1963) expressed this connection as follows:

$$IMP_{ij} = A \frac{Y_i^\alpha * Y_j^\beta}{d_{ij}^\gamma} \tag{3}$$

Where $Y_i$ and $Y_j$ are the GDPs of the countries, $\gamma$ shows the distance elasticity. By taking the log of Eq. (2), along with the addition of the disturbance term (error or residual term), the relationship can be expressed as follows:

$$\log(IMP_{ij}) = \log A + \alpha \, \log(y_i) + \beta \, \log\left(y_j\right) - \gamma \, \log(d_{ij}) + \varepsilon_{ij} \tag{4}$$

### 3.2 Empirical Connotation

Since the gravity framework experiences shortfalls, therefore, the usage in economic discourse needs to be explored. Having efficiency, the gravity framework is under investigation. For numerous causes, the theoretical foundation of the initial gravity framework needs a revisit and should be adequately outlined (De Benedictis & Taglioni, 2011; Head & Mayer, 2014; Novy, 2013; Theie, 2015; Yotov, 2022). The solution to this problem was proposed by Anderson and Van Wincoop in 2003, by including the 'Multilateral Resistance Term' (MRT). By MRT, we define it as the bilateral trade fluxes between two regions that are contingent upon the output of both regions and the bilateral trade costs in comparison to the trade costs encountered by the other regions. In simpler words, it is defined as the trade barrier that each country experiences while trading with other countries. The inclusion of MRT helped in revising the gravity framework in a symmetrical form making the inclusion of other key variables easy (Balassa, 1967; Clausing, 2001; Cipollina et al., 2016; Freund, 1999; Krueger,1999; Magee, 2008; Meade, 1955). Fixed effects for the exporter and importer years are one method for including MRT in the gravity equation (Feenstra, 2002).

Using fixed effects offers several advantages and makes the inclusion of variables feasible. These variables include the impacts of the economic cycle within a single year, shifts in local consumer tastes for imported commodities, exchange rate fluctuations and various other unobservable country-specific characteristics.

Studies done post-2000 have started including fixed effects methods. The use of a standard dummy variable strategy to incorporate MRT has the limitation of just providing a single TC and diversion figure. Preference, tariff rate and trade flow are the factors utilised to compute TC and diversion at the industry level. Omitted variable bias may result if the bilateral tariff rate, a fundamental component of international trade, is not incorporated (Hayakawa, 2011). The potential exacerbation of omitted variable bias can occur when the RTA dummy variable is eliminated (Hayakawa, 2011). The usage of the RTA as a dummy variable will enable us to estimate the overall equilibrium consequences (general) of RTA on imports from abroad.

*3.2.1 Framework-I*

The equation is as follows, after incorporating the previously enumerated variables and adjusting for fixed year effects for both the importer and exporter:

$$\text{imp}_{jkt} = e^{\left(\alpha_{oj} + \alpha_{ot} + \alpha_1 \text{TR}_{jkt} + \alpha_2 \text{TP}_{jkt} + \alpha_3 \text{RTA}_{jt} + \alpha_4 \ln(\text{GDP}_{jt})\right)} + \varepsilon_{jkt} \qquad (5)$$

The variable $\text{imp}_{jkt}$ denotes the volume of imports into Afghanistan by nation $j$ (at $a$ time $t$ in sector $k$). A standardised impact, denoted as $\alpha_{oj}$, is allocated to each exporter of commodities and considers all constant time components that could potentially impact trade between exporting country $j$ and importing Afghanistan. Time-constant factors include the distance between two nations that share the same language and contiguity. The time-fixed effect, denoted as $\alpha_{ot}$, accounts for variables such as the magnitude of the importing country's economy (specifically, Afghanistan), which may influence its trade relations across all countries that export goods at time $t$. The natural log of exporters' GDP is variable $\ln(\text{GDP}_{jt})$, and it shows the impact of macro factors in country $j$ (at time $t$). The variable $\text{TR}_{jkt}$ denotes the tariff rate agreed upon under RTA that the exporter of nation $j$ faces while exporting goods from industry $k$ to the importing country at time $t$. The $\text{TR}_{jkt}$ coefficient assesses the cost of increasing the rate of tariffs on a product purchased by partners in the region while taking into account tariff advantages provided to regional exporters over non-regional exporters. The variable's negative coefficient provides indications for TC.

$\text{TP}_{jkt}$ is a tariff preferential granted to the nation that exports products $j$ in sector $k$ at period $t$, and its positive coefficient indicates that trade is trending away from affordable extra-regional nations. In addition, it illustrates a more pronounced disparity between intra-regional and MFN tariffs that non-regional nations are required to pay. RTA's dummy nature equates to 1 if Afghanistan possesses a bilateral FTA or 0 when the countries don't enjoy FTA. The positive value of the coefficient of this variable demonstrates the overall equilibria consequences of RTA and BFTA ratification. It demonstrates that despite the regulation of tariffs as well as preferences by BFTAs and RTAs, trade flows between RTA members are greater. Finally, by concurrently combining the variable in question tariffs, tariff preferences and BFTA/RTA dummies, the derived equation differentiates the impacts of RTA reductions in tariffs from the general equilibrium consequences of BTAs and RTAs.

*3.2.2 Framework-II*

Countries with significant cultural and historical linkages are more inclined to enter into BFTA and RTA (Krugman, 1991; Mattoo et al., 2022; Wonnacott & Mark, 1989). Consequently, signing the BFTA and RTA is unlikely to result in greater bilateral trade. Instead, these are a result of increased trade ties. Thus, the gravity model estimate has the potential to incorporate previously unexplored interactions. One method is for determining the equation of gravity in the first difference, eliminating the two countries' invisible but time-constant elements (Bayoumi & Eichengreen, 1995; Cipollina et al., 2016; Rahman et al., 2006;

Romalis, 2007; Starck, 2012; Yang & Zarzoso, 2013). These studies used bilateral fixed-effect models to adjust for unnoticed features particular to both sets of countries. In the context of the normal gravity approach, each variable can be specific to either an importer or exporter (e.g. real exchange rate, GDP, GDP per capita) or to a dyad (distance, contiguity, shared language, colonial connections). Consequently, irrespective of which variable is omitted or included, the afore-mentioned fixed effects specific to dyad, exporter, and importer year govern all aspects of trade flows within the gravity framework, in addition to unidentified variables that are unique to each dyad, exporter, or importer (Ghost & Yamarikb, 2004). Our model will exclusively incorporate exporter-year fixed effects for all dyadic and importer-year variables, given that Afghanistan is the sole importer.

$$\text{imp}_{jkt} = e^{\left(\alpha_{ojt} + \alpha_1 \text{TR}_{jkt} + \alpha_2 \text{TP}_{jkt}\right)} + \varepsilon_{jkt} \qquad (6)$$

The constant term $\alpha_{ojt}$ differs with respect to every $j$th exporter in year $t$. It indicates the effect of any unique variables that affect the Afg-exporter pair during the time period '$t$'. Including the exporter-year fixed goods has one disadvantage: it limits the inclusion of the RTA dummy variable. As a result, the general equilibrium effects (GEE) are ignored in the above equation.

### 3.2.3 Framework-III

The previous model encourages us to adopt another model in which we may compute GEEs by incorporating exporter-year fixed outcomes.

$$\text{imp}_{jkt} = e^{\left(\alpha_{ojk} + \alpha_1 \text{TR}_{jkt} + \alpha_2 \text{TP}_{jkt} + \alpha_3 \text{RTA}_{jt} + \alpha_4 \, \ln\left(\text{GDP}_{jt}\right)\right)} + \varepsilon_{jkt} \qquad (7)$$

In this approach, $\alpha_{ojk}$ is a variable for each exporter and industry. It reflects any unnoticed factors (like geographic proximity) that are constant but impact $j$th nation's flow of exports to Afghanistan.

When utilising a simple ordinary least square (OLS) technique to calculate the gravity equation, there are two key difficulties to consider. Particularly at the 6-digit HS industrial level, the gravity equation is frequently log-linear, and the dependent variable, bilateral trade flow, may equal zero for bilateral trade. As is common knowledge, the logarithm of zero is undefined, which can lead to esti-mation issues. Second, the error component of the gravity framework is frequently heterogeneous, which distorts forecasts. The gravity framework's Poisson pseudo maximum likelihood (PPML) approximation can be derived from trade data (Silva & Tenreyro, 2006). This estimating approach accepts data with no trade flow. Its estimations are also consistent, even when there is hetero-skedasticity. As a result, the fixed effects of the PPML estimator are used to determine the three Eqs. (4) to (6). The reliable predictor computes the standard error, which offers reliable estimations (Huber, 1967; White, 1980).

### 3.3 Data

The analysis includes 14 years from 2008 to 2021 encompassing six countries. Out of these six countries, Afghanistan enjoys a South Asian FTA with four nations, the PTA with India and the APTTA with Pakistan. The data figures on GDP, trade flows and tariff data have been acquired from the World Bank, UN COMTRADE and WTO, respectively, at the 6-digit HS codes. The tariff data encompass the average ad valorem customs duties and denote the preferential tariffs pursuant to distinct tariff systems including BTAs and RTAs.

## 4. Findings and Analysis

Table 2 summarises the findings of the three models mentioned in the Data section. The coefficients from Eqs. (5) to (7)'s fixed effects Poison estimate are presented.

### 4.1 Model I

Model I is generated by solving Eq. (4) for all exporting countries. Given the single importer in the sample, all importer-exporter-fixed effects characteristics are governed by exporter-fixed effects. Considering characteristics of time-constant factors (such as distance, shared boundary, historical links and same language), and are thus regulated by importer-exporter fixed effects. As an illustration of how fluctuations in the exporter's economy affect Afghanistan's imports, an appended logarithm of the exporter's GDP is provided. By including 'year' as a dummy parameter in the analysis, the impacts of the importers on Afghanistan's economy are demonstrated.

#### 4.1.1 Estimates of the Full Panel

The elements representing TC and diversion are demonstrated through Model I. The analysis suggests that reducing tariffs by a percentage point boosts industry imports by 2.76% as shown by the coefficient of tariff rate in Table 2. Upon considering tariffs at the industry level, the coefficients of all FTAs (bilateral and regional) exhibit a positive sign, indicating the existence of TD. A 1% difference in tariff rates between MFN and preferential tariff rates applicable across all BFTAs and SAFTAs would increase Afghanistan's import level by 0.67%. The GDP of exporters is a statistically significant metric that indicates Afghanistan's import levels increase by 1% for every 1% increase in the GDP of an exporting nation. The coefficient of significance for all FTA dummy variables is 1%, suggesting that the introduction of BPTAs and RTAs has an overall equilibrium effect, as evidenced by the 19.12% increase in Afghanistan's imports. This positive change is a result of entering into trade agreements (BFTAs and RTAs).

### 4.2 Model II

The result of Eq. (6) estimations with exporter-year fixed consequences is presented via model II. It takes into account the exporting nation's macroeconomic indicator as the log of GDP and the reflection of the GEEs of other time-constant factors like establishing the RTA, the distance, common boundary and languages. The estimations for Tariff Rate (TR) and Tariff preferential (TP) are almost identical to the ones given in Model I. The analysis argues for a case that if MFN tariff rates are maintained accompanied by a 1% drop in tariff rates provided to BPTA and RTA members boosts Afghan imports by 2.7%, signifying the creation of trade (Table 2). Assume a 1% increase in tariffs for all FTAs (including BFTAs and SAFTAs). In such instances, the total FTA imports to Afghanistan would rise by 0.68%, showing a diversion of trade from non-regional nations.

Table 2. Factors Influencing Afghanistan's Imports.

| Ind Var | Simulation (Model) I Coeff | Simulation (Model) II Coeff | Simulation (Model) III Coeff |
|---|---|---|---|
| TR | $-0.023^{***}$ | $-0.032^{*}$ | $0.022^{***}$ |
| TP | $0.006^{***}$ | $0.006^{**}$ | $0.010^{***}$ |
| ln(GDP) | $0.874^{***}$ | | $0.377^{*}$ |
| All FTAs | $0.165^{***}$ | | $0.541^{**}$ |
| 2008 | $0.022^{***}$ | | $0.422$ |
| 2009 | $0.010^{***}$ | | $0.344$ |
| 2010 | $0.377^{*}$ | | $-0.196$ |
| 2011 | $0.541^{**}$ | | $-0.091$ |
| 2012 | $0.422$ | | $0.237$ |
| 2013 | $0.344$ | | $-0.081$ |
| 2014 | $-0.196$ | | $0.821$ |
| 2015 | $-0.091$ | | $0.812$ |
| 2016 | $0.237$ | | $-0.260^{**}$ |
| 2017 | $-0.081$ | | $-0.198^{*}$ |
| 2018 | $0.821$ | | $-0.393^{***}$ |
| 2019 | $0.812$ | | $-0.260^{**}$ |
| 2020 | $-0.260^{**}$ | | $-0.198^{*}$ |
| 2021 | $-0.198^{*}$ | | $-0.393^{***}$ |
| Observations | 73575 | 73575 | 558798 |
| Fixed effects | Exporter | Exporter year | Exporter-industry |

*Source:* Data output from EViews 8.0.

*Note:* The coefficients denoted by *, ** and *** are statistically significant at 10%, 5% and 1%, respectively. The complete panel dataset and all free trade agreements are incorporated in these results.

Regional trade agreements and bilateral free trade agreements with Afghanistan are incorporated into every FTA variable.

The results obtained from simulations I and II indicate that the impact of TC, including BPTAs and SAFTAs, is four times more significant than the impact of TD across all PTAs. At the 1% significance level, the chi-square test contradicts the hypothesis that the combined magnitude of both of these impacts (2 = 1) is identical. Consequently, from a statistical standpoint, the generation of trade exceeds the diversion of trade.

Eq. (7) forms the foundation of simulation III, which incorporates exporter-industry fixed variables. In simulation III, the total number of observations decreased from 623,435 in Models I and II to 587,498 when these fixed factors were considered. The change was the Poisson regression model requires import alterations within each exporter-industry connection.

The tariff rate coefficient is anticipated to decline from 2.7% to 2.1% while maintaining statistical significance at 1% (Table 2). As a result, a 1% reduction in tariff rates for all FTAs while maintaining MFN tariffs results in a 2.2% improvement in Afghan imports from these nations, thereby suggesting the creation of trade. The tariff preferences variable has increased and is now highly significant at one percent. It indicates that a 1% rise in tariff preferences offered to all FTA members led to a 1% increase in Afghan imports, suggesting the diversion of trade from non-regional nations. At a significance level of 5%, the chi-square statistic rejects the null hypothesis, indicating that the magnitudes of these effects vary. Consequently, the impact of TC remains roughly 1.2 times greater than the impact of TD.

The coefficient of the exporting nation's logarithmic GDP is statistically insignificant (meaning it is only significant at the 10% level). It illustrates that Afghan imports increase by 0.38% for every 1% increase in the exporter's economy. The presence of overall equilibrium effects is confirmed by the positive and statistically significant RTA coefficient of 5%, which indicates the existence of such effects. Furthermore, 72.9% of the trade expansion could conceivably be attributed to factors unrelated to a subsequent tariff reduction under the RTA.

### 4.2.1 Regional Trade Agreements (SAFTA)

In Table 3, the results are summarised based on the coefficients for Models I, II and III involving the Eqs. (5)–(7) utilised, correspondingly. $TR_{jkt}$ coefficients in Models I and II reveal substantial proof of TC, with values of 13% and 13.1%, accordingly. Model III accounts for the TC benefit of the SAFTA agreement. According to the GEEs of implementing the FTA with SAARC nations, the SAFTA is responsible for 43.3% of SAFTA TC. At 1%, the GDP coefficients in Models I and III are statistically significant and favourable, indicating that Afghanistan's imports increase by 0.88% and 1.7%, respectively, for every one percentage point increase in the exporter's economy.

### 4.2.2 Bilateral Free Trade Agreements (BFTAs)

An overview of the results of BFTAs is presented in Table 4 based on the coefficients derived from the models (I–III) acquired through the respective

Table 3. Factors Influencing Afghanistan's Imports: SAFTA.

| Ind Var | Simulation (Model) I Coeff | Simulation (Model) II Coeff | Simulation (Model) III Coeff |
|---|---|---|---|
| TR | −0.123*** | −0.132* | −0.002** |
| TP | 0.064*** | 0.069** | 0.004* |
| ln(GDP) | 0.879*** | | 1.607* |
| SAFTA | 0.175*** | | 0.356* |
| 2008 | 0.033*** | | 0.292 |
| 2009 | 0.019*** | | 0.564*** |
| 2010 | 0.387* | | −0.196 |
| 2011 | 0.641** | | −0.091 |
| 2012 | 0.322 | | 0.237 |
| 2013 | 0.304 | | −0.081 |
| 2014 | −0.186 | | 0.821 |
| 2015 | −0.071 | | 0.812 |
| 2016 | 0.217 | | −0.260** |
| 2017 | −0.081 | | −0.198* |
| 2018 | 0.821 | | −0.393*** |
| 2019 | 0.812 | | −0.260** |
| 2020 | 0.260** | | −0.198* |
| 2021 | 0.298* | | −0.393*** |
| Observations | 43,585 | 43,585 | 348,798 |

*Source:* Data output from EViews 8.0.

*Note:* *, ** and *** indicate statistically important levels of 10%, 5% and 1%, accordingly.

calculations of Eqs. (5)–(7). All three models provide indications of TC, with models I, II and III accounting for 16%, 15% and 1.7% of the total, respectively. In Models I and II, the inverse direction of $TR_{jkt}$ indicates that there is no indication of TD; in Model III, *it* approaches zero or 0.1%. The log exporter's GDP coefficient in Model II is set at 0.50%, whereas in Model III, it approaches unity while maintaining statistical significance. The BFTA component in Model III is positive and is statistically valid at 5%, indicating that the overall equilibrium impacts of adopting BFTAs with China, Malaysia and Sri Lanka constitute approximately 65% of the overall creation of trade.

TC coefficients are more important than TD coefficients in all three models. Despite the market failure, the consequences of trade formation are always welfare-enhancing, meaning that full panel FTAs, SAFTAs and BFTAs always have positive welfare effects. In this scenario, the impacts of TD are smaller than

Table 4. Factors Influencing Afghanistan's Imports: BFTAs.

| Ind Var | Simulation (Model) I Coeff | Simulation (Model) II Coeff | Simulation (Model) III Coeff |
|---|---|---|---|
| TR | −0.143*** | −0.136*** | −0.002** |
| TP | 0.014*** | 0.019** | 0.002*** |
| ln(GDP) | 0.406*** | | 0.850** |
| All BFTAs | −0.325*** | | 0.356* |
| 2008 | 0.033*** | | 0.292 |
| 2009 | 0.019*** | | −0.074*** |
| 2010 | 0.387* | | −0.196 |
| 2011 | 0.641** | | −0.091 |
| 2012 | 0.322 | | 0.237 |
| 2013 | 0.304 | | −0.081 |
| 2014 | −0.186 | | 0.821 |
| 2015 | −0.071 | | 0.812 |
| 2016 | 0.217 | | −0.260** |
| 2017 | −0.081 | | −0.198* |
| 2018 | 0.821 | | −0.393*** |
| 2019 | 0.812 | | −0.260** |
| 2020 | 0.260** | | −0.198* |
| 2021 | 0.298* | | −0.393*** |

*Source:* Data output from EViews 8.0.
*Note:* *, ** and *** show statistical significance at 10%, 5% and 1%, respectively.

those of TC and should be described more broadly. As a result of signing all FTAs, SAFTAs and BFTAs, Afghanistan's domestic consumers benefited (owing to increased consumption).

### 4.3 Evaluating Magnitudes of TC and Diversion

Afghanistan's actual imports from all FTAs (including BFTAs and SAFTA) are used to assess the degree of TC and diversion. Predicted on the continued existence of all FTAs, this framework can potentially be utilised to compute the anticipated volume of imports while neglecting the impact of international trade agreements. In this circumstance, all FTA tariff rates will return to the MFN tariff rate.

$$\widehat{imp}_{noFTAs,jkt} - imp_{jkt}/imp_{jkt} = e^{\widehat{\alpha}(TP_{jkt})} * e^{-\widehat{\alpha}(TP_{jkt})} - 1 \qquad (8)$$

where $\widehat{\text{imp}}_{\text{noFTAs,kt}}$ is the expected level of imports in the absence of an FTA (either bilateral or regional), and $\text{imp}_{\text{jkt}}$ is the actual imports. In the absence of trade, $\text{TP}_{\text{jkt}}$ is the discrepancy within MFN tariffs and tariff reductions granted through all FTAs.

Eq. (7) may be used to calculate the cash worth of RTA agreements, the trade impact in each industry $k$ and the period $t$. It anticipates the value of trade in Afghanistan.

$$\text{imp}_{\text{jkt}} - \widehat{\text{imp}}_{\text{noFTAs,jkt}} = \text{imp}_{\text{jkt}} \left( 1 - e^{\widehat{\alpha}_1 \left( \text{TP}_{\text{jkt}} \right)} * e^{-\widehat{\alpha}_2 \left( \text{TP}_{\text{jkt}} \right)} \right) \tag{9}$$

where $\widehat{\text{imp}}_{\text{noFTAs,jkt}}$ is the projected value of imports in the absence of an FTA. In Eq. (9), two implications are visible where $\widehat{a}_1$ and $\widehat{a}_2$ denote the creation and diversion of trade, respectively, and are reflected in the following two equations:

$$\text{imp} - \widehat{\text{imp}}_{\text{noTC,jkt}} = \text{imp}_{\text{jkt}} \left( 1 - e^{\widehat{\alpha}_1 \left( \text{TP}_{\text{jkt}} \right)} \right) \tag{10}$$

$$\text{imp} - \widehat{\text{imp}}_{\text{noTC,jkt}} = \text{imp}_{\text{jkt}} \left( 1 - e^{\widehat{\alpha}_2 \left( \text{TP}_{\text{jkt}} \right)} \right) \tag{11}$$

The implications of TC are shown in Eq. (10), whereas the effects of TD are shown in Eq. (11). The combined impact of the aforementioned equations is inconsistent with the total impact of the RTA in Eq. (9). The sum of Eqs. (10) and (11) scaled by the X-factor on the RHS equals Eq. (9) on the LHS resulting in the missing value:

$$\left\{ \text{imp}_{\text{jkt}} \left( 1 - e^{\widehat{\alpha}_1 \left( \text{TP}_{\text{jkt}} \right)} \right) \right\} X + \left\{ \text{imp}_{\text{jkt}} \left( 1 - e^{\widehat{\alpha}_2 \left( \text{TP}_{\text{jkt}} \right)} \right) \right\} X$$
$$= \text{imp}_{\text{jkt}} \left( 1 - e^{\widehat{\alpha}_1 \left( \text{TP}_{\text{jkt}} \right)} * e^{\widehat{\alpha}_2 \left( \text{TP}_{\text{jkt}} \right)} \right) \tag{Ai}$$

$$X \left( \text{imp}_{\text{jkt}} \left( 1 - e^{\widehat{\alpha}_1 \left( \text{TP}_{\text{jkt}} \right)} + 1 - e^{\widehat{\alpha}_2 \left( \text{TP}_{\text{jkt}} \right)} \right) \right) = \text{imp}_{\text{jkt}} \left( 1 - e^{\widehat{\alpha}_1 \left( \text{TP}_{\text{jkt}} \right)} * e^{\widehat{\alpha}_2 \left( \text{TP}_{\text{jkt}} \right)} \right) \tag{Aii}$$

$$X = \text{imp}_{\text{jkt}} \left( 1 - e^{\widehat{\alpha}_1 \left( \text{TP}_{\text{jkt}} \right)} * e^{\widehat{\alpha}_2 \left( \text{TP}_{\text{jkt}} \right)} \right) \Big/ \text{imp}_{\text{jkt}} \left( 1 - e^{\widehat{\alpha}_1 \left( \text{TP}_{\text{jkt}} \right)} + 1 - e^{\widehat{\alpha}_2 \left( \text{TP}_{\text{jkt}} \right)} \right) \tag{Aiii}$$

$$X = \left( 1 - e^{\widehat{\alpha}_1 \left( \text{TP}_{\text{jkt}} \right)} * e^{\widehat{\alpha}_2 \left( \text{TP}_{\text{jkt}} \right)} \right) \Big/ \left( 1 - e^{\widehat{\alpha}_1 \left( \text{TP}_{\text{jkt}} \right)} + 1 - e^{\widehat{\alpha}_2 \left( \text{TP}_{\text{jkt}} \right)} \right) \tag{Aiv}$$

$$X = \left( 1 - e^{\widehat{\alpha}_1 - \widehat{\alpha}_2 \left( \text{TP}_{\text{jkt}} \right)} \right) \Big/ \left( 1 - e^{\widehat{\alpha}_1 \left( TP_{\text{jkt}} \right)} + 1 - e^{\widehat{\alpha}_2 \left( \text{TP}_{\text{jkt}} \right)} \right) \tag{Av}$$

Eqs. (12) and (13) are obtained by adding up the values of $X$ in Eqs. (10) and (11).

$$\text{TC} = \left( \text{imp}_{\text{jkt}} \left( 1 - e^{\widehat{\alpha}_1 \left( \text{TPI}_{\text{jkt}} \right)} \right) \right) * X \tag{12}$$

$$\text{TD} = \left( \text{imp}_{\text{jkt}} \left( 1 - e^{\widehat{\alpha}_1 \left( \text{TPI}_{\text{jkt}} \right)} \right) \right) * X \tag{13}$$

### 4.3.1 Full Panel

Table 5 calculates the value of trade creation and diversion using Eqs. (12) and (13), and forecasts are based on a proportion of total Afghan imports. Table 5 shows the expected economic value of every industry for all of the years from 2008 to 2021. The initial column denotes the anticipated monetary value of the creation of trade, whereas the second column signifies the percentage of diverted trade relative to Afghanistan's total imports. It is anticipated that all Afghanistan FTAs will increase imports by $1.85 billion via trade expansion and $0.6 billion via TD between 2008 and 2021. All FTAs combined were predicted to boost the country's importing level by $4.3 billion via the creation of trade and $1.9 billion by means of diversion of trade in 2021. The worth of trade effects and impacts from all FTAs as a percentage of Afghanistan's has reached a new high.

### 4.3.2 Reginal Trade Agreement (SAFTA)

The $TR_{jkt}$ and $TP_{jkt}$ coefficients from Model II are utilised to compute the dollar value of the creation and diversion of trade by employing Eqs. (12) and (13). These figures for 2008–2021 enable us to calculate the average creation and

Table 5. Model II: Creation and Diversion of Trade Employing all Free Trade Agreements.

| Year | TC | (%) | TD | (%) |
|------|------|------|--------|------|
| 2008 | 143 | 0.31 | 47.2 | 0.41 |
| 2009 | 178 | 0.38 | 66.5 | 0.59 |
| 2010 | 169 | 0.36 | 56.7 | 0.50 |
| 2011 | 432 | 0.94 | 146 | 1.29 |
| 2012 | 4,419 | 9.63 | 143 | 1.27 |
| 2013 | 5,908 | 12.88 | 198 | 1.76 |
| 2014 | 4,956 | 10.81 | 138 | 1.22 |
| 2015 | 4,127 | 9.00 | 139 | 1.23 |
| 2016 | 3,421 | 7.46 | 1,367 | 12.15 |
| 2017 | 4,312 | 9.40 | 1,507 | 13.39 |
| 2018 | 5,326 | 11.61 | 1,511 | 13.43 |
| 2019 | 4,390 | 9.57 | 1,965 | 17.46 |
| 2020 | 3,751 | 8.18 | 1,978 | 17.58 |
| 2021 | 4,309 | 9.39 | 1,908 | 17.66 |
| 2001–2021 | 3274.35 | 7.14 | 11170.4 | 7.15 |

*Source:* Authors' compilation based on the data.

*Note:* Trade creation (TC) and trade diversion (TD) are expressed in millions of dollars, respectively.

diversion of trade in Afghanistan as a proportion of total imports. SAFTA costs Afghanistan an average of $0.14 billion each year or 0.7% of total imports. Trade growth surged in 2018, following the SAFTA agreement was reached, resulting in 1.33% of total Afghan imports. From 2008 to 2021, it is anticipated that SAFTA TD will account for $0.09 billion, or 0.49%, of Afghanistan's total imports. 17.66% was the all-time peak for diverted trade in 2021.

### 4.3.3 TC and Diversion in BFTAs

According to Tables 6 and 7, BFTAs create an average of $0.95 billion in trade for Afghanistan. The creation of trade contributes to 1.31% of total Afghan imports.

In Model III, the impact of the creation of trade originates from two distinct sources. As stated earlier, the initial benefit is the reduction in tariffs that exporters attain by entering into FTAs. The second can be attributed to the inclusion of GEEs in the RTA dummy variable. After accounting for these impacts, the TC equation is as follows:

$$\text{imp}_{jkt} - \widehat{\text{imp}}_{\text{noTC,jkt}} = \text{imp}_{jkt}\left(1 - e^{\widehat{\alpha}_1(\text{TP}_{jkt}) - \widehat{\alpha}_3(\text{FTAs}_{jt})}\right) \tag{14}$$

The TD equation will stay unchanged.

$$\text{imp}_{jkt} - \widehat{\text{imp}}_{\text{noTC,jkt}} = \text{imp}_{jkt}\left(1 - e^{\widehat{\alpha}_2(\text{TP}_{jkt})}\right) \tag{15}$$

The overall impact of FTAs will now be stated as:

$$\text{imp}_{jkt} - \widehat{\text{imp}}_{\text{noFTAs,jkt}} = \text{imp}_{jkt}\left(1 - e^{\left(\widehat{\alpha}_1 - \widehat{\alpha}_2\right)(\text{TP}_{jkt})} * e^{-\widehat{\alpha}_3(\text{RTA}_{jt})}\right) \tag{16}$$

In this case, TC and diversion have little influence on the overall effect of FTAs. Eqs. (14) and (16) may be multiplied with factor $X$ to get a similar result.

$$\text{TC} = \left(\text{imp}_{jkt}\left(1 - e^{\widehat{\alpha}_1(\text{TP}_{jkt}) - \widehat{\alpha}_3(\text{FTAs}_{jt})}\right)\right) * X \tag{17}$$

$$\text{TD} = \left(\text{imp}_{jkt}\left(1 - e^{\widehat{\alpha}_2(\text{TP}_{jkt})}\right)\right) * X \tag{18}$$

$$\text{RTA} = \left(\text{imp}_{jkt}\left(1 - e^{\left(\widehat{\alpha}_1 - \widehat{\alpha}_2\right)(\text{TP}_{jkt}) - \widehat{\alpha}_3(\text{FTAs}_{jt})}\right)\right) * X \tag{19}$$

This estimating technique calculates the volume of TC and trading diversion and separates TC from two distinct sources. The tariff reduction is one source and the general equilibrium impacts of FTAs are the other.

Table 6. Creation and Diversion of Trade in the South Asian Free Trade Agreement.

| Year | TC | (%) | TD | (%) |
|------|------|-------|-------|-------|
| 2008 | 54.5 | 2.55 | 37.7 | 2.78 |
| 2009 | 92.5 | 4.34 | 65.4 | 4.83 |
| 2010 | 76.3 | 3.58 | 54.6 | 4.03 |
| 2011 | 287 | 13.47 | 151 | 11.16 |
| 2012 | 198 | 9.29 | 138 | 10.20 |
| 2013 | 287 | 13.47 | 187 | 13.82 |
| 2014 | 109 | 5.11 | 143 | 10.57 |
| 2015 | 118 | 5.54 | 138 | 10.20 |
| 2016 | 136 | 6.38 | 65 | 4.80 |
| 2017 | 134 | 6.29 | 69 | 5.10 |
| 2018 | 144 | 6.76 | 81 | 5.98 |
| 2019 | 165 | 7.74 | 78 | 5.76 |
| 2020 | 176 | 8.26 | 76 | 5.61 |
| 2021 | 152 | 7.13 | 69 | 5.10 |
| 2001–2021 | 152.09 | 7.14 | 96.62 | 7.16 |

*Source:* Authors' compilation based on the data.

*Note:* These values are based on the estimates of Model II.

### 4.3.4 Estimates of Full Panel (Including All the FTAs)

The data in the initial two columns of Table 8 illustrate the degree of the creation of trade in relation to the overall value of imports. The intensity of the diversion of trade is expressed in the subsequent two columns as a percentage of overall imports from abroad. Further to note, column 5 displays the dollar amount of the overall equilibrium consequences, whereas the sixth column depicts the proportion of the overall imports. Column 7 presents the monetary value of the creation of trade resulting from tariff reductions, while column 8 calculates this figure as a percentage of Afghanistan's total imports. Compared to Models I and II, the predicted impacts of all FTAs on the creation of trade increased in Model III. Afghanistan's trade expanded by $9 billion on average between 2008 and 2021, attributable to the creation of trade (compared to $1.85 billion in Table 5). TD, on the other hand, increases by an average of $0.9 billion (compared to $0.6 million in Table 5).

Column 2 indicates that before the ratification of PTAs and TTAs (with India and Pakistan) and during South Asia Preferential Trade Agreement's (SAPTA's) tenure, the overall creation of trade as a proportion of Afghanistan's overall imports might have been higher. In 2008–2009, the dollar amount of the creation of trade fell to $1.7 billion, but a $21 billion gain is anticipated in 2011. Following that, the enactment of

Table 7. Creation and Diversion of Trade in Bilateral Free Trade Agreements.

| Year | TC | (%) | TD | (%) |
|---|---|---|---|---|
| 2008 | – | – | – | – |
| 2009 | – | – | – | – |
| 2010 | – | – | – | – |
| 2011 | 187 | 13.11 | 165 | 11.23 |
| 2012 | 197 | 8.66 | 138 | 9.39 |
| 2013 | 285 | 12.54 | 189 | 12.87 |
| 2014 | 179 | 7.87 | 193 | 13.14 |
| 2015 | 121 | 5.32 | 165 | 11.23 |
| 2016 | 145 | 6.38 | 69 | 4.69 |
| 2017 | 167 | 7.34 | 79 | 5.38 |
| 2018 | 156 | 6.86 | 88 | 5.99 |
| 2019 | 160 | 7.04 | 77 | 5.24 |
| 2020 | 179 | 7.87 | 76 | 5.17 |
| 2021 | 159 | 6.99 | 69 | 4.69 |
| 2001–2021 | 162.3 | 7.16 | 104.86 | 7.19 |

*Source:* Authors' compilation based on the data.

*Note:* These values are based on the estimates of Model II.

the South Asian FTA in 2011 resulted in a surge in imports. This surge of $30 billion record increase in imports is attributed to TC and was observed until 2014. Until SAFTA was adopted in 2011, the TD effect was insignificant in column 3. TD raised Afghanistan imports by $2 billion in 2021. Afghan imports exercised through diversion of trade have progressively grown but are anticipated to continue to hover around $3 billion in 2021.

Column 5 indicates the anticipated expansion of trade as a result of the ratification of FTAs. From 2008 to 2021, TC increased imports by $1.4 billion on average due to GEEs. These effects were minimal until SAFTA was enacted; in 2011, Afghan imports increased by $3 billion. The general equilibrium impacts of signing FTAs were estimated to reach $4.6 billion in 2021. As shown in column 4, from 2008 to 2021, the benefits of TC amounted to $7.7 billion primarily as a result of tariff reductions. During the SAPTA era, it was little again, but there was a $1.7 billion rise in 2006, right after Afghanistan signed its first Afghanistan Pakistan Preferential Trade Agreement (APPTA) with Pakistan. It remained unchanged in 2007; a $2.3 billion increase in imports represents the TC benefit of tariff removal in 2008. There was a $18 billion increase in 2011, the year SAFTA was adopted. Imports increased by $25.8 billion as a result of tariff reductions, according to reports.

Table 8. Expected Values of Creation and Diversion of Trade (Including All Free Trade Agreements).

| Year | Trade Creation | TC (%) | Trade Diversion | TD (%) | TC, FTAs | TC, FTAs (%) | TC, Tariff | TC, Tariff (%) |
|---|---|---|---|---|---|---|---|---|
| 2008 | 54.5 | 2.39 | 39.8 | 2.71 | 254 | 0.93 | 93 | 0.40 |
| 2009 | 93.5 | 4.11 | 62.5 | 4.25 | 383 | 1.41 | 141 | 0.61 |
| 2010 | 78.3 | 3.44 | 57.8 | 3.93 | 322 | 1.18 | 118 | 0.51 |
| 2011 | 298 | 13.11 | 165 | 11.23 | 92.3 | 0.34 | 1747.8 | 7.56 |
| 2012 | 197 | 8.66 | 138 | 9.39 | 147 | 0.54 | 1,721 | 7.44 |
| 2013 | 285 | 12.54 | 189 | 12.87 | 231 | 0.85 | 2,359 | 10.20 |
| 2014 | 179 | 7.87 | 193 | 13.14 | 126 | 0.46 | 1,632 | 7.06 |
| 2015 | 121 | 5.32 | 165 | 11.23 | 99.8 | 0.36 | 1,630 | 7.05 |
| 2016 | 145 | 6.38 | 69 | 4.69 | 3,032 | 11.19 | 18,171 | 7.86 |
| 2017 | 167 | 7.34 | 79 | 5.38 | 4,169 | 15.39 | 19,867 | 8.59 |
| 2018 | 156 | 6.86 | 88 | 5.99 | 3,671 | 13.55 | 19,431 | 8.39 |
| 2019 | 160 | 7.04 | 77 | 5.24 | 4,681 | 17.28 | 25,820 | 10.90 |
| 2020 | 179 | 7.87 | 76 | 5.17 | 4,408 | 16.27 | 26,415 | 11.44 |
| 2021 | 159 | 6.99 | 69 | 4.69 | 5,461 | 20.16 | 27,621 | 11.94 |
| 2001–2021 | 162.3 | 7.16 | 104.86 | 7.19 | 1934.07 | 7.14 | 11282.6 | 7.16 |

*Note:* The values of diversion and creation of trade are predicated on Model-III FTAs. A million dollars are invested in the trade creation, trade diversion, TC (RTA) and TC (tariff) columns. The percentages of trade creation, diversion, TC (RTA) and TC (tariff) are derived from the aggregate imports of Afghanistan.

The combined estimates encompassing all FTAs generate 9.79% of Afghanistan's total imports. The diversion of trade is projected to represent 0.97% of Afghanistan's total imports. The average general equilibrium impact of all FTAs that generate trade is projected to be 1.5% of the nation's total imports from 2008 to 2021. TC as a result of tariff reductions offered to BFTA and RTA partners, on the other hand, is estimated to be 8.31% on average. Based on the statistics, the trade generated from FTAs outnumbers the diversion of trade by a ratio of two.

*4.3.5 Regional Trade Agreements (SAFTA)*

The determination of the magnitude of diversion and creation of trade intensity, and the overall equilibrium impact in the context of SAFTA, requires the utilisation of Model III coefficients and Eqs. (17)–(19). TC has an average value of $2.4 billion, which corresponds to 2.61% of the total imports of Afghanistan. A TD rate of $0.2 billion, or 0.22% of total imports, is the mean value. TC and diversion reached their highest points in 2014, each contributing 0.27% and 0.37% to total imports, respectively. In this scenario, the GEE of signing SAFTA results in $1.6 billion in TC. Tariff cuts for partner countries create an average of $0.7 billion in trade (see Table 9).

*4.3.6 Bilateral Free Trade Agreements*

On calculating Eqs. Eqs. (17)–(19) and employing Afghanistan's bilateral trade agreements, we can estimate the intensity of TC and diversion. The calculations reveal that TC is hovering around $6.6 billion, or 7.15% of the country's overall imports (See Table 10).

The yearly value of TD is $0.01 billion or 0.14% of Afghanistan's total imports. In accordance with the source cited above, the overall equilibrium benefits of implementing the BFTA result in an average TC of $5.5 billion, rather than $1 billion owing to tariff reductions granted to member states.

# 5. Conclusions

This study examined the effects on Afghan imports of FTAs and associated preferential tariff reductions, with an emphasis on the welfare implications. Based on Models I and II, the results indicate that TC in Afghanistan exceeds TD by a factor of four. However, in Model III, the disparity is only 1.5 times. As per Model II, TC is valued at an average of $1.8 billion, which corresponds to 1.99% of the total imports of Afghanistan. TD accounts for an estimated $0.6 billion, or 0.65%, of the overall value of imports. Model III predicts that trade will generate an average of $9 billion, representing 9.79% of Afghanistan's total imports. Model III generates more trade than Model II when the GEEs of signing FTAs are accounted for, which amount to an average of $1.4 billion and 1.54% of total imports in Afghanistan. The remainder of trade expansion can be ascribed to the

Table 9. Expected Values of Creation and Diversion of Trade (Including All South Asia Free Trade Agreements).

| Year | TC | TC (%) | TD | TD (%) | TC, RTA | TC, RTA (%) | TC, Tariff | TC, Tariff (%) |
|------|------|--------|--------|--------|---------|-------------|------------|----------------|
| 2008 | 46.4 | 0.05 | 65.5 | 3.32 | 10.98 | 0.07 | 49.7 | 0.34 |
| 2009 | 62.9 | 0.07 | 67.8 | 3.46 | 11.67 | 0.08 | 54.9 | 0.49 |
| 2010 | 54 | 0.06 | 69.8 | 3.6 | 12.43 | 0.09 | 54 | 0.68 |
| 2011 | 46.8 | 0.19 | 70.8 | 3.63 | 11.76 | 0.08 | 55 | 0.68 |
| 2012 | 62.91 | 0.26 | 94.8 | 4.86 | 15.3 | 0.1 | 80.7 | 0.99 |
| 2013 | 51 | 0.21 | 82.8 | 4.24 | 13.2 | 0.09 | 40.7 | 0.5 |
| 2014 | 1150 | 4.91 | 211 | 10.82 | 1330 | 9.08 | 720 | 8.92 |
| 2015 | 2,164 | 9.24 | 206 | 10.57 | 1331 | 9.09 | 980 | 12.14 |
| 2016 | 2,806 | 11.98 | 286 | 14.67 | 1343 | 9.17 | 687 | 8.51 |
| 2017 | 1,807 | 7.71 | 187 | 9.59 | 2,328 | 15.9 | 643 | 7.96 |
| 2018 | 1,863 | 7.95 | 189 | 9.7 | 1,440 | 9.83 | 1,026 | 12.71 |
| 2019 | 3,130 | 13.37 | 191 | 9.8 | 2,430 | 16.59 | 1,150 | 14.24 |
| 2020 | 4,489 | 19.17 | 188 | 9.64 | 2,143 | 14.63 | 1,266 | 15.68 |
| 2021 | 5,840 | 24.966 | 242 | 12.42 | 2,254 | 15.39 | 1,423 | 17.63 |
| *2001–2021* | 1683.78 | *7.15* | 153.67 | 7.88 | 1048.16 | 7.15 | 587.85 | 7.24 |

*Source:* The calculations are the authors' compilation based on the data from WDI and UNCOMTRADE.

*Note:* Using Model III, the indicators of trade creation and diversion are derived from SAFTA. Trade creation and diversion columns contain values in the millions of dollars. Tariffs generate trade as a result of their influence on general equilibrium and tariff concessions in TC, RTA and TC, respectively.

tariff reductions that are a component of every FTA. The $0.9 billion in reported diverted trade represents 0.97% of the total imports of Afghanistan.

Based on Models II and III, TC is of greater significance than the diversion of trade in the case of SAFTA. In contrast to all prior FTA scenarios, the general equilibrium impacts of signing SAFTA generate greater trade compared to the tariff concessions offered to its member nations. For Models II and III, BFTAs provide similar outcomes, with the creation of trade surpassing the diversion of trade. Similarly, TC generated by the overall equilibrium impacts of the BFTA agreement is greater than the TC generated by tariff advantages granted to member nations.

Notably, once the agreements were signed, the volume of trade between Afghanistan and BFTA and SAFTA members expanded. Although policymakers in Afghanistan perceive the effects of such agreements to be negative, our estimations of TC and TD reveal that these figures typically overlook the total

Table 10. Expected Creation and Diversion of Trade (Bilateral Free Trade Agreement).

| Year | TC | TC (%) | TD | TD (%) | RTA | % | Tariff | % |
|---|---|---|---|---|---|---|---|---|
| 2008 | – | – | – | – | – | – | – | – |
| 2009 | – | – | – | – | – | – | – | – |
| 2010 | – | – | – | – | – | – | – | – |
| 2011 | 5,831 | 7.33 | 118 | 6.30 | 4,881 | 8.38 | 955 | 7.87 |
| 2012 | 6,281 | 7.89 | 127 | 6.78 | 5,302 | 9.10 | 980 | 8.08 |
| 2013 | 6,321 | 7.94 | 129 | 6.89 | 5,320 | 9.14 | 990 | 8.16 |
| 2014 | 8,150 | 10.24 | 169 | 9.03 | 5,330 | 9.15 | 1,120 | 9.23 |
| 2015 | 8,164 | 10.26 | 173 | 9.24 | 5,431 | 9.33 | 1,180 | 9.73 |
| 2016 | 8,066 | 10.14 | 176 | 9.40 | 5,343 | 9.18 | 1,187 | 9.78 |
| 2017 | 8,078 | 10.15 | 187 | 9.99 | 5,328 | 9.15 | 1,043 | 8.60 |
| 2018 | 7,663 | 9.63 | 189 | 10.10 | 5,440 | 9.34 | 1,066 | 8.79 |
| 2019 | 8,130 | 10.22 | 193 | 10.31 | 5,430 | 9.32 | 1,190 | 9.81 |
| 2020 | 6,320 | 7.94 | 198 | 10.58 | 5,143 | 8.83 | 1,209 | 9.69 |
| 2021 | 6,540 | 8.22 | 212 | 11.33 | 5,254 | 9.02 | 1,207 | 9.95 |
| *2001–2021* | *7231.27* | *9.09* | *170.09* | *9.11* | *5291.09* | *9.10* | *1102.45* | *9.07* |

*Source:* The calculations are the authors' compilation based on the data from WDI and UNCOMTRADE.

*Note:* Utilising Model III, the parameters associated with trade diversion and creation are determined in accordance with BFTA.

welfare impacts of consumption and production. Our results have substantial policy implications because they demonstrate that FTAs, whether bilateral or regional, are not always detrimental but rather beneficial. To summarise, the impacts of TC are beneficial, as seen by the growth of all FTAs.

### 5.1 Policy Suggestions

The study suggests that the SAFTA's business growth potential must be addressed. The trade relationships of SAARC members might be enhanced in favour of the region. SAARC countries need to demonstrate an unwavering determination to continue to transform their economic systems and liberalising their trading regimes by streamlining and enhancing tariff policies and processes, offering transit services for border-sharing nations and streamlining banking services for easier financing of trade so as to capitalise on the full benefits of SAFTA. The study calls for more integration with BFTA nations, in addition to eliminating mutual trade obstacles. Current regional FTAs and BFTAs have a considerable and beneficial welfare impact. The impact of implementing the treaties on the creation of trade has been much greater compared to the impact on the diversion of trade. Although TC improves well-being, on the other hand, TD has unclear benefits. Finally, the overall balancing impacts are significant and appropriate. All of these impacts must be preserved in Afghanistan's existing and future FTAs, since FTAs, whether regional or bilateral, improve well-being.

# References

Akbari, S. (2021). *The WTO transit regime for landlocked countries and its impacts on members' regional transit agreements: The case of Afghanistan's transit trade with Pakistan* (Vol. 17). Springer Nature.

Akhter, N., & Ghani, E. (2010). Regional integration in South Asia: An analysis in trade flow using gravity model. *Pakistan Development Review, 42*(2), 105–118.

Ali, E., & Talukder, D. K. (2009). Preferential trade among the SAARC countries: Prospects and challenges of regional integration in South Asia. *JOAA, 4*(1), 47–59.

Anderson, J. E., & Wincoop, E. V. (2001). *Gravity with gravitas: A solution to the border puzzle*. Working Paper No. 8079. National Bureau of Economics Research, Cambridge, MA.

Balassa, B. (1967). Trade creation and trade diversion in the European common market. *The Economic Journal, 77*(30), 1–21.

Bao, X., & Wang, X. (2019). The evolution and reshaping of globalization: A perspective based on the development of regional trade agreements. *China and World Economy, 27*(1), 51–71.

Bayoumi, T., & Eichengreen, B. (1995). *Is regionalism simply a diversion? Evidence from the evolution of the EC and EFTA*. Working Paper No.5283. National Bureau of Economics Research, Chicago.

Bergstrand, J. H., Egger, P., & Larch, M. (2016). Economic determinants of the timing of preferential trade agreement formations and enlargements. *Economic Inquiry, 54*(1), 315–341.

Bhagwati, J. N., Panagariya, A., & Srinivasan, T. N. (1998). *Lectures on international trade* (2nd ed.). The MIT Press.

Clausing, K. A. (2001). Trade creation and trade diversion in the Canada-United States free trade agreement. *Canadian Journal of Economics, 34*(3), 677–696.

Cheong, J., Kwak, D. W., & Tang, K. K. (2015). *It is much bigger than we thought: New estimates of trade diversion*. The World Economy.

Cipollina, M., De Benedictis, L., Salvatici, L., & Claudio, V. (2016). *Policy measurement and multilateral resistance in gravity models*. MPRA (Munich Personal RePEc Archive) paper.

De Benedictis, L., & Taglioni, D. (2011). *The gravity model in international trade* (pp. 55–89). Springer.

Deme, M., & Ndrianasy, E. R. (2017). Trade-creation and trade-diversion effects of regional trade arrangements: Low-income countries. *Applied Economics, 49*(22), 2188–2202.

Feenstra, R. (2002). *Advanced international trade: Theory and evidence*. Princeton University Press.

Freund, C. M. (1999). *The dynamics of trade diversion: Evidence from four trade blocs*. Columbia University.

Ghosha, S., & Yamarikb, S. (2004). Does trade creation measure up? A re-examination of the effects of regional trading arrangements. *Journal of International Economics*, *63*(4), 369–395.

Hayakawa, K. (2011). *How serious is the omission of bilateral tariff rates in gravity?* Discussion Paper No. 311. Institute of Developing Economies, Thailand.

Head, K., & Mayer, T. (2014). Gravity equations: Workhorse, toolkit, and cookbook. In *Handbook of International Economics* (Vol. 4, pp. 131–195). Elsevier.

Huber, P. J. (1967). The behavior of maximum likelihood estimates under non-standard conditions. In M. L. Le Cam & J. Neyman (Eds.), *Proceedings of the fifth berkeley symposium on mathematical statistics and probability* (Vol. 1, pp. 221–233). The University of California Press.

Krueger, A. (1999). *Trade creation and trade diversion under NAFTA.* Working Paper No. 7429. National Bureau of Economic Research, Cambridge, MA.

Krugman, P. (1991). The move toward free trade zones. *Economic Review*, *76*(6), 5.

Magee, C. S. (2008). New measures of trade creation and diversion. *Journal of International Economics*, *75*(2), 349–362.

Magee, C. (2016). Trade creation, trade diversion, and the general equilibrium effects of regional trade agreements: A study of the European community – Turkey customs union. *Review of World Economics*, *152*(2), 383–399.

Mattoo, A., Mulabdic, A., & Ruta, M. (2022). Trade creation and trade diversion in deep agreements. *Canadian Journal of Economics/Revue canadienne d'économique*, *55*(3), 1598–1637.

Meade, J. (1955). *The theory of customs unions.* North Holland.

Novy, D. (2013). Gravity redux: Measuring international trade costs with panel data. *Economic Inquiry*, *51*(1), 101–121.

Park, I. (2020). Regional trade agreements in East Asia: Past and future. *Development Policy Review*, *38*(2), 206–225.

Rahman, M., Shadat, W., & Das, N. (2006). *Trade potential in SAFTA: An application of augmented gravity model.* Working Paper No. 61. The Centre for Policy Dialogue Bangladesh, Dhaka.

Rodrik, D. (2018). What do trade agreements really do? *The Journal of Economic Perspectives*, *32*(2), 73–90.

Romalis, J. (2007). NAFTA's and CUSFTA's impact on international trade. *The Review of Economics and Statistics*, *89*(3), 416–435.

Silva, J. M., & Tenreyro, S. (2006). The log of gravity. *The Review of Economics and Statistics*, *88*(4), 641–658.

Starck, S. C. (2012). *The theoretical foundation of gravity modelling: What developments have brought gravity modelling into mainstream economics?* Report No. 182. 299. Copenhagen Business School, Denmark.

Theie, M. G. (2015). *Non-tariff barriers, trade integration and the gravity model.* Working Paper No. 843. Norwegian Institute of International Affairs NUIP Department of International Economics, Norway.

Viner, J. (1950). Full employment at whatever cost. *Quarterly Journal of Economics*, *64*(3), 385–407.

White, H. (1980). A heteroskedasticity-consistent covariance matrix estimator and a direct test for heteroskedasticity. *Econometrica*, *48*(4), 817–838.

Wonnacott, P., & Mark, L. (1989). Is there a case for free trade agreements? In J. Schott (Ed.), *Free trade areas and U.S. Trade policy* (pp. 59–84). Institute for International Economics.

Yang, S., & Martinez-Zarzoso, I. (2014). A panel data analysis of trade creation and trade diversion effects: The case of ASEAN–China Free Trade Area. *China Economic Review, 29*, 138–151.

Yang, S., & Zarzoso, I. M. (2013). *A panel data analysis of trade creation and diversion effects: The case of ASEAN- China Free Trade Area (ACFTA)*. Discussion Paper No. 224. Económicas Ibero-America Institute for Economic Research, Germany.

Yotov, Y. V. (2022). On the role of domestic trade flows for estimating the gravity model of trade. *Contemporary Economic Policy, 40*(3), 526–540.

# Chapter 8

# Impact of Non-Tariff Measures on Trade Within the SAARC Region: An Empirical Investigation of Afghanistan

## Abstract

The benefits of global trade are primarily attributed to reducing trade distortions between trading partners. The anticipated promise of a progressive diminution in tariffs throughout the globe was, regrettably, steadily superseded by non-tariff measures (NTMs). However, the impact of these NTMs is only sometimes evident since it occurs in various disguises. NTMs significantly influence trade in the SAARC, mandating prompt attention. The question is how much internal trade will expand if NTMs are repealed. Based on statistics from 2015 to 2020, the study endeavours to quantify the impact of NTMs on Afghanistan's trade volume within the SAARC region, primarily targeting four export destinations (Bangladesh, India, Pakistan and Sri Lanka). Using trade freedom scores as a proxy for trade distortions, it has been determined that Afghanistan's magnitude of export earnings is significantly lower due to NTMs imposed by its importing trading partners. According to the findings, a 1% rise in tariffs and NTMs applied by importing countries diminishes Afghanistan's exports by 1.23%.

In contrast, the impact of tariffs alone lowers Afghanistan's exports by 1.13%. The incidence of NTMs also devoid actual Afghanistan exports by US$ 5.70 million, equal to a 0.029% loss of Afghanistan's GDP. The calculations also reveal that lowering or eliminating non-tariff barriers has diverse trade growth effects in different trade groupings. The study recommends a serious NTM-oriented trade policy dialogue that is liberal and guarantees regional integration, thereby promoting and ensuring the future of Afghanistan's economic laurels and stability.

*Keywords*: Afghanistan; South Asian Association for Regional Cooperation; non-tariff measures; international trade; trade distortions; restrictions

*JEL Codes*: F14; F16; F18

**Policy Solutions for Economic Growth in a Developing Country, 181–200**
**Copyright © 2024 Nassir Ul Haq Wani**
**Published under exclusive licence by Emerald Publishing Limited**
**doi:10.1108/978-1-83753-430-220241009**

## 1. Introduction

> Tariff reductions have had the effect of emptying a swamp. The decreased water level has revealed all the snags and stumps of non-tariff obstacles that should be removed. (Robert Baldwin, 1970)

This statement highlights the repercussions of employing non-tariff measures (NTMs) and non-tariff barriers (NTBs). Even Edwin Newman, the newscaster and defender of the English language, objected to the term 'non-dairy creamer' because it tells you what it is not but not what it is. He may have had the same view of 'non-tariff measures', an elusive class of measures that inhabit the twilight zone between trade policy and national regulation. Many policies and regulations are classified as NTMs, from import licencing to technical regulations, procurement preferences, to subsidies. They are pervasive across countries and over time.

Furthermore, their variety makes them much harder to measure than tariffs. Since trade is deemed a vital precursor and agent of economic growth and thus policies targeting growth are of profound vitality. Trade is crucial in alleviating poverty worldwide (Clemens & Kremer, 2016), and NTMs hamper the welfare effect. The economic growth miracles in East Asia, Europe and North America owe a huge chunk of their laurels to robust trade ties with their neighbours and trading partners (Naseri & Wani, 2020; Sarel, 1995; Wani & Dhami, 2014, 2017). South Asian countries, on the other hand, have yet to gain from proximity (Ahmad & Wani, 2018; Akbari, 2021). Intraregional trade is slightly more than 5% of global trade in South Asia, parallel to consistent performance in Asia, the Pacific and Sub-Saharan Africa by 50% and 22%, respectively.

One of the reports published by the World Bank in 2018 vividly highlights the disparities between present and prospective trade in South Asia. South Asia's overall goods trade might be valued at $67 billion rather than the present value of $23 billion. For example, official trade between India and Pakistan may increase 15-fold from present levels. The incidence of high levels of informal trade reflects the force of gravity as these countries are neighbouring ones. It is estimated to comprise 50% of formal trade based on assessments from several investigations from 1995 to 2019. Since South Asian trade frameworks are prejudiced against one another, massive differences exist between actual and prospective trade (Kathuria, 2019). It is demonstrated by a trade restrictiveness index, as seen in Table 1.

Using trade statistics, the TRI index calculates a tariff implied that assesses a country's tariff and non-tariff import barriers. In India, Afghanistan, Pakistan and Sri Lanka, the index for imports from South Asia is two to nine times greater than for imports from the rest of the globe (Table 1). Furthermore, while the overall burden of NTMs appears to be low, it is considerable for certain goods and market combinations in South Asia. It ranges from more than 75% to more than 2,000%. Sri Lanka is routinely listed as having the region's highest trade restrictiveness index for product–market pairings. These restrictions (including

Table 1. Overall Trade Restrictiveness Index, Selected Countries in South Asia, 2019.

| Importing Country | Origin of Imports | |
|---|---|---|
| | South Asia | Rest of World |
| Afghanistan | 3.84 | 4.65 |
| Bangladesh | 10.59 | 6.87 |
| India | 4.59 | 0.50 |
| Pakistan | 3.00 | 0.51 |
| Sri Lanka | 1.01 | 0.33 |

*Source:* Authors' Calculations based on the overall Trade Restrictiveness Index.

tariffs and para-tariffs, actual and perceived NTBs and connectivity costs embodied in the expense of air travel) and the more significant trust deficit have hampered South Asian trade and investment prospects (UNCTAD, 2013).

Recent years have witnessed the involvement of government institutions and organisations towards liberalisation and augmentation of the world trade environment that facilitates the country's economic laurels (Henson & Loader, 2001; Johnson & Koyama, 2017; Koo & Kennedy, 2005). The vital manifestations and objectives of establishing GATT, and later on WTO, were to facilitate and secure freer trade accessibility and expand international trade vitalities through economic globalisation; this was possible if tariffs, other NTBs and NTMs impeding trade were reduced (Akintola et al., 2021; Jordaan, 2017; Torsekar, 2019). The trade agreements (bilateral or multilateral) globally have attempted to diminish the usage of tariffs, especially by developed ones. As a result, other forms of trade barriers have emerged (e.g. inadequate infrastructure and compliance with Sanitary and Phytosanitary regulations [SPS]), thus limiting their capacity to access latent markets (Ackerman, 2005; ITC, 2022). Even in the case of underdeveloped countries, the available knowledge, expertise and resources to comply with these trade distortion and restriction standards, specifically for exports, still need to be included (Bellanawithana et al., 2009). Therefore, it is interesting to measure the economic effect of NTMs, which restrict and hinder bilateral trade and, ultimately, the trade potential of Afghanistan in terms of exports and imports to/from the SAARC region. By doing so, we can track and assess the possible trade consequences if present non-tariff restrictions were decreased or removed, which is one of the SAARC free trade declaration's goals.

Given the trade's crucial importance in the economic arena, several studies have been conducted to identify the factors that influence and obstruct trade flows; however, the impact on underdeveloped countries is still being determined, and Afghanistan is almost non-existent. The present study includes the NTMs in assessing their impact on the international trade of Afghanistan within the SAARC region. The current study contrasts with other studies in several respects and adds to the existing literature in areas viz; firstly, it has included all the NTMs employed by SAARC countries about trade with Afghanistan and presents discussed analysis with the major trading partners (India, Pakistan, Bangladesh and Sri Lanka). In light of the results, the study further provides policy justification for the same.

The rest of the study is organised as per the structure as follows: the second part provides a brief economic overview of Afghanistan, highlighting the trade with BIPS (Bangladesh, India, Pakistan and Sri Lanka) and NTMs, while the third section discusses the extant literature on the NTMs. The fourth section provides the model specifications, data and approach to achieve the desired outcomes. The fifth section estimates the approach and model specification. Accordingly, the results are reported while the conclusions are established based on analysis and explained, along with policy implications, suggestions and the future scope of the study.

## 2. Afghanistan's Economy: Trade With BIPS

Afghanistan is a landlocked economy located at the crossroads of Central Asia and South Asia and is steadily transitioning from a war economy to a peace economy (Wani, 2019). With the population surpassing 40 million, having a gross domestic product (GDP) per capita of US\$ 21,00 is the lowest in the South Asian region. In Afghanistan, an aid-dependent country with looming poverty and other socio-economic challenges, trade can ensure more considerable welfare gains than aid. The recent debacle and journey story from 'Republic to Emirate' has also added new concerns. Based on the reports of IMF regional economic outlook report (2021), suggest that after the Taliban takeover, Afghanistan's GDP has witnessed a contraction of up to 30%. These shocks have caused 20–30% output contraction, with diminishing imports, a depreciating Afghani, and accelerating inflation. The trade since collapse has not been momentous even. Among the trusted trade partners of Afghanistan, 43.3% and 32.8% of Afghanistan's exports came from India and Pakistan. Its trade links with Central Asian republics and the Middle East are still in their infancy. Its involvement in the Economic Cooperation Organization (ECO), which includes certain nations from both areas, has not provided substantial benefits (Ahmad et al., 2018).

Since Afghanistan enjoys membership in SAFTA and has been a source of relief for the economy, the mandate of SAFTA through Article 7(6) stipulates that imports from LDCs will be duty-free by 2025, thus leaving a ray of hope for Afghanistan's exports. Thus, this guarantees that Afghanistan to reap benefits from this dispensation. The clauses of SAFTA in terms of Technical Assistance and Special and Differential (S & D) mechanisms might reinvigorate and facilitate Afghanistan's economic rehabilitation and boost governmental capacity building. Natural resources such as natural gas, petroleum, coal, copper, iron ore and precious gems are abundant in Afghanistan and might be exported under SAFTA concessions. Afghanistan now has 1.6 trillion cubic feet of natural gas, 95 million barrels of oil and 400 MT of coal – all essential resources for alleviating the regional energy issue (Siddiqui & Naeem, 2015). As a result, Afghanistan's strategic location as a trade transit hub with South Asia may be linked by land with the Central Asian Republics to promote commerce and energy security activities. Since 2001, the merchandise flow has been spectacular, with the value of Afghanistan's exports steadily increasing to US $ 991 million in 2020, up from US $ 700 million in 2015. Since most trade destinations are in South Asia (mainly India and Pakistan), Tables 2 and 3 illustrate the flow of exports from Afghanistan to BIPS and vice versa to help understand the trends and patterns of Afghanistan trade.

Tables 2 and 3 depict the impact on the actual value of exports from Afghanistan to its main trading partners, based on the flow to each country, to understand the trade phenomenon. In 2019, Afghanistan exported $313k to Bangladesh and imported $7.15M from Bangladesh. In the case of Bangladesh exports to Afghanistan, the flow has intensified at a yearly rate of 2.69%, from $3.99M in 1997 to $7.15M in 2019. Afghanistan's trading connections with India have been historic, exporting $499 million to India in 2020. The primary goods were tropical fruits ($132 million), insect resins ($111 million) and grapes ($96.9 million). Afghanistan's exports to India have increased at an annualised rate of 18.1% over the last 25 years, from $7.87 million in 1995 to $499 million in 2020, while India exported $855 million to Afghanistan (raw sugar [$174 million], synthetic filament yarn woven fabric [$113 million] and packaged medicaments [$70.7 million]). However, the economic picture with Pakistan is bleak since Afghanistan exported $492 million to Pakistan in 2020, including raw cotton ($114 million), grapes ($57.1 million) and dried legumes ($56.9 million). Afghanistan's exports to Pakistan have surged at an annualised rate of 17.9% during the previous 17 years, from $29.9 million in 2003 to $492 million in 2020. In contrast, Pakistan exported $870 million to Afghanistan (rice [$146 million], cement [$71.2 million] and packaged medicaments [$63.1 million]). Afghanistan exported $24.8k worth of goods to Sri Lanka in 2020, with exports dropping at an annualised rate of 7.34%, from $123k in 1999 to $24.8k in 2020, while Sri Lanka exported $168k (tea [$76.8k], coconuts, brazil nuts, cashews [$74.2k] and insect resins [$16.8k]) to Afghanistan.

Table 2. Exports From Afghanistan to BIPS, 2016–2021 ('000 US$).

| Year | X to Bangladesh | X to India | X to Pak | X to Sri Lanka | Total |
|---|---|---|---|---|---|
| 2016 | 669 | 276,000 | 407,000 | 16,800 | 700,469 |
| 2017 | 177 | 386,000 | 427,000 | 46.7 | 813223.7 |
| 2018 | 10.1 | 447,000 | 442,000 | 108 | 889118.1 |
| 2019 | 313 | 526,000 | 507,000 | NA | 1,033,313 |
| 2020 | 311 | 608,000 | 610,000 | 71.5 | 1,218,383 |
| 2021 | 310 | 499,000 | 492,000 | 24.8 | 991334.8 |
| **Total** | 1790.1 | 2,742,000 | 2,885,000 | 17,051 | **5645841.1** |

*Source:* Authors' compilation and the data figures have been collected from OEC.

Table 3. Exports From BIPS to Afghanistan, 2016–2021 ('000 US$).

| Year | X of Bangladesh | X of India | X of Pak | X of Sri Lanka | Total |
|---|---|---|---|---|---|
| 2016 | 615,000 | 560,000 | 2,140,000 | 1,050 | 3,316,050 |
| 2017 | 142,000 | 508,000 | 1,680,000 | 1,400 | 2,331,400 |
| 2018 | 286,000 | 705,000 | 2,020,000 | 1,260 | 3,012,260 |
| 2019 | 582,000 | 783,000 | 1,670,000 | 354 | 3,035,354 |
| 2020 | 715,000 | 1,040,000 | 1,690,000 | 1,230 | 3,446,230 |
| 2021 | 783,000 | 855,000 | 870,000 | 168 | 2,508,168 |
| Total | 3,123,000 | 4,451,000 | 10,070,000 | 5,462 | **17,649,462** |

*Source:* Authors' compilation and the data figures have been collected from OEC.

## 3. Scholarship Review on NTMs to Trade in the SAARC Region

The barriers to trade, like NTMs and NTBs, initially came on the scene in the early 1960s (Carrère & De Melo, 2011). According to the degree of effect, the full range of NTBs may be categorised into three broad categories: legislative protection via government intervention, administrative protection and private groups and organisations such as trade associations and trade unions (Quambusch, 1977). Among these three categories, the government's effect is often the greatest and most direct as it is based on law. The other categories, like administrative protection, entail management adopting political action within the administrative domain and includes consumer protection rules, protection of human, animal and plant life and health, copyright protection, standard specifications and safety restrictions as policy discourses, whereas the intervention through private groups and organisations engage in discriminatory activities against foreign rivals, a practice known as emotional protectionism. The most prevalent are appeals to purchasers' patriotism to boycott foreign items (Quambusch, 1977). As NTMs and NTBs to trade are increasingly commonly regarded as more essential, the impact incidence is much more skewed towards NTMs or NTBs than tariff barriers. Although the economic impact of NTBs has received a great deal of attention in the literature, only a few studies present statistical estimates of the effect of specific NTBs on bilateral trade volumes.

Most earlier research has concentrated on broad agricultural trade and overall protection (Akintola et al., 2021; Bacchetta & Beverelli, 2012; Beghin & Bureau, 2001; Bora et al., 2002; Egger et al., 2015; Gonzalez-Mellado et al., 2010; Haveman & Thursby, 1999; Henson & Loader, 2001; Hillman, 1991; Niu et al., 2018; Trabelsi, 2013). The studies of NTMs and NTBs have not kept up with their increasing complexity, resulting in a knowledge gap. Depending on the nature of trade barriers, McCarty (1999) offers a line of differentiation between NTMs and NTBs, thus presenting that NTBs are not a synonym for NTMs, but rather a subset of NTMs. NTBs are also NTMs, but only sometimes the other way around. Non-tariff distortions are defined by Baldwin (1970) as 'any policy (public or private) that causes globally traded products and services, or resources committed to the production of these goods and services, to be allocated in such a way as to lower potential real-world revenue'. Although the policy's objective is vital, determining whether NTMs are also NTBs can be difficult. The purpose sometimes needs to be addressed, and even uneasy when policy discourse comes into play (Laird & Yeats, 1990). The usage of NTMs, countries have engaged voraciously in employing NTMs, like in Indian Ocean Rim Association (Akintola et al., 2021) and Regional Comprehensive Economic Partnership (RCEP) countries (Zainuddin et al., 2020), while some studies have focused on the post-recession rise of non-tariff-measures (Torsekar, 2019).

As a relatively fragile economy, Afghanistan constantly faces trade barriers in the form of NTMs. The primary concern is the difficulty in discovering these often undetectable constraints, which progressively appear in various forms and shapes. NTM constraints in Afghanistan are usually determined by availability and political ties. For NTMs, Afghanistan imports have a coverage ratio of 22.74% and a frequency ratio of 13.30%. For NTMs, Afghanistan's exports have a coverage ratio of 69.92% frequency ratio of 11.38%. While there are many other forms of NTBs, the most common are three, two of which are administered at the border. Export subsidies, prohibitions and quotas are examples of export obstacles, whereas import licences, restrictions and customs processes are examples of import barriers. Fuels (99.8%), food goods (4.63%), apparel (64%), animals (textiles and leather) (42.78%) and other transportation are the export industries primarily impacted by NTMs in Afghanistan (27.1%). As a landlocked economy, Afghanistan is particularly sensitive to NTMs, making it challenging to increase competitiveness and boost export development when faced with overwhelming deterrents.

Depending on the incidence of impact, five categories have been identified: measures to restrict import volume; measures to regulate import price; monitoring measures, such as price and volume assessments; production and export restrictions; and technology barriers for health and safety concerns (Bora et al., 2002). However, specific issues arise in distinguishing NTMs from regulations that safeguard consumers. Although certain NTMs contribute to trade restrictions, they should not be considered NTMs if the primary goal is to remedy market inefficiencies (Baldwin, 1970). Some studies omit measures such as NTMs if they are primarily geared toward the domestic economy (Maskus et al., 2001; UNCTAD, 2013).

The only precise framework of NTMs is provided by the UNCTAD, which states that 'Non-Tariff Measures are policy measures that, unlike typical customs tariffs, can affect international trade in products by modifying quantities traded, prices, or both' (Basu et al., 2012; Bratt, 2017). According to a UNCTAD study, most NTMs fall into TBTs and SPS measures. Concerns about the predominance of SPS measures and TBTs related to exports from developing countries have been raised. The TBTs are much more prevalent than SPS, as specific countries levy TBTs on around 30% of their products and trade compared to SPS regulations that apply to around 15% of trade (UNCTAD, 2013).

On the analytical, technical note, the capacity to measure the set of NTMs is vivid, as there exists a broad diversity of formal and informal NTMs (Bora et al., 2002; Disdier & Fugazza, 2020; Jakab et al., 2001; Maggi & Rodriguez-Clare, 2007; Ronen, 2017). Since analysing NTMs differs from analysing tariffs, there are various challenges although. A fundamental difference exists between a trade-oriented and a welfare-oriented definition of NTMs. Some techniques consider the trade impact, while others consider the welfare elements (Beghin & Bureau, 2001; Deardorff & Stern, 1998). This study focuses on the trade impact of NTMs. In this study, we shall adhere to the basics and define 'non-tariff barriers' or 'non-tariff measures' as any economic intervention that purposefully discriminates against foreign competitors. NTMs will be used as a collective term that embraces all NTBs to keep things simple.

## 4. Research Methodology

This study follows the positivist philosophy as the links between variables have been tested. The study is quantitative, and the data are collected from different agency sources like UN COMTRADE, WITS, IMF and Global Heritage Foundation. The investigative approach to this study is deductive. Measuring the cost of protection at the national level is feasible. However, considerable data about each economic domain and import restrictions are required. The partial equilibrium approach is commonly used to estimate the costs associated with protection. However, the empirical cost estimates have been low (De Melo & Tarr, 1992). The possible reason is that the cost of protection for large sectors is evaluated individually, and the assessment of the cross-sector impacts needs to be included. The amount for each area is then combined to produce an overall protective effect. Wall (1999) subsequently developed an alternate estimating approach that required considerably less information while providing the same benefits as a general equilibrium assessment of the impacts of protection. This study uses a gravity model technique, similar to that suggested by Wall (1999), to assess the impact of NTMs on the trade in Afghanistan. The basic model is specified as shown in Eq. (1), expressed in log form:

$$\ln X_{ij} = \beta_0 + \beta_1 \ln Y_i + \beta_2 \ln Y_j + \beta_3 \ln D_{ij} + \beta \ln A_{ij} + \mu_{ij} \tag{1}$$

where $X_{ij}$ denotes the export of products from the country I to country $j$, $Y_i$ and $Y_j$ denote the GDPs of the exporter and importer countries, $D_{ij}$ denotes the distance between the two countries, $A_{ij}$ denotes any additional factors impacting commerce between the countries and it denotes the error term. The study under consideration includes a selection of Afghanistan's four primary trading partners based on the SAARC trade situation (India, Pakistan, Bangladesh and Sri Lanka). The period is from 2015 to 2020; hence the panel data technique is used.

### 4.1 Data Specification, Instrumentation and Operationalisation of Variables

In looking at the multiplicative gravity trade model, the Ordinary Least Squares (OLS) regression methodology is commonly employed to calculate the coefficients of this model in its log-linear form (Shepherd, 2013; UNCTAD, 2012). Fixed effect estimate is preferred over random effect estimation for assessing bilateral trade flows between specified sets of trading states (Baltagy, 2008; Dinçer, 2014; Egger, 2000; Greene, 2013; Martinez-Zarzoso & Nowak-Lehman, 2003; Wani et al., 2016). Given that there is no relationship between the country-specific effects and the regressors in the panel data set, the fixed effect estimation technique is more effective and coherent than the random effect estimation method. The heteroscedasticity of the dataset is addressed by doing an Ordinary Least Squares (OLS) regression with robust standard errors (Yamano, 2009). Thus, in heteroscedasticity, Best Linear Unbiased Estimators (BLUE) and error terms with constant variance help in estimating using OLS with standard errors (Yamano, 2009). A Panel Unit Root Test (PURT) has been used to check for unit roots in panel data. The Augmented Dickey–Fuller (ADF) and Levin et al. (2002) (LLC) PURT tests are the most commonly reported tests for unit roots employing panel data (Banerjee & Wagner, 2009).

Although at least any of the possible panel unit root tests reject the null hypothesis (described below), it is possible to conclude that the variables in the data series are indeed stationary (Gujurati, 2006). Consequently, this study assumed stationarity based on at least one test rejecting unit roots. The LLC test was run on the data set using EViews software for each variable. The choices selected in each variable for the LLC unit root test are shown in Table 4. The findings of the LLC test rejected the null hypothesis (H0), indicating that the data series was stationary. After evaluating the panel data for each variable in the basic model, the gravity trade model employed in this work has been estimated using fixed effect and OLS regression approaches. As a result, the difference is not required, and the coefficients can be interpreted as elasticities. The static data

Table 4. Levin, Lin and Chu (LLC) Unit Root Test Results.

| Variable | $t$-Statistic | $p$ Value |
|---|---|---|
| $X_{ij}$ | $-3.3291$ | $0.000^{***}$ |
| $Y_i$ | $-1.6753$ | $0.0412^{**}$ |
| $Y_j$ | $-3.1486$ | $0.0000^{***}$ |
| $D_{ij}$ | $-23.6353$ | $0.0000^{***}$ |
| $A_{ij}$ | $-13.1291$ | $0.0000^{***}$ |
| ER | $-11.6793$ | $0.0000^{***}$ |
| $T$ | $-11.2934$ | $0.0000^{***}$ |

*Source:* Calculations using EViews software.

*Note:* \*\*\*/\*\*/\* indicate the rejection of the null hypothesis at 1%, 5% and 10% levels.

were then used to estimate the model(s), and the empirical results are provided in the results section.

Table 4 shows that all variables are significant at the 5% significance level. Each data set has 12 observations, comprising 6 yearly observations for each of the four countries. Specific key estimating concerns must be addressed before applying the gravity trade equation. As a result, the variables in the study have been operationally defined as follows in Table 5:

Table 5. Operationalisation of Variables.

| Variable | Definition | Source of Data |
|---|---|---|
| Exports $(X_{ij})$ | The export of products from country $i$ to country $j$ | UN COMTRADE, WITS and IMF |
| GDP ($Y_i$ and $Y_j$) | GDP of exporting and importing nations | UN COMTRADE, WITS and IMF |
| Distance $(D_{ij})$ | The distance between the two nations is $D_{ij}$ | IMF |
| $A_{ij}$ | Other factors impacting international trade | Global Heritage Foundation |
| $ER_{it}$ | It is the exporting country's real exchange rate concerning the US dollar at time $t$ | IMF |
| $T_{jt}$ | It indicates trade freedom for the importing country at time $t$. | Global Heritage Foundation |

*Source:* Collected from different works of literature and compiled by the Author.

### 4.2 Empirical Estimation

This section outlines the model's functional forms and explains the variables that best suit the model. The model is analysed for panel data as country-specific factors impact the dependent variable. By Wall (1999), the general gravity equation is modified and presented as follows:

$$\ln X_{ij} = \beta_0 + \beta_1 \ln Y_{it} + \beta_2 \ln Y_{jt} + \beta_3 \ln ER_{it} + \beta_4 T_{jt} + \mu_{ijt} \tag{2}$$

$ER_{it}$ is the exporter country's real exchange rate compared to the US dollar at time $t$, and $T_{jt}$ is the importing country's trade freedom score index at time $t$. A higher currency rate (depreciation) usually increases exports, whereas a lower exchange rate (appreciation) usually decreases exports. Increased import protection typically reduces export levels for the exporting country and vice versa. The data statistics are readily available, but the only problem is identifying a proxy for the NTMs indicated by trade freedom ratings, which is examined more below. This study's trade freedom rankings are based on two inputs: trade-weighted average tariff rates and NTBs or NTMs. Tariffs are often levied on various commodities entering a nation. Weighted average tariffs are a purely quantitative statistic that accounts for the score's basic computation (Riley & Miller, 2013):

$$\text{Trade Freedom}_i = \left\{ \frac{\text{Tariff}_{\text{Max}} - \text{Tariff}_i}{(\text{Tariff}_{\text{Max}} - \text{Tariff}_{\text{min}})} \right\} * 100 - \text{NTM}_i \qquad (3)$$

$\text{Tariff}_{\text{max}}$ and $\text{Tariff}_{\text{min}}$ indicate the top and lower boundaries for tariff rates, respectively, while tariff represents the weighted average tariff rate in the country $i$. The equation includes a standard NTM penalty (5, 10, 15, 20 and no penalty) for the degree of NTMs used in a specific nation (3). Based on the scale of NTMs in a specific nation, this NTM penalty is deducted from the base score. The amount of NTMs in each country's trade policy framework is established using qualitative and quantitative data. NTMs examined in the trade freedom penalty include quantity constraints, pricing limits, regulatory restrictions, customs restrictions and direct government intervention such as subsidies, taxes and regulations. The Heritage Foundation's databank was used to compile the trade freedom ratings (Riley & Miller, 2013), and because data for Afghanistan for 2021 and 2022 are unavailable, data for 2015 and 2020 were used instead. The World Bank provides each nation's trade-weighted average tariff rates (2022).

# 5. Results, Analysis and Discussions

This section entails the results of the models applied for analysis purposes. The section offers an analysis of the gravity model and explains the equations discussed in the methodology.

## 5.1 Model Estimation and Results

This section discusses the results obtained by employing a gravity trade model to evaluate the study's overall objectives. In the Afghanistan trade scenario, BIPS nations were chosen based on import levels from Afghanistan, and the fixed effect approach was implemented appropriately. The fixed effect method has several appealing features since it adjusts for extraneous variables that are unobservable or difficult to measure, improves estimate heterogeneity and allows the intercept and other parameters to vary between countries as an unconstrained model (Wall, 1999). Regarding commercial ties, the fixed effects technique works best with various countries (Egger, 2000; Martinez-Zarzoso & Nowak-Lehman, 2003). For analysis purposes, two estimations were employed to assess the impact of NTMs on Afghanistan's exports. The first estimation uses trade freedom ratings based on two inputs, trade-weighted average tariff rates and NTMs. Table 6 shows the preliminary estimation results.

This model worked well, with an $R^2$ of 0.976, and all estimated coefficients bear the expected signs and are statistically significant. The coefficient of interest is the one that combines the impact of tariffs and NTMs on Afghanistan's exports to determine the amount of 'protectionism' by importing nations. According to

Table 6. Afghanistan Exports: Impact of Tariffs Plus NTMs.

| Variable | Coefficient | *t*-Statistic | Prob-Value |
|---|---|---|---|
| C | 30.399 | 2.101 | 0.038 |
| Exchange Rate | −1.243 | −2.345 | 0.0120* |
| Tariffs plus NTM | −1.1832 | −1.546 | 0.123* |
| $R^2$ | 0.976 | | |
| Adjusted $R^2$ | 0.995 | | |
| *F*-Statistic | 768.435 | | |
| Prob (*F*-stat) | 0.000000 | | |

*Source:* Author's calculations.

*Note:* */**/***/significant at 10%/5%/1% level.

the data, a 1% increase in tariffs and NTMs imposed by importing countries would result in a 1.183% decrease in Afghan exports. The second estimate is based only on each importing nation's trade-weighted average tariff rates, with no respect for NTMs. The second estimate presents the results of the impact on Afghanistan's exports without any NTMs by importing nations.

Table 7 shows the results of the second estimation. The model performed well with an $R^2$ of 0.93; all predicted coefficients had the anticipated signs and were statistically significant. The 'protectionism' variable in this model examines the impact of tariffs imposed only by importing nations on Afghan exports. According to the data, a 1% increase in tariffs imposed by importing countries would result in a 1.131% drop in Afghan exports. When evaluating the coefficient amount when tariffs combined with NTMs are implemented, there appears to be a considerable difference in the level of 'protectionism' compared to a case where the importing country merely applies tariffs. The country-specific impact

Table 7. Afghanistan Exports: Impact of Tariffs Only.

| Variable | Coefficient | *t*-Statistic | Prob-Value |
|---|---|---|---|
| C | 29.432 | 2.301 | 0.036 |
| Exchange Rate | −1.123 | −2.135 | 0.0190* |
| Tariffs only | −1.131 | −1.675 | 0.213* |
| $R^2$ | 0.935 | | |
| Adjusted $R^2$ | 0.996 | | |
| *F*-Statistic | 678.135 | | |
| Prob (*F*-stat) | 0.000000 | | |

*Source:* Author's calculations.

*Note:* */**/***/significant at 10%/5%/1% level.

Table 8. Fixed Effects on Afghanistan's Exports.

| Country | Tariffs + NTM | Tariffs Only |
|---|---|---|
| Bangladesh | −1.430921 | −1.649926 |
| India | 2.812279 | 1.978680 |
| Pakistan | 2.782054 | 2.138680 |
| Sri Lanka | −0.027654 | −1.931113 |

*Source:* Authors compilation.

estimates for both estimations are derived from these two estimates and are provided in Table 8.

The cross-sectional effects highlight the impact of country-specific characteristics that the model does not quantify. It demonstrates how trade between Afghanistan and its trading partners varies depending on the characteristics of each country. Table 8 demonstrates that certain components in specific countries stimulate Afghan exports to India and Pakistan (because of the combined influence of tariffs and NTMs) (countries with positive signs). However, it has been established that unobservable country characteristics limit Afghan exports to specific countries, especially Bangladesh and Sri Lanka (countries with negative signs). Furthermore, Table 8 demonstrates that there are characteristics in some countries that boost Afghan exports to India and Pakistan (based only on tariff impact) (countries with positive signs). However, it has been discovered that unobservable country attributes limit Afghan exports to select countries, especially Bangladesh and Sri Lanka (countries with negative signs). Even though individual nation signals are typically consistent, the value of country-specific impacts is frequently more significant in the first estimation (tariffs and NTMs) than in the second estimation (tariffs only).

Table 9. Effects of NTMs Protection on Afghanistan Exports (2015–2020).

| | Actual value ('000 of US$) | Effect of Protection ('000 US$) | Effect as % of Exports |
|---|---|---|---|
| Afghanistan exports to countries in the sample (Tariffs + NTMs) | 5645841.1 | −69556.7624 | −1.23 |
| Afghanistan exports to countries in the sample (Tariffs only) | 5645841.1 | −63854.4628 | −1.13 |
| Loss in export value due to NTMs | | −5702.2996 | |

*Source:* Authors Compilation.

The actual value of Afghanistan's total exports to the sample countries from 2015 to 2020 is presented in Table 9 at US$ 5645.84 million. The aggregate adverse consequences of tariffs and NTMs on this amount are also indicated in real export value (second row, third column). Without tariffs and NTMs, an additional US$69.55 million in exports may have occurred over the 6 years. This figure is obtained by dividing the regression coefficient by the total value of actual exports. The value of Afghanistan's total exports to the sample nations is displayed in US dollars in the third and second columns. As a result, the third row, the third column, solely depicts the negative impact of tariffs on this amount in real export value. Without tariffs, an additional $63.85 million in exports may have happened for 6 years. The last row looks at how tariffs and non-tariff obstacles affect the actual value of exports. It is done to determine the effect of NTMs on the actual value of Afghan exports. Over 6 years, the real value of Afghan exports to the sample nations is $5.70 million lower due to the impact of NTMs. The prevalence of NTMs also reduces actual Afghanistan exports by US$ 5.70 million, amounting to a 0.029% loss in GDP.

## 5.2 Discussions

This study increases our capacity to estimate the impact of NTMs on Afghanistan–BIPS trade. The model's results were rather good. The factor of interest is the variable assessing the level of 'protectionist measures' by importing countries, which combines the impact of tariffs and NTMs on Afghanistan's exports. According to the data, a 1% increase in tariffs and NTMs enforced by importing countries would result in a 1.233% drop in Afghan exports. These findings correlate to the gravity equation, in which NTMs and tariffs reduce the willingness to trade by increasing trade costs. This finding is consistent with the literature, as NTMs are frequently used as a proxy for trade costs in empirical research. These findings are consistent and in agreement with what Balistreri and Hillberry (2006), Jordaan (2017) and Jordaan and Kanda (2011) discovered in prior research investigations based on the economic intuition that NTMs and tariffs impede trade flow. The second estimation is carried only on trade-weighted average tariff rates employed by each importing nation without regard for NTMs. The model worked rather well, and the 'protectionism' coefficient satiates that a 1% rise in tariffs implemented by importing nations results in a 1.13% decline in Afghan exports. Other research in diverse national settings, primarily concentrating on tariffs, has shown similar results (Anders & Caswell, 2009; Disdier et al., 2008; Fontagné et al., 2005; Furceri et al., 2018; Jordaan, 2017; Li & Beghin, 2012; Moenius, 2006) (2017). The results of both estimations are startling as there exists a considerable difference in the degree of protectionism based on the magnitude of coefficients, as the coefficient of NTMs + Tariffs is greater than the Tariffs. The actual value of exports from Afghanistan to the sample countries over the 6 years is, therefore, US$ 5.70 million lower because of the incidence of NTMs. The incidence of NTMs also devoid actual Afghanistan exports by US$ 5.70 million, equal to a 0.029% loss of Afghanistan's GDP. These findings are consistent with earlier research in which NTMs and tariffs reduce the inclination to trade by increasing trade costs. This finding aligns with the literature, as empirical research frequently uses NTMs as a proxy for trade costs; this is also consistent with what Jordaan (2017), Jordaan and Kanda (2011) and Balistreri and Hillberry (2006) discovered in their research investigations based on the economic intuition that NTMs and tariffs impede trade flow. The conclusions of this study are stunning, although there is still some discrepancy with the findings of other investigations. Despite these limitations, the extant empirical research concludes that, at the aggregate level, NTM indicators are unrelated to reduced trade and that standards have a negligible influence on trade (Kee et al., 2009; Trabelsi, 2013). Despite their disparate outcomes, both types of research contradicted the belief that national norms stifle trade. According to studies based on disaggregated trade data, the impact of NTBs/NTM measures varies by industry. According to one of these studies, Moenius (2006), import-specific regulations hinder non-manufacturing imports (mainly food, beverages, raw materials and mineral fuels) but boost manufacturing imports (including oils, chemicals, manufacturing and machinery). Several investigations back up Moenius' (2006) findings like that of Bhunia and Nataraj (2014); Clemens and Kremer (2016); Disdier et al. (2008); Li and Beghin (2012); Maskus et al. (2001).

## 6. Conclusions

NTMs, along with tariffs and protectionism procedures, have only recently received attention as factors impacting trade flow, albeit in a narrower sense. Thus, this study justifies a detailed examination of the influence of NTMs on trade flows from Afghanistan to the SAARC region, with a primary focus on BIPS. Using a gravity trade model technique, we analysed the possible trade effect of various NTMs of trade on Afghanistan's exports from 2015 to 2020. The study was inspired by the fact that developing nations, such as Afghanistan, have turned to NTMs in conjunction with tariffs (their usage has been controlled and curtailed) to defend their domestic industries. The model output was obtained using a basic model with only the target country's exchange rate, NTMs and tariff rate equivalents as explanatory variables. In the first estimation, a rise of 1% in the tariffs and NTMs causes exports to decline by 1.23%, whereas a rise in 1% in the tariffs causes exports to decline by 1.13%. When evaluating the coefficient amount when tariffs combined with NTMs are implemented, there appears to be a considerable difference in the level of 'protectionism' compared to a case where the importing nation merely applies tariffs. The impact of NTMs is evident. The actual value of Afghan exports to the sample nations is US$ 5.70 million lower due to NTMs, equating to a 0.029% loss of Afghanistan's GDP annually over the 6 years. In other words, the higher the import tariff imposed by the importing nation, the smaller the exporting country's average profit margin supplied to the related country. As a result, this will hurt the total amount of exports to this market sector, functioning as a trade-limiting barrier. If the impact of NTMs on Afghan exports is studied, it resembles a severe negative influence on the country's economic growth. The impact of NTMs thus has a negative influence on Afghanistan's perceived export gains, resulting in trade chaos in the nation.

## 6.1 Recommendations

In terms of policy discourse and recommendations, facilitating more significant free trade and reducing NTMs and NTBs should be undertaken with the goal of not only regional economic integration and growth but also community engagement, employment and alleviating poverty across South Asia, highlighting the significance of removing trade barriers in South Asia. NTMs are the primary impediment to intra-regional trade in South Asia. As a result, regional intra-regional commerce must be expanded through bilateral and regional initiatives. It is critical for Afghanistan exporters to continually launch fresh items in non-traditional export areas in response to changing customer tastes. Afghanistan exporters must vary their export destinations to keep pace with ever-changing consumer choices to stay afloat and remain competitive in the current global export environment. Government institutions such as the Ministry of Commerce, Industry, and Trade (MoCIT) and the Ministry of Economy (MoE) must resolve these NTMs/NTBs during trade discussions at both the regional and global levels to ensure that certain NTMs/NTBs do not continue to obstruct trade, facilitate exporters and producers by providing pertinent data on newly implemented NTMs/NTBs and maintain market penetration databases. Such NTB databases and statistics may be utilised by exporters to identify prospective trade-impeding NTMs/NTBs and to plan how to absorb the unique conformity costs associated with NTMs/NTBs enacted by importing nations. Even on the policy front, the state of affairs is dismal as the Afghanistan trade policy sans the rigorous touch as to how to set a mechanism that needs to be transparent and comprehensive in terms of stakeholder involvement, by nations' responsibilities under WTO, SAARC and other regional agreements, as well as trade policies aimed at boosting international commerce. Greater regional integration will help its economic growth and institutional stability if trade policy is reoriented towards a more open trade policy.

## 6.2 Limitations and Future Scope of the Study

The speculation surrounding quantitative assessments of these NTMs and NTBs should not preclude research that evaluates and documents trade impediments. There is still more work to be done, notably in extending and improving the gravity trading model. Future research in the export industry that employs the gravity trade model approach should focus on developing proxies to incorporate other parameters in the model. There needs to be more literature on licencing and qualifying criteria, processes and technical standards in services. It will be intriguing to see how these variables affect Afghanistan's exports. In future studies, conventional issues like tariffs, proximity from markets and market needs regarding customer choices can be investigated. The study must evaluate the benefits of SAARC policy actions to remove NTBs and increase internal trade. Instead, we quantify the current effect of NTMs on trade within the SAARC area, emphasising Afghanistan, and examine the prospective trade growth implications of reducing or eliminating existing NTBs.

# References

Ackerman, F. (2005). *The shrinking gains from trade: A critical assessment of Doha round projections* (No. 1434-2016-118837).

Ahmad, B., Ghafoor, A., & Maqbool, A. (2018). Regional trade Pakistan's perspective. In *Developing sustainable agriculture in Pakistan* (pp. 833–856). CRC Press.

Ahmad, S. S., & Wani, N. U. H. (2018). Trade potential of Afghanistan against SAARC: An application of gravity model approach. *Kardan Journal of Economics and Management Sciences*, *1*(4), 1–19.

Akbari, S. (2021). *The WTO transit regime for landlocked countries and its impacts on members' regional transit agreements: The case of Afghanistan's transit trade with Pakistan* (Vol. 17). Springer Nature.

Akintola, A., Boughanmi, H., Antimiani, A., Zaibet, L., & Kotagama, H. (2021). Estimating the impacts of non-tariff measures in the Indian Ocean Rim Association. *Sustainability*, *14*(01), 68.

Anders, S. M., & Caswell, J. A. (2009). Standards as barriers versus standards as catalysts: Assessing the impact of HACCP implementation on US seafood imports. *American Journal of Agricultural Economics*, *91*(2), 310–321.

Bacchetta, M., & Beverelli, C. (2012). *Non-tariff measures and the WTO*. VOX CEPR's Policy Portal. Research-Based Policy Analysis and Commentary from Leading Economists.

Baldwin, R. E. (1970). *Non-tariff distortions in international trade*. Brookings Institution.

Balistreri, E. J., & Hillberry, R. H. (2006). Trade frictions and welfare in the gravity model: How much of the iceberg melts? *Canadian Journal of Economics/Revue canadienne d'économique*, *39*(1), 247–265.

Baltagy, B. H. (2008). *Econometric analysis of panel data*. John Wiley & Sons.

Banerjee, A., & Wagner, M. (2009). Panel methods to test for unit roots and cointegration. In *Palgrave handbook of econometrics: Volume 2: Applied econometrics* (pp. 632–726). Palgrave Macmillan.

Basu, S. R., Kuwahara, H., & Dumesnil, F. (2012). *Evolution of non-tariff measures: Emerging cases from selected developing countries*. United Nations Conference on Trade and Development.

Beghin, J. C., & Bureau, J. (2001). *Quantification of sanitary, phytosanitary and technical barriers to trade for trade policy analysis* (Working Paper No. 01-WP 291). Ames, Iowa, US: Centre for Agricultural and Rural Development (CARD), Iowa State University.

Bellanawithana, A., Wijerathne, B., & Weerahewa, J. (2009). Impacts of non-tariff measures (NTMs) on agricultural exports: A gravity modelling approach. In *Asia–Pacific Trade Economists Conference*. ESCAP.

Bhunia, A., & Nataraj, G. (2014, March 14). *East Asia Forum*. https://eastasiaforum. org/. https://eastasiaforum.org/2014/03/14/break-down-the-barriers-to-trade-in-south-asia/#:~:text=First%2C%20export%20subsidies%2C%20prohibitions%

2C,the%20free%20flow%20of%20trade. https://eastasiaforum.org/2014/03/14/break-down-the-barriers-to-trade-in-south-a

Bora, B., Kuwahara, A., & Laird, S. (2002). *Quantification of non-tariff measures.* United Nations Conference on Trade and Development. Division for International Trade in Goods and Services and Commodities. Trade Analysis Branch (Geneva).

Bratt, M. (2017). Estimating the bilateral impact of non-tariff measures on trade. *Review of International Economics, 25*(5), 1105–1129.

Carrère, C., & De Melo, J. (2011). Non-tariff measures: What do we know, what might be done? *Journal of Economic Integration, 26*(1), 169–196.

Clemens, M. A., & Kremer, M. (2016). The new role of the World Bank. *The Journal of Economic Perspectives, 30*(1), 53–76.

De Melo, J., & Tarr, D. G. (1992). *A general equilibrium analysis of US foreign trade policy.* MIT University Press.

Deardorff, A. V., & Stern, R. M. (1998). *Measurement of non-tariff barriers* (Vol. 179). University of Michigan Press.

Dinçer, G. (2014). *Turkey's rising imports from BRICS: A gravity model approach.* MPRA Paper (61979). https://mpra.ub.uni-muenchen.de/61979/

Disdier, A., Fekadu, B., Murillo, C., & Wong, S. A. (2008). *Trade effects of SPS and TBT measures on tropical and diversification products.*

Disdier, A. C., & Fugazza, M. (2020). *A practical guide to the economic analysis of non-tariff measures.* United Nations.

Egger, P. (2000). A note on the proper econometric specification of the gravity equation. *Economics Letters, 66*(1), 25–31.

Egger, P., Francois, J., Manchin, M., & Nelson, D. (2015). Non-tariff barriers, integration, and the transatlantic economy. *Economic Policy, 30*(83), 539–584.

Fontagné, L. G., Mimouni, M., & Pasteels, J. M. (2005). Estimating the impact of environmental SPS and TBT on international trade. *Integration and Trade Journal, 22*(3).

Furceri, D., Hannan, S. A., Ostry, J. D., & Rose, A. K. (2018). *Macroeconomic consequences of tariffs (No. w25402).* National Bureau of Economic Research.

Gonzalez–Mellado, A., Gay, S. H., M'Barek, R., & Ferrari, E. (2010). Evaluation of non-tariff measures for African agricultural exports to the EU in a CGE framework. In *Research in Agricultural and Applied Economics, Conference Paper Presentation.* https://ageconsearch.umn.edu/record/332012

Greene, W. (2013). *Export potential for US advanced technology goods to India using a gravity model approach* (pp. 1–43). US International Trade Commission. Working Paper, 2013-03B.

Gujurati, D. (2006). *Essentials of econometrics.* McGraw-Hill Education.

Haveman, J., & Thursby, J. G. (1999). *The impact of tariff and non-tariff barriers to trade in agricultural commodities: A disaggregated approach.* http://docs.lib.purdue.edu/ciberwp/143

Henson, S., & Loader, R. (2001). Barriers to agricultural exports from developing countries: The role of sanitary and phytosanitary requirements. *World Development, 29*(1), 85–102.

Hillman, J. S. (1991). *Technical barriers to agricultural trade.* Westview Press.

IMF. (2021). Regional economic outlook Middle East and Central Asia. In *Trade-offs today for transformation tomorrow.* International Monetary Fund.

ITC. (2022). *Trade map.* International Trade Centre (ITC).

Jakab, Z. M., Kovacs, M. A., & Oszlay, A. (2001). How far has regional integration advanced? An analysis of the actual and potential trade of three Central and European countries. *Journal of Comparative Economics*, *29*(2), 276–292.

Johnson, N. D., & Koyama, M. (2017). States and economic growth: Capacity and constraints. *Explorations in Economic History*, *64*, 1–20.

Jordaan, A. C. (2017). Impact of non-tariff measures on trade in Mauritius. *Foreign Trade Review*, *52*(3), 185–199.

Jordaan, A., & Kanda, P. (2011). *Analysing the trade effects of the EU-SA & SADC trading agreements: A panel data approach*. Department of Economics. The University of Pretoria.

Kathuria, S. (Ed.). (2019). *A glass half full: The promise of regional trade in South Asia*. World Bank Publications.

Kee, H., Nicita, A., & Olarreaga, M. (2009). Estimating trade restrictiveness indices. *The Economic Journal*, *119*(534).

Koo, W., & Kennedy, P. L. (2005). International trade and agriculture. *Management of Environmental Quality: An International Journal*, *16*(5), 566–567.

Laird, S., & Yeats, A. (1990). *Quantitative methods for trade-barrier analysis*. New York University Press.

Levin, A., Lin, C., & Chu, C. J. (2002). Unit root tests in panel data: Asymptotic and finite-sample properties. *Journal of Econometrics*, *108*(1), 1–24.

Li, Y., & Beghin, J. C. (2012). A meta-analysis of estimates of the impact of technical barriers to trade. *Journal of policy modeling*, *34*(3), 497–511.

Maggi, G., & Rodriguez-Clare, A. (2007). A political-economy theory of trade agreements. *American Economic Review*, *97*(4), 1374–1406.

Martinez-Zarzoso, I., & Nowak-Lehman, F. (2003). Augmented gravity model: An empirical application to Mercosur-European Union trade flows. *Journal of Applied Economics*, *6*(2), 291–316.

Maskus, K. E., Wilson, J. S., & Otsuki, T. (2001). An empirical framework for analysing technical regulations and trade. In K. E. Maskus, J. S. Wilson, & A. Arbor (Eds.), *Quantifying the impact of technical barriers to trade*. University of Michigan Press.

McCarty, A. (1999). *Vietnam's integration with ASEAN: Survey of non-tariff measures affecting trade* (United Nations Development Project, VIE 95/015). Ministry of Trade.

Moenius, J. (2006, May 28–30). *The good, the bad and the ambiguous: Standards and trade in agricultural products*. International Agricultural Trade Research Consortium.

Naseri, M. E., & Wani, N. U. H. (2020). Export competitiveness of Afghanistan with Pakistan: An economic evaluation. *Kardan Journal of Economics and Management Sciences*, *3*(2), 1–12.

Niu, Z., Liu, C., Gunessee, S., & Milner, C. (2018). Non-tariff and overall protection: Evidence across countries and over time. *Review of World Economics*, *154*(4), 675–703.

Quambusch, L. (1977). Non-tariff barriers to trade. *Intereconomics*, *3*(4), 79–83.

Riley, B., & Miller, T. (2013). *Index of economic freedom: No boost in trade freedom* (Special Report from the Center for International Trade and Economics, No. 123).

Ronen, E. (2017). Quantifying the trade effects of NTMs: A review of the empirical literature. *Journal of Economics and Political Economy*, *4*(3), 263–274.

Sarel, M. M. (1995). *Nonlinear effects of inflation on economic growth.* International Monetary Fund.

Shepherd, B. (2013). *The gravity model of international trade: A user guide.* https://hdl.handle.net/20.500.12870/128

Siddiqui, M. S., & Naeem, T. (2015). *Investment opportunities in Afghanistan.* The Islamic Republic of Afghanistan Ministry of Commerce & Industry.

Torsekar, M. (2019). *The post-recession rise of non-tariff measures.* Office of Industries, US International Trade Commission.

Trabelsi, I. (2013). Agricultural trade face to non-tariff barriers: A gravity model for the Euro-Med area. *Journal of Studies in Social Sciences, 3*(1).

UNCTAD. (2012). *Classification of non-tariff measures.* February 2012 Version. United Nations Conference on Trade and Development.

UNCTAD. (2013). *World investment report 2013: Global value chains: Investment and trade for development.* UN.

Wall, H. J. (1999). Using the gravity model to estimate the cost of protection. *Review Federal Reserve Bank of St. Louis, 81*(1), 33–40.

Wani, N. U. H. (2019). Nexus between openness to trade and economic growth: An empirical investigation of Afghanistan. *South Asia Economic Journal, 20*(2), 205–223.

Wani, N. U. H., & Dhami, J. K. (2014). Economic concert, collaboration, and prospective of trade between India and Brazil. *Foreign Trade Review, 49*(4), 359–372.

Wani, N. U. H., & Dhami, J. K. (2017). India's trade linkage with BRCS economies: Trends, patterns and future potentialities. *Journal of International Economics,* (0976–0792), *8*(1).

Wani, N. U. H., Dhami, J. K., & Rehman, A. (2016). *The determinants of India's imports: A gravity model approach.* MPRA Paper-74700. https://mpra.ub.uni-muenchen.de/74700/

World Bank. (2022). *Trade weighted average tariff rates per country.* World Integrated Trade Solution. https://wits.worldbank.org/countrysnapshot/AFG/textview

Yamano, T. (2009). *Lecture notes on advanced econometrics: Heteroskedasticity and robust estimators.* https://www.yumpu.com/en/document/view/41049107/lecture-9-heteroskedasticity-and-robust-estimators

Zainuddin, M. R. K., Sarmidi, T., & Khalid, N. (2020). Sustainable production, non-tariff measures, and trade performance in RCEP countries. *Sustainability, 12*(23), 9969.

# Glossary of Afghan Expressions

**Bank-i Milli:** National Bank
**Loya Jirga:** Grand Council, 'Grand Assembly of elders'
**Walayat:** Province
**Jirgas:** Local Consultation Meetings
**Hawala:** Unofficial money transferring system

# Index

Printed in the USA
CPSIA information can be obtained
at www.ICGtesting.com
JSHW011356250624
65367JS00004B/40